A Palace
for the
Antichrist

A Palace for the Antichrist

Joseph R. Chambers

New Leaf Press

First printing: October 1996
Second printing: November 1996

ISBN: 0-89221-333-7
Library of Congress Catalog Number: 96-69688

All Scripture references are from the King James Version.

Acknowledgments

The study of prophecy has been a breathtaking experience for this servant of Jesus Christ. I was privileged to be converted in a classical Pentecostal church where prophecy teaching was merged into the whole of biblical truth. Saved in March of 1952, I immediately began to hear about the Rapture, the Tribulation period, the Millennium, and other dispensational doctrines. My heart was awakened by my conversion to an unsatisfiable hunger for truth.

One of the first things I remember learning was that the Bible was verbally inspired of God and that it was to be interpreted as literal. This truth, above all else, has protected me through the years. Learning that there is no private interpretation kept me from the vice of arrogance and humanistic ego. Listening to some of the greatest preachers of my day inspired my heart to keep on digging, reading, praying, fasting, and learning.

I was already pastoring when I learned to supplement my Bible study with other books. The first study books were teacher training courses, which I still have, with the many notes of dictionary meanings for words I had never seen. These books opened up my life to the world of great Christian literature. From these church study courses, I moved to every autobiography and biography I could get in my possession. I will not try to name all of these authors, but they impacted my life.

The classical Pentecostal church that I was blessed to be a part of deserves much appreciation for the biblical foundation they gave to me. Someday I will be able to tell each person face to face of my love. The local churches Juanita and I have pastored have always been a joy to us. Every truth in my heart was hammered out in those church pulpits. No man is an island unto himself, but each of us reflects the influences of many wonderful people who have impacted our lives.

I acknowledge the many great Christians I have known who blessed me by their godly lifestyle; the many authors who have written books full of truth and the theology they inspired to my heart; my wonderful family at our church in Charlotte, North Carolina, and my personal family, the greatest joy of my physical life. Special appreciation goes to my daughter Tanya Turner, who typed all the manuscripts over and over until they were perfect, and my daughter-in-law Anne Chambers, who meticulously proofread for the same perfection. They are both great daughters.

Dedication

This book is dedicated to our church family at Paw Creek Ministries in Charlotte, North Carolina. They have loved me as their pastor for 28 years. They are not blind followers, but servants of Jesus Christ who love my family, Juanita, and myself, because we love the infallible Word of God and the Lord Jesus Christ revealed in its pages.

The local church is the center of all manifestations of His glory. Nothing in God's earthly kingdom supersedes the church. Everything I represent owes its strength to the local church where I serve and the anointing that rests in its authority.

Table of Contents

Foreword

This world has not seen the last of the city of Babylon! Not only is Saddam Hussein working furiously to rebuild it in an effort to perpetuate his place in history, the Hebrew prophets saw it as an important part of end-time events. But few world leaders today expect it to be the center of world government, finance, and ultimately world religion, which is its chief destiny.

The city of Babylon is among the most ancient cities of the world and could well be the very cradle of civilization. Historically it has had a greater influence on the world than any city on earth except the city of Jerusalem — and it took the life, death, and Resurrection to make Jerusalem the most influential place on earth. But all of Babylon's influence has been evil. My long-time colleague and friend Dr. Henry Morris, in his masterful book *The Long War Against God*, proves that every modern evil had its earthly origin in Babylon. He also points out that it was Satan himself, using Nimrod and his mother, Semiramis, who introduced those evils, from the Tower of Babel to goddess worship to "Pontifix Maximus," the supreme pontiff of every false religion in the world.

You cannot name a prominent evil in this world that did not have its origin in Babylon, from false religions, cults, goddess worship, rebellion to God, drugs, immorality, and the list goes on endlessly. Even today its biblical name,

"Mystery Babylon," reeks with intrigue as it walks with a heavy footstep through the pages of prophetic writing, which guarantees it a future and a prominent place in end-time events.

Admittedly, confusion exists today about the future destiny of that city, even among faithful Bible teachers who are generally regarded to be good students of prophecy. They were lulled into thinking that the city had been destroyed centuries ago — but that is not true. The Hebrew prophets said it would be destroyed in a single day. It may come as a surprise for you to learn that never happened. Babylon did lose its position of prominence, but was alive and well in the days of our Lord. In fact, the apostle Peter wrote his first epistle from that city (1 Pet. 5:13-14) during the first century. Historically, the city was just abandoned and left to ruin in the ravages of time, not the destruction that was predicted by the prophets "in a single day." That destruction is yet to come and is detailed in Revelation 17 and 18. Obviously, however, the city must be rebuilt and become the governmental and financial capital of the world in order to be destroyed.

When I wrote my commentary on Revelation some 20 years ago, called *Revelation: Illustrated and Made Plain*, I had a very difficult time finding anything really worthwhile on the subject, particularly pertaining to its current status. In fact, I even contemplated a trip to the place just to investigate it for myself.

Dr. Joseph Chambers did just that. He was a special guest of the Iraqi government (before the Gulf War) and literally saw the place for himself. When I first read his daily journal written on that trip, it was almost like being there. I found it fascinating!

Few people in our country know more about the city of Babylon than Dr. Chambers. He has studied it for years, including all the prophecies that pertain to that ancient city. I have read his book carefully and feel it is closer to my view of the past, present, and future of the city than anything now in print. I cannot recommend it too highly. In fact, I predict that this book will become the definitive word on the subject for the next 20 or more years if Jesus tarries. When you finish it, you will look over the world scene for the emergence of that man of sin and charisma-like cunning who will mold the One World Order we hear so much about into the ten-toed kingdom of Daniel and Revelation. Then it will be only a step to deciding that New York City is too dangerous and too unrepresentative of the countries of the world to serve as the UN headquarters of the future. He will move it to Babylon, the future capital of the world.

Where will the money come from? Very simple. The present leadership of the UN is already asking for a ten cent tax for every electronic financial transaction in the world. That would net them over one and a half trillion dollars a year — more than enough to finance such a project. In addition, they are asking for a one dollar tax on every barrel of oil, plus one dollar for each airplane landing fee, and much more.

The first 50 years of history of the United Nations has been a mockery of ineptitude and impotence. That is about to change! Probably in the lifetime of many of us reading this book. For a cunning politician will soon arise with cleverness and craft in his mouth, and like the rider on the white horse in Revelation 6 he will wear a crown and go forth to conquer with a bow in his hand that has no arrows, meaning he will by diplomacy and the promise of "world peace," save the world for self-destruction by established autocratic control.

His next move will be to rebuild the city of Babylon, including a palace for himself. Read this book and see if you agree. Keep in mind as you read, however, that eventually our Lord will destroy "with the brightness of His coming," both the new city of Babylon, which will then be the international headquarters of the world, and that cunning leader who established it.

— Tim LaHaye

Introduction

There are no ideas of the human experience more electrifying than the prophecies of future events. Every major religion or philosophy has some futuristic development in its thinking. We all want more than a few troublesome years of this present fleshly sojourn. It does not fit the "highly developed facts of human experience" that we end our total existence under six feet of clay.

The modern New Agers are predicting a "Crystal Kingdom" to begin in A.D. 2012.[1] Kingdom Dominion theorists are preaching a golden age in which the Church takes dominion over the earth. In fact, they blame the doctrine of the pre-Tribulation Rapture as the culprit that has hindered the Church from this ill-conceived task. The hope of a golden age was so embedded in the Jewish mindset that the disciples of Jesus could not grasp His kingdom concepts. They wanted an earthly kingdom, but He came to establish a spiritual one. Even at His ascension in the Book of Acts, they were still asking the question, "Wilt thou at this time restore the kingdom to Israel?" (Acts 1:6).

Pharaoh Cheops of Egypt had two elaborate ships buried beside his pyramid. He believed that these ships were his passport to the realm of the gods. Although he spent 23 years of his reign preparing for this final trip using multi-millions of man hours of his slaves and literally the wealth of the great nation of Egypt; when it was finally over and his mummified body was buried in his cathedral tomb, his ships never sailed. They were recently unearthed and put on display in a beautiful museum behind his pyramid. What a revealing testimony to the hopelessness of pagan religions and their counterpart in our modern day, the New Age movement.

Thanks to the one supreme and only true God and the revelations of both His Son Jesus Christ and His unchanging Word; we are not left without hope. There is a future for all men and a glorious one for those who dare to trust the saving sacrifice of Christ's blood at Calvary.

Babylon

This book starts in Babylon, the pagan city, but ends up in the eternal city of Jerusalem and its eccelesiastical counterpart, New Jerusalem, coming down from God out of heaven. It is a book about hope. Paganism is real and it threatens every step of the human experience, but it will be judged and hope will prevail. Life is not a trip to nowhere unless you chance to follow the path of darkness that has Babylon for its capital. There is an antithesis or opposite to Babylon and it is Jerusalem and all of her children. "But Jerusalem which is above is free, which is the mother of us all" (Gal. 4:26). The children of light are the children of Jerusalem, while the children of darkness are the children of Babylon.

The country of Iraq, where Babylon is located, and the city of Jerusalem are in the absolute center of world attention and movements. That is not an accident! Human history has recorded the same at many intervals and will unquestionably end in like manner. Babylon is the original capital of all pagan religions. The first tower to a false god was built in this city. As the Great Tribulation period progresses and the sixth angel sounds the sixth trumpet, "I heard a great voice from the four horns of the golden altar which is before God, Saying to the sixth angel which had the trumpet, Loose the four angels which are bound in the great river Euphrates" [which flows beside the city of Babylon] (Rev. 9:13-14).

From this act by the angel are unleashed upon the earth 200 thousand thousand or 200 million demon spirits. They are bound in the dark regions beneath Babylon, the wicked city, and will be unleashed upon an unsuspecting world. Their reign is a reign of sheer hell and destruction. Babylon will be judged for her wickedness.

Jerusalem

The second city is Jerusalem, which is hated by anyone and everyone that has been captured by the spirit of Babylon. Every revelation of God, from the day of Abraham to the present, has focused on this eternal city. God himself has declared Jerusalem His earthly capital and beloved city. New Jerusalem will hover over the earthly city while Jesus Christ himself will sit on the throne of David and will be the light of the heavenly city, both at the same time.

It is our goal to unveil end-time events in this book. From the pre-Tribulation Rapture to the golden Millennium, all are seen in contrast with Babylon and Jerusalem and the final revelation of Jesus Christ.

New World Order Capital

The European Common Market will have future ties to the Antichrist kingdom and may well be a kind of prelude to the coming world government, but Babylon must become the primary capital. The revival of the Roman kingdom is biblical and this kingdom will be the last great act of human government. Each worldwide kingdom foretold by Daniel's interpretation of Nebuchadnezzar's dream and Daniel's own dream both identify Babylon as the final capital of world government. Both Nebuchadnezzar's dream and Daniel's dream were focused in Babylon and interpreted to suggest that this city would be the center. The first three of those world kingdoms all made Babylon their capital. I believe that the fourth kingdom will do the same. Babylon is the biblically designated city of every effort of Lucifer to establish his government to control the world. It all started in Babylon when Nimrod built the Tower of Babel. It will end in the same geographic location by its burial in the Euphrates River.

New World Religion Capital

The city of Rome has held central position as the false religious capital for much of the New Testament Church history. That is likely to change either before or after the rapture of the Church. Rome will share its apostate glory with Jerusalem when the ultimate false prophet and harlot woman of Revelation 17 are manifest to the world. It will be in Jerusalem that the abomination of desolation is erected at the middle point of the coming seven years of hell on earth. The Antichrist will seek to make God's chosen city a pagan paradise of evil. Already the Vatican is talking of becoming the principle government in the city of Jerusalem. There are many wonderful Catholics who honestly love the Lord and love the United States, and we are not talking about them.

In spite of the dark information, this is a book about hope. We are not left to human speculation, but serve a God who has prepared for us a city. We do not follow blind alleys leading to an undetermined destiny. The children of God are awaiting a future that exceeds the wildest dreams of all the utopians. One cannot learn of the future as marvelously revealed in our Holy Bible and meet its author without being filled with expectancy for His appearing. We await the manifestation of the Son of God with unspeakable joy. As we await His coming, let us learn of those movements and activities that signal the approaching hour.

[1]José Arguelles, "The Crystal Earth Papers." Reprinted from *NRI Trumpet,* July 1987.

Chapter 1

Babylon Rises from the Dust

The only biblical fulfillment in our generation that surpassed the rebuilding of ancient Babylon is the regathering of Israel to their God-given homeland. Babylon represents to the world system what Israel represents to biblical ideas and Christianity. The climax of all the ages is at hand. Everything must be in order. Judicial excellence must be perfectly satisfied. The Creator is ready to conclude the period within eternity that we call time. Human systems of religious and civic order have failed, but from that failure God has redeemed a remnant of godly men and women and it is time for their vindication. They will be His new kings and priests and will reign under His complete Holiness and perfect government forever and ever.

Babylon was the world system that popularized the vices of paganism and government control over the masses. Man was created to be the Creator's family and to live under His sovereign and spiritual Lordship. When our early fathers rejected His commandments, they accepted control by an evil system designed by Lucifer and carried out by the basest of men. Satan has always sought base men to be his emissaries. That is why carnal and worldly persons are found in high places of government. An evil system will lift the shrewd into positions of power to gain control over human lives. That is what the liberalism of America represents today. The ultimate struggle is between good and evil, godliness and godlessness.

William Buckley, one of America's foremost conservative thinkers, said the same in his book, *God and Man at Yale:* "But there was a nice rhetorical resonance and an intrinsic, almost nonchalant suggestion of an exciting symbiosis, so I let pass: 'I believe that the duel between Christianity and atheism is the most important in the world. I further believe that the struggle between individualism and collectivism is the same struggle reproduced on another level."[1]

Babylon of the Past

It is absolutely imperative that Babylon be rebuilt and once again heralded as the great city. God's final judgment cannot be complete unless the judgment equals the offense. It is not acceptable for Him to judge someone or something that symbolizes the offender. His judicial excellence requires perfect justice in complete harmony with the sin and rebellion that is judged. (i.e., He cannot judge you for someone else because you are similar to them.) The province and city of Babylon will be judged for her sin and stubbornness against the government and holiness of God.

The Babylonian wickedness introduced three major systems in opposition to God's rule of His creation. All three of these systems have continued from that day and have been the means of great evil and human catastrophe. Every cruelty known to man has sprung from one of these systems. They were expressed in earlier towns of Sumer, Assyria, Persia, and Egypt, etc., but were made fashionable by Babylon. Understanding these systems is imperative to this book and the rise of Babylon.

First System: Babylon made pagan religions fashionable. They took the base and deplorable idea of pantheism (matter as a series of gods representing every act or expression of nature) and elevated all of it to an art form. They incorporated art, drama, and music until the pagan ideas were beautifully represented in the highest expression of their culture. These ideas literally overwhelmed the populace and they gave to it their souls. Then they added sexual and carnal satisfaction with great feast days, celebrations, and pleasurable religious expressions, including sexual orgies and temple prostitution. The religious life became the center of the cultures and the king or queen was transformed into a god or goddess. The whole idea is a perfect picture of the New Age religion so popular today. It is religious Babylon seen in Revelation 17 and being joined by every religious system of our present world. Any religion that becomes primarily celebration, pomp and emotional titillation is following the Babylonian system.

Second System: Babylon then took the ideas of the city-states as known in Ur, Erech (Uruk), and many other small cities and gave it a philosophical and intellectual form. They raised government to a system of bureaucracies which permanently established control over the populace. They brought in representation from conquered small states and trained them to serve as their bureaucrats and then used them to control their own people. Building giant forms of bureaucracies, they made the people dependent on government. As government met human needs, it took on a god-like form. The state became all powerful, and the people gave up their independence.

Third System: Iraq today brags about the kind of educational system and inventions it gave the world through the Sumerian and Babylonian periods. Here is their own description:

> What is known is that they were a tremendously gifted and imaginative people. Their language, linguistically related to no other, ancient or modern, is preserved for us through the thousands

of clay tablets on which they inscribed and developed the first writing as yet known to man. Fortunately, the Sumerians were prolific writers and meticulous record-keepers: these tablets richly describe their existence. With the invention of writing, the simple village life could evolve into complex civilization. They developed schools for an educated elite and for the many scribes who were needed for all the record-keeping and letter-writing they liked to do. Not only business records were written down but also the first numbers, calendars, literature, laws, agricultural methods, pharmacopoeias, personal notes, maps, jokes, curses, religious practices, and thousands of lists and inventories of all manner of human interests.[2]

They made education a responsibility of the state and used it to promote state control. The educated elite came to claim authority and wisdom above the common people. Through the elitist educational system they were able to control thought and intellectual development. When government operates the educational program you have the fox in the hen house. This kind of a governmental run program takes on the form of the all-powerful state and squelches independent thinking so intrinsic to personal responsibility and true faith in God. These three systems are destined to be judged in the very geography of their origination.

Babylon Rises Again

A recent booklet published by the Iraqi government best describes their dream for rebuilt Babylon. The booklet's title itself is quite revealing: *From Nebuchadnezzar to Saddam Hussein, Babylon Rises Again.* (An edited form of this book is presented in chapter 3.) Let me quote the first five paragraphs.

Babylon rises again. Glorious in a glorious time. She is the lady of reviving centuries. Rising dignified and holy. Showing the great history of Iraq. Adding to its magnificence. And emphasizing its originality. The Phoenix of the new time rising alive from the ashes of the past to face the bright present that places it on a golden throne and bringing back to it its charming youth and unique glory.

Babylon was not a city made of rocks and bricks and full of events. It was not a forgotten place of the ancient past. In fact, Babylon is something else. Since its birth Babylon has stretched its arm to the future to be the place of wisdom and to represent the civilization and to remain as a glittering lighthouse in the dark nights of history. Here is Bab-ilu. . . .

It survived the ages, defied all times and overcame whatever threatened its existence. It won the battles by virtue of its great heritage and the formidable men, who carried that heritage, and defended it throughout the ages that produced unique heroes who know the originality of their city as it rises and revives to add to human civilization something new in writing, law, astronomy, medicine, arts, literature, commerce, agriculture, education, and mathematics. So history can start with it so that it remains the compass throughout the ages.

When Babylon was consisted of small city-states and separate dynasties, Hammurabi waged successive wars to unite these city-states so that Babylon remains as one city, as the bright light of civilization.

However, it suffered more and more from repeated attacks until Nebuchadnezzar came to power and reconstructed it. He built temples and high walls as he realized it was the pulpit of the first Iraqi civilization.

Today looks exactly like yesterday. After

long periods of darkness that enveloped the land of Babylon and concealed its characteristics, Saddam Hussein emerges from Mesopotamia, as Hammurabi and Nebuchadnezzar had emerged, at a time to shake the century old dust off its face. Saddam Hussein, the grandson of the Babylonians, the son of this great land is leaving his fingerprints everywhere. (*From Nebuchadnezzar to Saddam Hussein, Babylon Rises Again,* printed by Iraqi government.)

When you couple this dream of Iraqi President Saddam Hussein with present facts it makes an impressive picture. *World Press Review* ran a story in the February 1990 edition. Let me quote a few excerpts from that review. Here's how they described ancient Babylon:

And yet, for almost two millennia, Babylon was the most important city in the world. It was the commercial and financial center for all of Mesopotamia — the link connecting the Orient with the Mediterranean, Egypt with Persia. Its scribes and priests spread the cultural heritage of Sumeria, Chaldea, Assyria, and Ur — the arts of divination, astronomy, and accounting; private commercial law; and even the chariot — through the ancient world.

Then they gave a description of what is actually happening now:

Today, thousands of workers are reconstructing the ancient city of Babylon in the middle of the Iraqi desert. More than that of Marduk or even of Nebuchadnezzar, the new Babylon, expected to be finished in 1994 (the date has been revised because of the war), will be the city of Iraq's President Saddam Hussein. Though he has not had the martial successes of his distant predecessors, he is having his name stamped into the bricks with which the city is being restored. Every six feet along the new walls, there is a brick with an inscription in Arabic provided by the Iraqi president: "The Babylon of Nebuchadnezzar was reconstructed in the era of Saddam Hussein." Sixty million bricks have been laid so far.

It is very clear from this *World Press Review* that archaeologists (at least outside Iraq) think this is an unjustifiable adventure. They called it a "megalomaniacal Disneyland." Regardless, the Iraqi ruler continues. The progress was described in these words:

> Besides the palace of Nebuchadnezzar, which is almost complete, he plans to rebuild the summer palace, the temple of Hammurabi, the Greek theater, the processional way, and even the controversial Hanging Gardens, which many historians believe never existed. Three artificial hills, each almost 100 feet high, are being built on the plain. They will be planted with palm trees and vines. At the foot of the hills will be restaurants and perhaps a casino.

It is certainly exciting to preach a prophesied biblical truth for over 20 years and then watch as the great God of this universe fulfills all that you have preached. That is exhilarating, but the glory goes to God who has proven himself so completely faithful that every nuance of His Word is to be perfectly fulfilled. Living in a day of religious intellectualism, most ministers and teachers have given Bible truths relative interpretation. We are not searching for those hidden gems of revelation as the great reformers and revivalists of the past. We are satisfied with warmed-over homiletics.

The rebuilding of Babylon has caught the church leaders of our day by surprise and most of the ones I know are still denying that there is any significance. Very soon there will be no doubt. Here are some things you can watch for that will help strengthen this powerful biblical truth.

- Iraq will continue to be in the world news.
- This small nation will continue to be a sore spot in the Middle East and will gain political dominance.
- The rhetoric between Iraq and Israel will come and go until the fateful hour.
- Watch for a peace initiative between Iraqi leaders and Israeli moderates. This will eventually lead to a covenant of peace.
- Don't set a timetable on what is happening. Leaders could well come and go before the ultimate events in this nation of destiny.

Babylon Yet to be Destroyed in Biblical Fulfillment

A few brave souls have preached that the prophesied destruction of Babylon is yet future. Most Bible scholars have chosen the least controversial route of the convenient interpretation. They have taught that the great prediction of her destruction was complete and this city would never have a future. They cited such passages as, "And Babylon, the glory of kingdoms, the beauty of the Chaldees' excellency, shall be as when God overthrew Sodom and Gomorrah. It shall never be inhabited, neither shall it be dwelt in from generation to generation: neither shall the Arabian pitch tent there; neither shall the shepherds make their fold there" (Isa. 13:19-20). It certainly sounds convincing on the surface.

As we pointed out earlier in this chapter, Babylon is the human source of every foul institution that Satan has developed to control men. The pagan institutions of religion, the design of a governmental bureaucracy to control civil institutions and state controlled education are certainly his (Satan's) methods to establish his own government. God created men to be ruled by His theocracy. The invasion of sin changed that. Satan did not just induce men to slip up. Man fell into his arms and he became the god of this world. Every true believer has been a pilgrim and remnant since that day. We are not of this world, neither its systems.

Such debauchery, as I have described, must be judged. To think that judgment is complete in the past is to ignore many great biblical principles. Not only do we have direct scriptural proof that her judgment is future, the very idea of a final hour of restitution and revelation demands it. When the reconciliation of all things is at hand, both systems, God's and Satan's, must be seen in contrast. It will be forever and indelibly etched in man's mind that evil does not pay. Satan and sin will be seen in the light of eternal purity and justice and the elect will never desire the opposite of the Creator. After this impending judgment, there will never be another "Garden of Eden" catastrophe.

The Mystery Babylon, Mother of Harlots

The 18th chapter of Revelation is the picture of a revived political system, while chapter 17 is Babylon's pagan system of religion. The harlot decked with gold and precious stones and pearls, arrayed in purple and scarlet represents all false religions and the entire ecumenical religious crowd. Every religious idea from the crudest paganism to the pomp of Rome will be united in lust for wealth and political power. They will serve the political system and gain the allegiance of the multitudes. Religion is the most powerful unifying force on this earth. The Antichrist will use the harlot and then destroy her.

Here is the picture of the Babylonian political system destroying her religious ally, the harlot.

And he saith unto me, The waters which thou sawest, where the whore sitteth, are peoples, and multitudes, and nations, and tongues. And the ten horns which thou sawest upon the beast, these shall hate the whore, and shall make her desolate and naked, and shall eat her flesh, and burn her with fire. For God hath put in their hearts to fulfil his will, and to agree, and give their kingdom unto the beast, until the words of God shall be fulfilled (Rev. 17:15-17).

Just as Babylon under Hammurabi and Nebuchadnezzar used pagan religion to unify their control, the revived Babylon will do the same. But, remember, the political system always turns on the religious system when it has finished using her to gain the desired control over the people.

The Revived Political System of Babylon

Now we come to the actual rebuilding of this original city and her establishment as the leader of the world nations. Here are a few pertinent verses from Revelation 18:

> And after these things I saw another angel come down from heaven, having great power; and the earth was lightened with his glory. And he cried mightily with a strong voice, saying, Babylon the great is fallen, is fallen, and is become the habitation of devils, and the hold of every foul spirit, and a cage of every unclean and hateful bird. For all nations have drunk of the wine of the wrath of her fornication, and the kings of the earth have committed fornication with her, and the merchants of the earth are waxed rich through the abundance of her delicacies (Rev. 18:1-3). How much she hath glorified herself, and lived deliciously, so much torment and sorrow give her: for she saith in her heart, I sit a queen, and am no widow, and shall see no sorrow. Therefore shall her plagues come in one day, death, and mourning, and famine; and she shall be utterly burned with fire: for strong is the Lord God who judgeth her. And the kings of the earth, who have committed fornication and lived deliciously with her, shall bewail her, and lament for her, when they shall see the smoke of her

burning. Standing afar off for the fear of her torment, saying, Alas, alas, that great city Babylon, that mighty city! for in one hour is thy judgment come. And the merchants of the earth shall weep and mourn over her; for no man buyeth their merchandise any more: The merchandise of gold, and silver, and precious stones, and of pearls, and fine linen, and purple, and silk, and scarlet, and all thyine wood, and all manner vessels of ivory, and all manner vessels of most precious wood, and of brass, and iron, and marble (Rev. 18:7-12).

And a mighty angel took up a stone like a great millstone, and cast it into the sea, saying, Thus with violence shall that great city Babylon be thrown down, and shall be found no more at all. And the voice of harpers, and musicians, and of pipers, and trumpeters, shall be heard no more at all in thee; and no craftsman, of whatsoever craft he be, shall be found any more in thee; and the sound of a millstone shall be heard no more at all in thee; And the light of a candle shall shine no more at all in thee; and the voice of the bridegroom and of the bride shall be heard no more at all in thee; for thy merchants were the great men of the earth; for by thy sorceries were all nations deceived. And in her was found the blood of prophets, and of saints, and of all that were slain upon the earth (Rev. 18:21-24).

To read these passages leaves little doubt that the Holy Spirit is talking about a literal city. When Babylon is cited, the language is not symbolic language. To create symbolism by interpretative fiat is a horrible method of scriptural exegesis. It leaves the Holy Bible open to many intrusions that weaken its message. Once you accept the premise that this city is literal, then supportive truths emerge to strengthen the facts. Let us deal with a list of clear biblical support.

"Babylon the Great Is Fallen, Is Fallen"

"Babylon the great is fallen, is fallen." This is an incredible statement. If it appears only once in the Bible it would be powerful and dependable, but it is more than a statement, it is a theme. Babylon is destined for a specific act of God that will cause the whole earth to wonder. No doubt will be left that God the Creator had the last word. Look at the expression in this statement, "And he [the angel] cried mightily with a strong voice, saying, Babylon the great is fallen, is fallen" (Rev. 18:2). Our God intends to show this act to the whole world.

Again in Revelation 14 we have almost the exact words. The setting of this expression is an overview of the time of judgment. The exact words are, "And there followed another angel, saying, Babylon is fallen, is fallen, that great city, because she made all nations drink of the wine of the wrath of her fornication" (Rev. 14:8). This statement was made in conjunction with the worship of the Antichrist and his image, the mark of the beast, given to Satan's initiates and to God's great wrath against those who worship the devil and his cohorts.

What is striking is that these same words appear in Isaiah's treatment of the judgment of Babylon. "And behold, here cometh a chariot of men, with a couple of horsemen. And he answered and said, Babylon is fallen, is fallen; and all the graven images of her gods he hath broken unto the ground" (Isa. 21:9). Whenever such exact phraseology is used in Scripture we know that the Holy Spirit is arresting our attention. The wording is powerful proof that Isaiah and John are talking about the same judgment. We cannot ignore this fact.

Jeremiah made a similar statement by saying, "Babylon is suddenly fallen and destroyed: howl for her; take balm for her pain" (Jer. 51:8). In all four of these predictions of destruction, suddenness is clearly a factor. Babylon is to be destroyed in a devastating blow of judicial expression.

Historical facts clearly demonstrate that this has never happened. Her finely baked bricks have been used for centuries to build other buildings in the vicinity. A large town within visible sight named Hilliah is almost completely constructed of bricks with the name Nebuchadnezzar stamped in them. The area is a lively community of businessmen, professionals, educators, farmers, herdsmen, and Iraqi governmental functions. God's Word is specific when describing the final and complete judgment. It has not happened.

Even Saint Peter, when writing his first epistle, made mention of the church at Babylon. He said, "The church that is at Babylon elected together with you, saluteth you" (1 Pet. 5:13). Some have tried to establish that he was talking about Jerusalem or Rome, but such language would have been utterly foreign in Peter's day. If he had meant spiritual Babylon, the Holy Spirit would have inspired him to say that. That is the kind of confidence we can have in our verbally inspired, infallible Word of God.

The Arabs to be Judged in Babylon

The Holy Scripture clearly states that Arabians will be the occupants of this nation in the final hour of judgment. In previous times when Babylon was attacked and defeated, its occupants were Sumerians, Assyrians, Chaldeans, Persians, or Grecians, but never Arabians. In fact, it was in A.D. 637 that the first Arab empire was established in Mesopotamia. A northern city of Hatra was built and inhabited by Arabs about the time of Christ, but it was never more than a city state. The first Arab government in Iraq was called the Abbasid Empire.

Here is another great evidence of biblical prophecy stating names and places hundreds of years in advance. Isaiah spoke by the Holy Spirit and prophesied, "And Babylon, the glory of kingdoms, the beauty of the Chaldees' excellency, shall be as when God overthrew Sodom and Gomorrah. It shall never be inhabited, neither shall it be dwelt in from generation to generation: neither shall the

Arabian pitch tent there; neither shall the shepherds make their fold there" (Isa. 13:19-20). Isaiah even called Babylon the beauty of the Chaldees yet saw it occupied by the Arabians. This clearly puts the final judgment of this evil city after A.D. 637 and no such event has taken place in these intervening years. Another example of a small "jot or tittle" awaiting fulfillment in God's pre-established hour.

Israel to Possess the Babylonians

The judgment of Babylon goes beyond the destruction of the city itself. Very important details can easily be seen as we view the larger picture. Those small details give specific information. Israel is destined to possess the Babylonians as servants even as they were once possessed. Isaiah said:

> For the Lord will have mercy on Jacob, and will yet choose Israel, and set them in their own land: and the strangers shall be joined with them, and they shall cleave to the house of Jacob. And the people shall take them [Babylonians], and bring them to their place: and the house of Israel shall possess them in the land of the Lord for servants and handmaids: and they shall take them captives, whose captives they were; and they shall rule over their oppressors (Isa. 14:1-2).

This has never been fulfilled. The golden kingdom of Israel is immediately after the tribulation of the last days when Babylon will be destroyed. Israel will possess the promised land stretching all the way to the Euphrates River and those whom she served will then be her servants and handmaids. Not one promise of the Word can fail and this will be fulfilled.

Companion Prophecies (Isaiah 47, Revelation 18)

The 47th chapter of Isaiah is his most vivid description of Babylon's judgment, filled with clear details and descriptive events. Revelation 18 is equally descriptive and similar beyond accident. There is no comparison in the two testaments more striking than these. Many quotes from the Old Testament by New Testament writers are far less similar than we see in these. Neither should be doubted because the New Testament is the completion of the Old Testament.

Let's compare several passages. We will list the Isaiah text on the left and the Revelation text on the right.

Isaiah Text

Come down, and sit in the dust, O virgin daughter of Babylon, sit on the ground: there is no throne, O daughter of the Chaldeans: for thou shalt no more be called tender and delicate (Isa. 47:1).

Revelation Text

For all nations have drunk of the wine of the wrath of her fornication, and the kings of the earth have committed fornication with her, and the merchants of the earth are waxed rich through the abundance of her delicacies (Rev. 18:3).

Therefore hear now this, thou that are given to pleasures, that dwellest carelessly, that sayest in thine heart, I am, and none else beside me; I shall not sit as a widow, neither shall I know the loss of children (Isa. 47:8).

How much she hath glorified herself, and lived deliciously, so much torment and sorrow give her: for she saith in her heart, I sit a queen, and am no widow, and shall see no sorrow (Rev. 18:7).

But these two things shall come to thee in a moment in one day, the loss of children, and widowhood: they shall come upon thee in their perfection for the multitude of thy sorceries, and for the great abundance of thine enchantments (Isa. 47:9).

Therefore shall her plagues come in one day, death, and mourning, and famine; and she shall be utterly burned with fire: for strong is the Lord God who judgeth her (Rev. 18:8).

Thou are wearied in the multitude of thy counsels. Let now the astrologers, the stargazers, the monthly prognosticators, stand up, and save thee from these things that shall come upon thee (Isa. 47:13).

And the light of a candle shall shine no more at all in thee; and the voice of the bridegroom and of the bride shall be heard no more at all in thee: for thy merchants were the great men of the earth; for by thy sorceries were all nations deceived (Rev. 18:23).

I suggest that you read these two chapters several times and do a verse by verse study. They will yield many more similarities.

Babylon, The Seat of Sorceries and Paganism

This infamous city has provided the world with Satan's clever duplication of the true faith and the one true God. The account of the Genesis creation is matched with the epic of creation, Babylonian style. The Flood of Noah has its counterpart in the epic of Gilgamesh. Even the biblical jurisprudence given by God to Moses has its contrast in the Code of Hammurabi. All of these satanic counterparts are far inferior and always filled with theological, moral, and philosophical distinctions that leave no doubt to their origin. Satan is the idiot god that rebelled against the Holy God.

Satan is having his last fling. Babylonian-style mythologies are experiencing worldwide interest. America has its New Age religion with multitude expressions of the occultic. From hit movies like "Pocahontas" to the metaphysical charismatic churches, our nation is on a binge of pleasure, riches, and superstition. Even jewelry is no longer simple worldiness. It is now an intimate part of the seduction scheme. New Agers are reproducing the Babylonian spirit in every conceivable idea. The very "elect" will be deceived if possible. The words "if possible" means if you do not have the guards of the "Word" upon the frontlets of your spiritual eyes you are in grave danger of being deceived.

Babylon Rises Again!

Go with me on a visit to the actual city of Babylon where workmen are busy laying brick and rebuilding the walls. Two of America's foremost television personalities were in Babylon just before the Middle East War of 1990-91 (more in chapter 3). They documented on American television the facts of this emerging ancient city in the plains of Iraq. After our visit to the city and the Babylonian festival, we will explore additional biblical support for this city's future and its judgment.

[1] William Buckley, *God and Man at Yale* (New Haven, CT: Yale University, 1977), page xviii.

[2] *Historical Iraq*, newsletter published by the Iraq Education & Tourism Department as Information Series No. 02 [no date given].

Chapter 2

A Personal Visit

To visit Iraq and see the walls of the ancient city of Babylon towering out of the dust of its long decay is beyond description. The spirit you encounter among those walls is the exact opposite of what one feels in Jerusalem, but nonetheless breathtaking. Biblical and spiritual discernment easily identifies the spirit of Babylon as the same diabolical spirit this city has represented since the days of Nimrod. It is a city of unclean spirits and dark deeds that has opposed the true God and His eternal revelations.

When you listen to the modern Iraqi music in the rebuilt theater, you understand why Abraham quickly obeyed the voice of God and left this demonic, cursed region to seek a land of promise and the new city that God would choose. It is clearly God-forsaken and eternally cursed. The future of this city is set in biblical immutability, nevertheless it must fulfill its final chapter. And fulfill it it will.

The Antichrist is clearly connected to this city in biblical prophesy. He will be an Assyrian from the ancient empire of Assyria (probably a man of mixed ancestry from Assyrian and Jewish decent) according to Micah the prophet.

And this man shall be the peace, when the Assyrian shall come into our land: and when he shall tread in our palaces, then shall we raise against him seven shepherds, and eight principal men. And they shall waste the land of Assyria with the sword, and the land of Nimrod [Babylon] in the entrances thereof: thus shall he deliver us from the Assyrian, when he cometh into our land, and when he treadeth within our borders (Mic. 5:5-6).

Here he is unquestionably connected with Babylon (land of Nimrod), but clearly called "the Assyrian." The ancient empire of the Assyrians included much of present day Syria, Turkey, Iraq, Iran, and parts of other Arab countries at different intervals.

It is my clear conviction that the rebuilt city of Babylon will be his chief capital and palace. While he will become a world dictator, his beloved Babylon will be his favorite attraction for his wealth and grandeur. Its former glory will be eclipsed and the world will wonder with "great admiration." Saddam Hussein is probably just a flash in the pan, but his ability to survive and continue to build this ancient city suggests more for the city of Babylon itself. The Bible is always to be taken literally unless it clearly indicates otherwise. Every discussion of Babylon or the land of Shinar in futuristic prophecy is clearly literal. Let us visit this ancient city together and share the "International Babylonian Festival" that was held again, starting in 1992, after two years of cancellation.

Journal of My Trip to Babylon, Iraq

After preaching for 20 years that Babylon would be rebuilt, I was measurably thrilled to witness the actual evidence in person. The Iraqi government has already invested over 100 million dollars in the new city. With the war between Iran and Iraq ending, there was clear evidence that the pace would increase significantly.

The famous Hanging Gardens were being rebuilt, but we were not allowed into that section.

Ishtar, the famous goddess of Babylon, was the star of the "Babylonian Festival." I heard such words as "Ishtar has come again to Baghdad" (capital city). She was worshiped in the dramas and extolled in music. The mood was such as to suggest that an Ishtar cult was developing.

This goddess (Ishtar) is the same as Issi (Egyptian) which is experiencing a revival in America. A prominent witch in Salem, Massachusetts, leads a coven of 2,000 followers of Issi. She was declared the official witch of Salem by a former governor in 1977 and has taught classes on witchcraft at the Salem University. Right on the streets of Charlotte, North Carolina, a ceremony with a golden calf, priest, incense, and chants to the Egyptian gods (Issi included) was offered as an opening for the Rameses II exhibit. (I was in Iraq when this happened.) The title for this event was listed in the Mint Museum as the following: "Netherworld Spirits Invited to Join Charlotte Jubilee Festival."

Please join with me as I share with you a day by day account of my trip, a diary of sorts. We'll start in Charlotte, North Carolina, where I boarded a Pan Am flight for New York. Welcome aboard!

12:45 p.m., September 20: Just seated on Pan Am 588, Charlotte, North Carolina. Juanita and I have never been apart for two weeks. Once I was in Israel for ten days. That was horrible. Telling my family goodbye for two weeks was rough for me. Christa came over with her mom (my daughter, Theresa) from Tennessee for a few hours. Tanya, my daughter, came to the airport to spend a few minutes before I got on the plane. She is a sweet daughter indeed. Tiffany, Caleb, and Curtis (my three older grandbabies) loved me "bye" at the church. My son, Terry and his wife, Anne, along with Tanya's husband, Rick, were very special. Mike, my other son-in-law, would have been present if he had been able to come from Tennessee.

The entire school seemed to make something special out of my trip. That was really nice. There is a wonderful fellowship in our entire ministry. Praise the Lord!

Trip To Babylon: Iraq was called Mesopotamia in prior history. When Abraham left that area for the Promised Land, it was said he was from "Ur of the Chaldees." This is the place where civilization began. The Garden of Eden was located in the southern tip where the Tigris and Euphrates Rivers meet. Apparently, God himself touched His feet upon the plains of Shinar, for it was said that He visited Adam in the cool of the day.

I am reading the Book of Hebrews again as I travel toward my destination. "And, Thou, Lord, in the beginning hast laid the foundation of the earth; and the heavens are the works of thine hands" (Heb. 1:10). It seemed that our Creator must have seen this area as a garden spot and blessed it with special blessings. One can only imagine the beauty that met the eye when Iraq was seen in its pristine glory.

I shared Christ with a lovely lady named Carol on my way from Raleigh to New York. Just before we landed the Holy Spirit allowed me to break through and reach her heart. She was quite an intellectual (raised a Catholic) but had left her faith. She was so hungry for real bread. As she cleared the tears, I told her where the "safe haven" was found. She will be saved within a short time, no doubt about it. Jesus never fails!

5:25 p.m., September 20, John F. Kennedy Airport cafeteria: My plane leaves at 7:00 p.m. A Royal Air Maroc plane is taxiing down for takeoff ("Swiss," someone said.) I just sent my family (all four houses) their first card from Paw-Paw. What a family I've got! Yesterday (in Charlotte) the Holy Spirit showed me that a man's children are an extension of himself. When they are in ministry, he is in ministry. When any of my children have lived in other cities I have suffered terribly. Yet, this gives us peace when we must be separated. We want to see every little antic of our grandchildren. I guess they would survive without Paw-Paw's constant hand. (NOTE: These kids just don't know how to raise our grandbabies.)

The Paw Creek family is so special. I'm more convinced than ever that a pastor must be able to love every individual in his congregation. Super churches (Wal-Mart centers) just don't meet the needs of people. When a church outgrows the pastor, they should divide and start a new church in another part of town. Really, a Bible-centered and Jesus-centered church will be sending people all over the world in ministry and will never become cloistered behind four walls. My perspective of this has been so wrong. I believe God is cleansing me of this ego-trip mentality. A Northwest and Scandinavian plane just passed my window. This is certainly an international airport.

7:10 p.m., September 20, JFK Airport, New York, New York: Pan Am Flight #2 is ready for takeoff to London, England. It is a jumbo jet 747, seating 407 passengers, not counting the crew. It looks like a giant hotel lobby inside (two aisles with ten seats across). The stewardess just told us to set our watches up for London time. I moved my watch from 7:10 p.m. to 12:10 a.m. (September 21, 1988). Joshua commanded the sun to stand still. The jet age moves it forward (or backward), at least as you travel into time (time zones).

We have a hearty dinner and then I try to sleep. I lay on the floor, across two seats (hostess seats without hostesses), cuddled up in my seat many ways, but finally give up. We have breakfast at 5:30 a.m. (12:30 p.m., Charlotte time). We are moving into the sunrise, which means it is getting light at about double the normal rate. London is just ahead. We are still over the ocean. The calm of the sea beneath (and in this giant plane) appears unreal. What a world my Father has created!

The calm and rest I feel does not compare with the promise of Hebrews 4:1: "Let us therefore fear, lest, a promise being left us of entering into His rest, any of you should seem to come short of it." His rest is a gift of grace for those who can trust that His redemption work is finished and our duty is unquestioning faith.

9:30 a.m. (Charlotte, 4:30 a.m.), September 21, London, England, Flight 238 to Baghdad, Iraq: We are leaving for our destination at approximately 10:00 a.m. Then it will be time to move the watches ahead to 1:00 p.m. I'm exhausted. Making it to Baghdad, through customs, and the trip to our hotel will certainly finish me off. It is an unusual world for me. I just met a professor from Dallas Theological University. This is his second trip to study Babylon from a biblical perspective. Everyone else appears to be Iraqi or at least Arab. Their culture is different, but I plan to enjoy getting acquainted. Off to Baghdad, Iraq.

3:30 p.m. (Baghdad time), September 21: I've met several very kind people on the plane. They have been very friendly and helpful. Everybody is asking about the International Babylon Festival.

5:05 p.m., Istanbul, Turkey: We are making a refueling stop. As we taxi to the airport, we pass a Turkish plane named Bogasigi and come to a full stop beside a Saudi Arabian Airlines 747. It was in Turkey at Mt. Ararat that the ark came to rest. After unboarding, Noah and his family began their migration that eventually brought them back to the plains of Mesopotamia or Iraq. It was in this same land where God made the promise to Abraham and swore by himself that He would make his seed to be as the sand of the sea.

8:55 p.m. (12:55 p.m. Charlotte), Hossad Airport, Baghdad, Iraq: Approximately 24 hours and 10 minutes after leaving Charlotte, North Carolina, USA, we arrive at our destination. Mahasen Yono from the Iraqi Embassy meets us at the airport. She zips us through customs and all the red tape. Very simple. The Iraqi Airport is one of the most beautiful I have ever seen. It is an elaborate international hub. Evidence of Babylonian artifacts is everywhere expressed in art forms; especially in large murals on the walls.

We arrive at our hotel, "Al-Mansour Melia," about 11:00 p.m. After a good soaking in hot water, I go to bed.

That is all I can remember. *Immediate comatose!*

5:00 a.m., Thursday, September 22: The International Babylon Festival begins today. I finally reach Juanita at 5:50 a.m. (9:50 p.m. Wednesday evening, Charlotte). She and I are both delighted to tell each other, "I love you." She is a sweetheart. The phone goes dead after four minutes. They tell me that the only time to make connection with the USA by phone is between 4:00 a.m and 6:00 a.m. That is going to be rough for me. Breakfast in a few minutes. I'm still in Hebrews:

> Saying, Surely blessing I will bless thee, and multiplying I will multiply thee. And so, after he had patiently endured, he obtained the promise. For men verily swear by the greater: and an oath for confirmation is to them an end of all strife. Wherein God, willing more abundantly to show unto the heirs [that's all of us] of promise the immutability of His counsel, confirmed it by an oath. That by two immutable things, in which it was impossible for God to lie, we might have a strong consolation, who have fled for refuge to lay hold upon the hope set before us: Which hope we have as an anchor of the soul, both sure and steadfast, and which entereth into that within the veil; Whither the forerunner is for us entered, even Jesus, made an high priest for ever after the order of Melchisedec (Heb. 6:14-20).

What a blessing (historical facts included) to read this the first morning in Iraq, just a few miles from where Abraham heard God's Word and started his walk of faith. Remember, because "he believed God" he became the father of faith. Oh, how our Father wants us to believe and trust Him. He counts it for righteousness and we then inherit all His promises. This trip is a faith venture for me and already I'm sensing I'll not be the same.

My first Iraqi breakfast: It is delicious! Boiled eggs, fresh olives, beef, chicken, boiled beans, milk, juice, all kinds of sweet rolls, coffee — I try everything.

This morning we visit two places of extreme importance to modern Iraq. A memorial to the unknown soldier is our first stop. This monument is said to honor all men who have given sacrificially to defend their country. It is an elaborate ceremony. Hundreds of young people dressed in uniforms, waving flags and other ceremonial items line the elevated processional to the top of this multi-million-dollar memorial. They chant what is interpreted to mean, "We will die for our president (Saddam Hussein) and our country." It is expressive of a very military mindset.

Our second stop is at an unfinished but grandiose memorial called "Saddam Martyrs' Monument." At a cost of 40 million dinars (approximately 50 million dollars), this elaborate show of wealth and national pride is presented as a memorial to the Iraq-Iran War martyrs. President Saddam Hussein is clearly the show.

It is the most beautiful and ornate expression of nationalism I have ever witnessed. The main design is patterned after the dome of a Moslem prayer tower. It is constructed of multi-colored ceramic tiles (approximately 2 x 4 inch pieces, 40 meters wide and 45 meters high — one meter = 3'10"). Promenades in polished marble are going in all directions. Two levels of museum and historical space are beneath (underground) the main area. It is a magnificent edifice.

Back at our hotel we have a tasty Iraqi buffet lunch that no American restaurant could surpass. No food (meats, vegetables, etc.) is used unless it is fresh. The pastries and breads are exceptional. I spend the afternoon resting (comatose would be a better word). Remember, it's Thursday; I left home on Tuesday, 12:45 p.m., lost eight hours in time change, did not go to bed on Tuesday evening, and only slept five hours Wednesday night.

And now the opening ceremonies of the "Second Babylon International Festival." The theme of this second annual event is *"From Nebuchadnezzar to Saddam Hussein, Babylon Rises Again."*

We ride by Iraqi bus from our hotel in Baghdad to the city of Babylon (100 kilometers; 60 miles). Riding in buses with the Iraqi is an experience. Each driver must prove that he is more brave and courageous than the next. The horn is the most important part of the bus. It is an instrument of intimidation and it works! Once on site we join a large throng of people and march by torchlight to the Procession Street of the ancient city. This particular street, at least 75 feet wide by 300 feet long, with its high restored walls is the location for the opening ceremony.

After a brief statement in Arabic, the mystic-sounding event begins. Background music with a mythological ring heralds the drama of a returning monarch. "King Nebuchad-nezzar" enters with great fanfare. Paganistic incense fills the air as the worshippers of this god-like king march to his tune. The ceremonial dress is the ancient Babylonian attire. Other than the amplification, strobe lights and fireworks, it is very authentic. The air is pregnant with excitement (or evil, depending on your perspective).

Clearly, President Saddam Hussein is believed by the Iraqis to be the new Arabic Messiah ready to lead the Arab people to unparalleled greatness. This nation, with the world's second largest production of oil, has the wealth and means to affect the entire world's economy. Will they be part of the Antichrist's world government and help produce unparalleled prosperity for a short period? I have no doubt they will.

After the opening ceremony, we move down (literally) through the old excavated streets where Daniel actually walked 2,500 years ago. Beneath the torches, along the top of these massive walls with Babylonian-costumed torch-bearers lining the passageways, we walk beside ceramic lions inset in the masonry. Words hardly describe one's feelings. A courtyard area provides the location for refresh-ments as we view the artistic renderings of Babylon's heyday. A museum is adjacent to this area and open for a look at ancient artifacts and a model presentation of Babylon's past glory. From here, we move to the restored amphitheater for music and more drama. After a performance by the Iraqi National Symphony Orchestra and the Bayarih Musical Band (music in many languages), a fashion show begins.

I am surprised when this drama by the Iraqi House of Fashion becomes a mythological presentation of everything from the Babylonian epic of creation to a breathtaking picture of Ishtar, the goddess of fertility. Incense and worship are dramatically blended into a glowing history of Iraq's past. The cradle of creation is evident, but the God of creation is missing. I am so glad I have Him in my heart!

Again, this drama highlights the comparison of Nebuchadnezzar and Saddam Hussein. I have no doubt that this ancient city will play a strategic part in the future kingdom of the coming Prince. Whether President Hussein will be an intimate personality, the future must reveal.

We arrive back at our hotel at 1:30 a.m. on Friday. After soaking for a little physical relief, I have the privilege of five hours of sleep before another day begins.

8:00 a.m., Friday, September 23: I'm all confused. The sense of what day it is has escaped me. They say I am okay and this is all normal. Nothing else seems okay, so why should this? See, I told you I am confused. Forget it.

To add to all this I am having an Iraqi breakfast of lamb kidneys smothered in mushrooms. Honest, the meals are excellent! Absolutely, I'm not lying. I'm confused, but I'm still honest.

After breakfast, they tell us it is a Moslem holy day and there will be no trips. In a few minutes they change their minds and off we go to an Iraqi museum. No one has any idea that we are about to see a fabulous collection of ancient discoveries. We have one hour to see thousands of pieces of the artifacts of the ages. It is an archaeological haven. I sure hope my pictures are good. No flashes are allowed and the lighting is very poor. I do my best.

We travel through Baghdad for a look at this massive city. Next to gold-capped mosque domes, we see impoverished souls hawking their goods for survival. It is a contrast between panting hearts and misguided spirits. It testifies that greatness is not wealth nor is poverty particularly weakness. Human wealth is surely in the soul. I am spending the rest of today putting it all together and reading.

7:10 p.m., Saturday, September 24: Sleep is not an easy task when your schedule is all fouled up. I am living eight hours ahead of my normal time frame.

I was able to reach Juanita about 6:00 a.m. It was our second time to talk since I left home Tuesday. My family is a special part of my life. I miss being able to call my children and the grandbabies on this trip. Phone service out of Baghdad to the USA is almost impossible and both times we are cut off in the middle of conversation.

I plan to make contact this morning for a special guide and driver to places of extreme importance to my trip. It is suggested I give my first two days to their schedule since I am a guest of the Iraqi government with all expenses paid. Tomorrow I have an appointment with our American Embassy. They have promised a special briefing and tour of the compound. I am reading everything I can get my hands on about Iraq.

Charlie, my new friend from Dallas Theological University, and I have breakfast together. Each morning is a bit different; several meats (hamburger, beef liver, chicken), vegetables, and pastries. Everything is cooked with onions (no wonder my stomach keeps burning) and mushrooms. The egg omelet is light and filled with mushrooms today. A nice breakfast!

I decide to make some things happen toward my research efforts. After a call or two, I have an appointment with the directorate general of the External Department (Iraqi Information News Agency), Mr. Al Mukhtar. It is for 1:30 p.m. I use the time before my appointment to go shopping in the streets of Iraq. This is going to be an adventure into the unknown. The protocol agent from the news agency gives me instructions: No cameras, nothing to fear, cross over the Tigris River (by bridge), turn right, and you'll be there.

There are hundreds of little shops in a honeycomb of streets and alleyways. There are very small restaurants, bread shops (baking bread), vendors selling yogurt right out of tin tubs, fresh grapes, garages, and woodworking shops all blended together. I decide to buy some fruit to eat. I hold up an Iraqi coin and point to a basket of beautiful grapes. The man seems very unhappy and lets me know - no sale. I try at the next vendor and his treatment is equal. Suddenly, I realize he thinks I want to buy the whole basket for one small coin. Then I cup my hand to indicate a small amount. After this, he gives me a bunch and will not take any money. How foolish I feel!

At one point, I decide to cross the main street (six lanes). After waiting for clear traffic and watching brave souls dashing between cars, I decide to keep shopping on the same side. I want to go to heaven, but not from the port of Baghdad. You would probably need to watch them drive and hear the incessant blowing of horns to understand. They even blow their horns when nobody is in front. Can you imagine what they do in crowded traffic?

My appointment is in a new ten-story government building. The entire compound in which the building is located is fenced, guarded by soldiers carrying AK47 machine guns, and has an anti-aircraft platoon on top. (There is a very fragile cease-fire between Iraq and Iran at the moment, and this area has been shelled in the past.) By the way, my hotel is across the street.

Mr. Al Mukhtar is very cordial and extremely intelligent. I share my plans for my book. After we discuss what I have already seen in his country and how little of this information is known by the outside world, he agrees that the archaeological significance must become available to other cultures. He makes some calls to subordinates and tells me I am going to see everything from north to south. We plan a meeting for dinner at the end of my stay in Iraq with a promise to share information. His subordinate tells me to make a list of everything I want to see and return early Sunday morning. It looks like it is going to happen.

Back in my hotel I call my Iraqi friend, Mr. Jamil, whom I met on the plane from London. I had met his family at the airport and he had given me his phone number. He and his son, Jamal, come to the hotel to pick me up and give me a beautiful private tour of the city (very different from a crowded bus with no English translator). Jamal speaks perfect English and is presently graduating with an engineering degree from the University.

After the tour, they take me to their home. Beautiful! They live on the Tigris River with a large patio overlooking the water: three stories, garage underneath, and cooled with a water cooler. It is very evident that Mr. Jamil is a successful businessman. His family became my dear friends. They take me out to a Lebanese restaurant located in an old landowner's mansion that also faces the Tigris. When we enter, I immediately spot Senator Gary Hart (probably spending taxpayers' money). I go over to speak only to find he is with our American Ambassador. He is very friendly. She (Madam Ambassador April Glaspie) immediately says she had been awaiting my call because Senator Jesse Helms had written her that I was coming. (Later, I called her office and made an appointment to meet with her Sunday morning; Friday and Saturday is the weekend in Iraq.) The meal is delicious. This day has been very eventful, and I'm ready for bed.

I am awake at 3:00 in the morning, writing in bed in the middle of the night. I'm totally alone, except for Jesus.

7:30 a.m., Sunday, September 25: The breakfast is nice, but the same as previous mornings. I spend considerable time in the "news agency" getting the necessary information for research. Now I am waiting for a call. The directorate general is supposedly assigning me a guide from the Archaeological Department with driver and car for the next few days. It is very evident that my Heavenly Father is in control.

The American ambassador has just invited me (11:30 a.m.) to her official residence that is provided for our American representative in Iraq. She sounds very hospitable, and I look forward to hearing how our country is represented in this Islamic nation.

Most of my Sabbath day is spent in my room with the Word of God. About 6:30 p.m. (10:45 a.m., Sunday, Paw Creek Church), I experience a wonderful time with the Lord. During church time in Charlotte, I am having church time in Baghdad. Praise the Lord!

Old-fashion sanctification (a definite second work of grace) is booming big in my heart. I believe a new revival of holiness and dedication is coming to my beloved country. It is the only answer for the compromise, worldliness, and ego-churchism of the present. Jesus is life, and that life is available as we partake of His very nature. Listen to Jesus:

> I pray not that thou shouldest take them out of the world, but that thou shouldest keep them from the evil [tendency to follow fleshly and carnal things]. They are not of the world, even as I am not of the world. Sanctify (set apart from the profane unto His holiness) them through Thy truth: Thy word is truth (John 17:15-17).

The only solution to a worldly and world pleasing church is living in the sanctification experience. The apostle Paul said, "But I keep under my body, and bring it into subjection: lest that by any means, when I have preached to others, I myself should be a castaway" (1 Cor. 9:27).

The ability we have to sanctify ourselves (set ourselves apart from doing evil) is when His sanctification power is working in our life. In other words, our definite experience (second work of grace) in holiness becomes His grace for our personal obedience to all that is commanded for the godly walk in righteousness. It is all by grace and unmerited favor, yet our free choice of surrender will never be transcended in our present bodies. We joyously obey because

His divine nature is at work in our hearts.

6:45 a.m., Monday, September 26: I dedicate myself to a new fellowship in the divine life of my Saviour. "Likewise reckon ye also yourselves to be dead indeed unto sin, but alive unto God through Jesus Christ our Lord" (Rom. 6:11). It is a finished work and I receive it. Breakfast time!

After breakfast, we go on an official tour to see the display of weapons that the Iraqi army had taken from the Iranians. It is awesome — worth in the billions of dollars and most of it built by America. This represents military equipment we sold to the Shah before the Ayatollah Khomeini came to power in Iran. It is frightening to be in the midst of this kind of weaponry. I could see, in my mind's eye, the Iranians mutilated and piled up all over this war machinery.

When the Prince of Peace sets up His kingdom, war will cease. Swords will become reaping tools for the gathering of barley and wheat. Tanks will become tractors for cultivating the well-watered soil, while the wealth of nations will create a paradise on earth. What a day that is going to be!

Lunch! Too much Iraqi food. My stomach hurts, and hurt it does for two days. All my new friends are trying to help. Please forgive the break in information unless you want to know some very private details.

Tuesday, a.m.: I struggle out of bed long enough to go to the Iraqi News Agency. I have waited two days for a guide and the plans for my research. After waiting three hours in and out of the director's office, I decide to use the Iraqi method. Acting very upset, I pace around, go up to the desk, argue, try to call the directorate general, and finally I take off toward the elevator to go to the eighth floor where his office is located. Remember, those guards with AK47's outside? They come after me with a questionable look on their faces, I do not want to go to jail, but neither do I like wasting my time. In 10 minutes I have a guide for the next several days. It works. You have got to act like one of them!

One hitch is that I have to furnish my own transportation. I am feeling terrible, but I make calls until I have a car, driver, and the time is set. We will leave for Nineveh (440 km. north) at 3:00 a.m. I go to bed and sleep most of the time until about 2:20 Wednesday morning, and away we go.

We arrive in Nineveh about 7:15 a.m. We have a nice breakfast at a beautiful new hotel on the Tigris River. Our guide takes us to the External Information Department. In a few minutes we have a police escort with three guards and the directorate general from the Mosul (modern Nineveh) Museum. We are traveling in style. I am treated as a special guest in their city.

Our first stop is at the Palace of Ashurnasispal in Nimrud. Can you imagine walking through the rooms and halls where a famous king of the Assyrians lived almost 3,000 years ago? We pass the mammoth lions with human faces while we are awed by carved alabaster walls with continuous lines of writing perfectly straight around the perimeter of the entire inside. The palace itself is 200 x 130 meters (666 ft. x 432 ft., over 6 acres) The alabaster walls (6" thick, plus the support) have thousands of beautifully carved life-size reliefs of the king, angels, warriors, gods, and strange mythological creatures.

Inscriptions that have been deciphered reveal this description of the palace: "A palace of cedar, cypress, juniper, box wood, mulberry, pistachio wood, and tamarind, for my royal dwelling and for my lordly pleasure for all the time I found therein. Beasts of the mountains and of the seas of white limestone and alabaster I fashioned and set them up in its gates — Door leaves of cedar, cypress, juniper, and mulberry I hung in the gates thereof; and silver, gold, lead, copper, and iron, the spoil of my hand from the lords which I had brought under my sway in great quantities I took and placed therein."

The palace is still being excavated, with new discoveries taking place regularly. Four months earlier a marvelous find was made. A grave of a princess was unearthed under the palace floor. Millions of dollars worth of gold jewelry was still in her tomb. I descend into the grave and witness the actual clay tomb in which she was buried. This jewelry represents a breathtaking discovery revealing the refined capability of the goldsmiths of that period. The results are on display in the Iraqi museum which we had witnessed earlier.

Very few individuals have been allowed to visit this unfinished excavation. Words are not expressive enough to describe what we see.

Immediately behind the old palace is the main temple (three temples set around the palace) where King Ashurnasispal is said to have worshiped. Apparently, very few individuals have been allowed in this area. We have to wait a considerable time for someone to unlock the gate. A statue of a fish is on the left just before the main entrance. The main structure is divided to allow for an outer court, an inner court, and then the holy of holies containing the altar, etc. Apparently, a family of three gods was worshiped in this temple.

From here we visit the Mosul Museum. It is filled with treasures from ancient Nineveh history. Close by the museum are portions of the original Nineveh city walls with the mammoth western gate. Not far away stands a northern corner gate equally impressive. This city in its day of greatness covered hundreds of acres and was completely enclosed for protection.

As we return toward Baghdad we stop at another unfinished excavation: the 2,000-year-old city of Hatra. Hatra was built by the first Arab chieftains to rule in Mesopotamia (modern Iraq). The original walled city was 9 kilometers (5.4 miles) around the perimeter with a second inside wall of 6 kilometers (3.6 miles). The chieftain's or kinglet's palace was enclosed with a third wall with at least 12 temples to different gods. These were magnificent sculptures, complete with many statues. The arches over the temple entrance were simply exquisite with carved figures, apparently of other local gods.

A last stop is at Sammarah where the tallest minaret in

Iraq is located. Each Moslem mosque has a minaret where the leader calls the followers to prayer five times a day. This particular tower appears to have been designed after Babel, as built by Nimrod. We arrive back in Baghdad, having spent an exhilarating 19-hour day.

My room has become so lonesome I can hardly stand to walk into it. I need my two families: my personal family and the wonderful folks of the Paw Creek Church.

Thursday a.m.: I enjoy breakfast with two new friends, Tom and Lynn Abercrombie. They represent the world's largest publication, the *National Geographic Magazine.*

Today will have to be a slow day to recover from the exhausting trip to Nineveh. I make contact with the directorate general of Antiquities and receive an invitation to attend sessions of a three-day seminar on "The Code of Hammurabi." This is a legal set of jurisprudence that a famous Babylonian king (1792-1750 B.C.) by the same name made the law of his kingdom. This document antedates our Old Testament laws, but certainly does not compare to its quality. However, for the pagan world of that day it expressed an unusual height in human rights and justice.

The original code, carved in polished basalt and measuring eight feet high, was found at Susa. It was carried to Susa by the Elamites as war booty in the 12th century B.C. It is presently on display in the Louvre Museum in Paris, France.

My guide from the Iraqi Information Ministry, Thymil, takes me through an old Ottoman Empire building located on the Tigris River that is being restored and will become a museum. It is a mammoth sculpture being decorated with great skill. It will make an outstanding location for the purpose as planned. I am spending the afternoon and evening reading and deciphering what I have learned on the trip to Nineveh. I can hardly wait to present what I am experiencing to others.

Friday, September 30: After trying to down a little breakfast (yogurt, bread, coffee — my stomach just won't act right), I'm off to the seminar. At 1:30 p.m. my Iraqi friend Jamal and I head for ancient Babylon for a second visit.

The city of old Babylon was a mammoth monument to the kings who ruled the Babylonian Empire. (It has taken me about 10 days to get to see this old city in the daylight.) While it is not evident that there are plans for the city to become more than a historic center specifically designed to attract tourism, the amount of expense would suggest much, much more.

We walk down into the hallways and rooms where the slaves or soldiers of Nebuchadnezzar lived centuries ago. We visit the throne room and meander around the numerous walls now being reconstructed. The huge bull with a man under his feet was apparently the symbol of Babylon and has become the new symbol of Iraq. There is no question that this country intends to become the great world-influencing nation that old Babylon was in its day.

The Ishtar (goddess) gate has been reconstructed. Originally, it was much larger and built of baked enameled brick with lavish colors. One can imagine the great king Nebuchadnezzar coming into the city through this gate with King Jehoiakim and his captured noblemen (606 B.C.). Daniel, Shadrach, Meshach, and Abednego were among the slaves destined to make their God the most celebrated God of this city. Marduk or Ishtar and their pantheon of gods could not defend themselves against godly men who would not bend, bow, nor burn. Oh, for men like that today!

In the evening I watch a presentation in the rebuilt theater. Again, the star of the show is Ishtar, the goddess of old Babylon. Everywhere, her name is appearing. It is becoming more and more evident that she is the queen of all the goddesses from the earliest recorded history of the Mesopotamian valley. She was called Inanna by the earliest Sumerians and Issi by the later Egyptians. Almost every capitol or palace representing the early empires had her temple somewhere in the inner sanctum. In the war of the gods (Babylonian mythology), Marduk, the male god, and Ishtar, the female god, were the final victors. Is there any significance to the revival of these names in modern Iraq? I would suggest that time will make the final report.

Saturday, October 1: My night is very trying. My body will not adapt to this new culture. I'll be going home in two days, so why worry? Mom will make me some potato soup and I will get well. My breakfast is light by necessity.

Thymil takes me to the Department of Antiquities where I am able to get a few books about ancient matters. We visit the Abbasid Palace dating back to the seventh century A.D. Very nice! It seems so different in this country to talk about history. Buildings or historic sites that are only a few hundred or a thousand years old are insignificant. Only two or three millennia make things of special interest. Our American history suddenly appears to be in its infancy and near at hand.

I have arranged a car to leave at 4:00 a.m. tomorrow to go to Ur where Abraham left for the Promised Land (approximately 4,120 years ago). I am doing some reading, writing, and am trying to shop for my loved ones, with no progress in the latter. Tomorrow will be a special day.

Sunday, October 2: My last day in Iraq begins with a jolting wake-up phone call from the desk. It is 3:15 a.m. We are off at 4:00 a.m. I read from Daniel as we fly toward the southern portion of this emerging Third World nation. Everywhere I look there is evidence of a mad pace of modernization. We drive on an unfinished six-lane super highway that is unsurpassed anywhere in the world, complete with modern picnic areas, center and side rails, and street lights.

As the south looms in sight, the morning life is everywhere. Bedouin tent homes are interlaced with country homes, along with shepherds and their many sheep. As in any developing country, children are on their way to school. They are nicely dressed, with the girls especially pretty in their dresses, always either long or well below the knees.

There are no crudely dressed youths in the crowds I see.

The sight of the ruins of the ancient city Uruk (biblical name Erech, Gen. 10:10), rising breathtakingly ahead, sets my heart to racing. This city came into existence between 5,300 and 5,500 years ago. The mound or tell (archaeological name for the raised mounds of ancient cities) is visible 20 to 30 miles across the plains of Shinar (Sumer). Within a short distance of this city the civilization of man began. Ur is a few miles away but (to my surprise) presently off limits because of the Iraq-Iran War. Just below these two cities is where the Garden of Eden was placed by the Creator himself. I am within the area where Adam and Eve and their family walked or lived and from where Abraham left for Canaan.

I climb the Uruk mound to take pictures and witness firsthand the ruins. This ancient city was enclosed within a 9 kilometer (5.6 mile) wall and apparently filled the entire area. It was mammoth. The city's main sculptures were baked brick, but the years of decay have rendered most of them to piles of oddly-shaped mud. The lines of the brick are usually evident. Here and there excavators have unearthed foundations, arches, walls, temples, and finally, the palace.

The ziggurat (an elevated temple tower), where the worshippers could climb the ramps or stairs to offer sacrifices and make incantations to their many gods, is the most conspicuous part of the ruins. Some of the slanted support pillars are remarkably well-preserved. You can determine the ramps leading toward the top. From its peak, the countryside is visible for many miles.

It is apparent that the city was rich and highly cultured. Inside walls were decorated with different sized cylinders laid with the round ends exposed. This created an unusually elaborate mosaic design. Some of the walls were circular. Pottery pieces are abundant and high in quality. These early cities were not inhabited by cavemen. The human family of that early history was probably more intelligent than now. When man was created, it was in the Father's likeness.

Whether the temples representing the polytheist religions of this city were part of its earliest history is probably not discernible. They may have been built later. No doubt Cain, the son of Adam, continued his rebellion after his false worship and murder as revealed in Genesis, and was a part of these human inventions of gods. Under any circumstance, man had already departed from the eternal God when this city was at its peak of power. This is the very reason God called Abraham to leave Ur and walk by faith in search of a city and nation whose God would be the Lord.

Not far from Uruk and Ur is the location of a contemporary city, Tell-al-Ufaid, where mother-goddess figurines have been located with one goddess bearing a child in her arms. This is one of the earliest examples of the Madonna cult in ancient paganism. I have already learned of several similarities in the ancient religions that have continued throughout history, but are experiencing a breathtaking revival in the present. Paganism will be judged, and I believe it will be judged in the very place it was born (ancient Mesopotamia, Ur, Uruk, Babylon, etc.).

Driving back to Baghdad is my most unpleasant experience in Iraq. My guide has lost interest in what I am doing and is only concerned with getting back to the city. I cannot communicate with anyone except through him, and he is not helping. The driver drove like Jehu on our way south, but gets worse on the way home. I have to get angry to get the car I am renting slowed up. It is very disturbing. I am in the Lord's hands, not the driver's. We certainly make good time at the devil's expense.

The books I have acquired are filled with information, so my research continues. I am being careful to interlace my studies with the Word of God and some other spiritual books. I have almost re-read the history of the holiness movement that began in the Methodist church during the 19th century. The intellectuals in the church finally became too big for this spiritual awakening and the separated lifestyle. They clamped down in 1896 at the annual conference.

Churches like the Church of God, Church of the Nazarene, and many others were born out of that period. There had been no interest in beginning a new organization until it became evident that the Methodists had outgrown the "work of sanctification" preached by John Wesley. My heart pants for a revival of old-fashioned holiness.

Saying goodbye to friends is always a special time. Joseph is the floor manager in the restaurant and from India. He has become a special friend, always willing to help; and I show him special kindness. There are several others, also. I check out in the evening since we leave at 6:00 a.m. for the airport.

Monday morning, October 3: We are off to the airport. A professor of archaeology from the University of Chicago has been recommended to me by the American ambassador. I have learned of his presence in the hotel, and he is leaving on the same flight. We ride to the airport together and spend considerable time talking. As we discuss Iraq's future role, it is clear that he certainly feels this nation has the capacity to become the leader of the Arab world. The morning paper has just announced that Iraq has already verified oil deposits totaling more than 100 billion barrels with research continuing. Her farmland is experiencing renewed expansion with new canals for natural irrigation. Something momentous is happening to this land.

During the last two days, I also meet Dr. Anneters Kammenhubur, a Hittite archaeological specialist from the University in Munich, Germany. She promises help in her field. Remember, this was a lost culture until a few years ago. The Bible was the only source that mentioned this nation, and critics said the Word of God was in error. No such nation had ever existed. As always, the "Word" had the last word when this civilization suddenly appeared in archaeological discovery. Now it constitutes an important study in ancient history.

As the plane ascends over the countryside, I see miles of beautiful fields with the patchwork of canals. This extends almost without a break as we fly south along the Euphrates River. We fly past and over Babylon (modern Hilla) and other small cities until we turn west and over the deserts. It is five hours to Frankfurt, Germany, and another new culture for me.

West Germany is my stop for the night. After calling our military servicemen's center, I catch the train for a visit with Rev. Russell Ward and his wonderful family. What a wonderful American dinner Mrs. Ward prepares. There is a service at a U.S. Air Force base, and he asks me to speak. I accept, and we have a wonderful time. He takes an offering, and the Holy Spirit directs me to add 50 francs and give it to his son-in-law and daughter who pastor at another center some 50 kilometers away. This is a joy. After banana pudding and decaffeinated coffee (the Iraqis didn't know what that was), I am ready for bed.

After a nice breakfast, we take the kids to their Christian school and me to the airport. The Lord moves my heart to share with this family making such a beautiful sacrifice (they would deny that) for Christ. I give Mrs. Ward 50 francs (approximately $32) for each of the children at home (two) and $100 for her and Rev. Ward. My heart explodes with joy for several hours after flying out of Frankfurt on my way to New York. What a joy it brings when you obey the Spirit's prompting!

My airline from Frankfurt, Germany, to New York is the German airline Lufthansa. The service is beautiful and the food delicious. As always on the transatlantic flight, they show a film. The scenes are beautiful; but when I plug in the earphones, the language is horrible. I ask for a form to complain and am given an envelope and stationery to express my displeasure. My word to this airline is how it violates the rights of pure-minded people when they air this kind of dirty language during flight. Parents have a right to fly with their young children without being confronted with gutter entertainment. I wonder if I'll get a reply. (I do.)

New York, USA, is not the most exciting city; but for

a weary American, it is close to heaven. After I get the remainder of my flight taken care of (the Iraqis have not bothered to schedule a flight from New York to Charlotte), I call Paw Creek Church. It is a joy just to be able to pick up a phone and dial home.

I arrive home at 9:38 p.m., three minutes after the scheduled arrival. It is great to travel 14,000 miles over 14 days and only be three minutes late. What a joy to see my family! Tiffany, Curtis, and Caleb do not let me get out of the flow of passengers before they maul me. Praise the Lord for a godly wife! Juanita is such a patient lady and is God's gift to this God-called minister. Terry, Anne, and Tanya are there with all kinds of love. My committed family is my prized possession. Three additional grandchildren have joined our family since my trip to Iraq: Christa, Andrew, and Cami Anne.

It is great to be back with the family at Paw Creek Church. I love all of them. Hooray for home! There is much to tell about this trip and what I have learned. I hope to be ready shortly to have the entire story of Babylon, and the biblical facts in book form. Most of the Christian church has no idea of the part this ancient city will play in the future. It is the antithesis of Jerusalem. What Jerusalem means to the Christian world, Babylon means to the pagan world.

It is absolutely imperative that we search the Scripture for the biblical facts. Does Babylon have a literal worldwide future or is Saddam Hussein playing with his imagination? Let us take an unbiased trip into Holy Scripture. The Bible alone is the basis for all doctrinal answers.

Chapter 3

Babylon, the Land of Shinar, and the "New World Order"

The great city of Babylon, the same city that Nebuchadnezzar proudly called "the great city which I have built," shall soon be the capital of a new world leader. While Jerusalem is being prepared to be the capital of the King of kings, Babylon is being readied for the impostor who wants to take His place. These two cities are the two capitals or the two central cities of the universe. Their connection is fixed until the second city, Babylon, is judged by the great God Jehovah and sinks into the Euphrates.

> And it shall be, when thou hast made an end of reading this book, that thou shalt bind a stone to it, and cast it into the midst of Euphrates: And thou shalt say, Thus shall Babylon sink, and shall not rise from the evil that I will bring upon her: and they shall be weary. Thus far are the words of Jeremiah (Jer. 51:63-64).

This has never been fulfilled, but it certainly will be in the near future.

A great prophet by the name of Zechariah set forth a precise picture of Babylon's rise in the last days. He called it "An house in the land of Shinar." This refers directly to Genesis 10:10 where the scripture says, *"And the beginning of his* [Nimrod] *kingdom was Babel* [Babel = babilu, Babylon] *... in the land of Shinar."*

The term "land of Shinar" is symbolic in Scripture with the name "Babylon." When Nebuchadnezzar brought Daniel from Jerusalem to Babylon, the Scripture stated:

> And the Lord gave Jehoiakim king of Judah into his hand, with part of the vessels of the house of God: which he carried into the land of Shinar to the house of his god; and he brought the vessels into the treasure house of his god (Dan. 1:2).

Nebuchadnezzar's capital was Babylon, the house of his gods was in this city, and it was to that city he brought Daniel and the vessels of the temple in Jerusalem. It was a mighty triumph for Nebuchadnezzar to actually rob the temple of the true God in Jerusalem and carry the temple treasures belonging to the revelations of truth and deposit them in the dark temple of Lucifer and demon spirits. Even before this fateful hour the future of Babylon was set. Without question, this act by Nebuchadnezzar would fix forever the ultimate fate of such a dark and blasphemous deed. The city of God, beautiful Jerusalem, would one day be vindicated. Babylon, in the land of Shinar, represents everything that is contrary to Jerusalem. This deed by Nebuchadnezzar and many additional acts of blasphemy since that date have yet to be judged. God is literally raising up a city from ruins to prepare for His final answer to the god of rebellion, Lucifer. Please look at the 11 verses of Zechariah 5 for a picture of this resurrected city.

> Then I turned, and lifted up mine eyes, and looked, and behold a flying roll. And he said unto me, What seest thou? And I answered, I see a flying

roll; the length thereof is twenty cubits, and the breadth thereof ten cubits. Then said he unto me, This is the curse that goeth forth over the face of the whole earth: for every one that stealeth shall be cut off as on this side according to it; and every one that sweareth shall be cut off as on that side according to it. I will bring it forth, saith the Lord of hosts, and it shall enter into the house of the thief, and into the house of him that sweareth falsely by my name: and it shall remain in the midst of his house, and shall consume it with the timber thereof and the stones thereof. Then the angel that talked with me went forth, and said unto me, Lift up now thine eyes, and see what is this that goeth forth. And I said, What is it? And he said, This is an ephah that goeth forth. He said moreover, This is their resemblance through all the earth. And, behold, there was lifted up a talent of lead: and this is a woman that sitteth in the midst of the ephah. And he said, This is wickedness. And he cast it into the midst of the ephah; and he cast the weight of lead upon the mouth thereof. Then lifted I up mine eyes, and looked, and behold, there came out two women, and the wind was in their wings; for they had wings like the wings of a stork: and they lifted up the ephah between the earth and the heaven. Then said I to the angel that talked with me, Whither do these bear the ephah? And he said unto me, To build it an house in the land of Shinar: and it shall be established, and set there upon her own base (Zech. 5:1-11).

Before we continue, please note the clear prophecy that this city will be resurrected and rebuilt. The prophet Zechariah was so emphatic that he stated that this prophecy was to "build a house in the land of Shinar." But that is not all he said. It was to be built upon the original foundation. He stated, "it shall be established, and set there upon her own base." You cannot be more plain than that.

Is that happening already? Absolutely! I have walked through those ruins and have seen repeatedly the ancient bricks of Nebuchadnezzar with the bricks of Saddam Hussein laid on top and workers proceeding to erect wall after wall and building after building. Every nuance of God's infallible Word is being fulfilled. I have never doubted that it would happen as God by revelation said that it would. I do not need the world's confirmation; nonetheless, two American news personalities have confirmed this story. Diane Sawyer and Sam Donaldson did an ABC "Primetime" special on June 28, 1990, from Iraq just before Saddam Hussein invaded Kuwait. Here are Sawyer's words from the transcript of that program:

> And now, Saddam Hussein dreams of rebuilding that grandeur, reclaiming the vision. This is Babylon. Twenty-five hundred years ago, it was the dazzling center of a rich civilization. There were the Hanging Gardens, the palaces, all built by a man who managed to unite the country and rule with an iron hand. In fact, right over here there are bricks that bear an ancient stamp. It says, "I am King Nebuchadnezzar, King of Babylon, king of everything from sea to far sea." But there are new bricks here, too, imprinted with a different stamp. This one says, "I am Saddam Hussein, president of the Republic of Iraq."

I watched Mrs. Sawyer and Mr. Donaldson actually show Saddam Hussein's bricks on top of the foundation laid by the workmen of Nebuchadnezzar. Absolutely incredible! The perfection of God's eternal revelations is exactly what we should expect of God's infallible Word in every instance. Isn't it amazing to see two skeptical American journalists confirm prophecy that is 2,500 years old? They had no idea what they were doing, but our great God did.

Now, let's look at the entire passage of revelation by

Zechariah. First, he saw a flying roll which the angel identified as "the curse that goeth forth over the face of the whole earth". This is the end-time wickedness which will totally envelope the world and has already begun. This world is going to have a baptism of filth unparalleled. The lie being told about worldwide revival is designed to mislead and confuse worldly professing Christians. True biblical believers are going to be fewer and fewer in number as we near the end. In verse five, he speaks of judgment against those, "who sweareth falsely by my [God's] name."

False prophesies, false visions, and false dreams have never been as multiple as our present time. A pastor in Colorado Springs, Colorado, recently testified that God showed him a vision in which the Beatles' damnable music was called the "music of the end-time revival from God." A *Prophetic Perspective* publication carried a vision by the wife of that minister that was called *"Off to See the Wizard."* She said the Holy Spirit said to her that he (the Holy Spirit) was Toto, the dog in the "Wizard of Oz" story, and that Oz, the wizard (a sorcerer), was God. All of this is said by this publication to have come from God.[1] This kind of demonic activity is more and more being attributed to visions, revelations, and events taking place in apostate churches. Even sadder is the fact that people will believe such tales.

This wickedness is centered in an "ephah" which is a commercial symbol. An ephah is a grain container of one bushel and three pints. The picture of this ephah suggests that wealth, trade, and riches, including the divination of the prosperity gospel, will be the vehicle that propels this worldwide wickedness. It will be human desire for things totally out of control. It is amazing how the whole Middle East crisis and recent war relate to one thing, "Our lifestyle of the abundance of things centered in oil."

The entire One World Order that is developing is basically a lust for money, control, and power. Every aspect of our worldwide economy is uniting together for unprecedented growth and wealth. The developing identification systems are already being connected worldwide. Mass control of everything of value is not just possible, it is almost final.

This commercial system destined to control the whole world will be carried to Babylon by two women with the wind (speed and haste) in their wings. It will happen with great speed. The whole world systems will first focus their attention on this area (already happening) and will then swiftly move its political and military operations to be centered in the vicinity of Babylon. It will happen so fast that no one will have time to resist or even prepare an argument. While we must never set dates, I believe it will happen so swiftly that there is at best a few years before it will all culminate and the seven years of wrath begin. That judgment will end at the "Battle of Armageddon" and the glorious return of Jesus to establish His earthly kingdom.

Let us identify these two women in the text who bear the commercial systems (ephah) to their destiny in Babylon. They are the two women of Revelation 17 and 18. One is Mystery Babylon, the mother of religious harlotry; while the second is the political systems and the One World government that will eventually give their powers to this god-king and coming Antichrist.

Mystery Babylon is the pagan religions of the world united with apostate Catholicism and Protestantism. The religious world is in worse shape than the political. Deception, compromise, false unity, and tolerance are the basic motivations of the church. Denominations in the past have existed to sustain themselves and have directed almost their whole powers in self-centered pursuits. This is changing. Now, everything is centering on unity and ecumenicalism and all convictions and distinctions are giving way to total tolerance. It is amazing to watch as the Catholic Pope, the Dalai Lamas of the Buddhists, the New Agers, and the Pentecostals/Charismatics, plus many other strange religious leaders, meet together to promote peace and world harmony. This is Mystery Babylon already uniting for her present and future role.

The second woman is the political systems of many stripes, including democracies, dictators, kings and Communists all working together to create a New World Order. Their goal is world peace, international trade, and prosperity, but the ultimate design is a one world government headed by the last world dictator. Almost every political figure of note is involved in this idea of a "New World Order." Many of our past and present presidents have been dedicated to a worldwide discussion of this idea. Former President Bush's top foreign advisor, Brent Snowcroft, said on prime time news, "We are watching the emergence of a 'New World Order.' " This is the second of the two women that bear the commercial system on her wings to build it a house in Shinar.

Even more amazing is to see President Saddam Hussein with his godless religious zeal as a prime mover in this whole scenario. This man shows all the signs of being a John the Baptist of the Antichrist kingdom. He is either *the forerunner* or at least *one* of the forerunners.

An article in the *Chattanooga New-Free Press* of April 5, 1987, stated the following.

> From Genesis to the last chapters of Revelation, Babylon was a byword for splendor and sin to the biblical authors, whose views were colored by the Hebrews' forced exile here under King Nebuchadnezzar II, the last great Babylonian king.
>
> But to modern Iraqis, Babylon is a monument to the region's history as the birthplace of writing and law, and they have begun a task likely to take many years to restore the city that dates from around 2000 B.C. Officials have set no time limit nor do they give any idea how much it will cost.
>
> The Iraqis have begun rebuilding several major structures from Nebuchadnezzar's time and plan to unveil them this summer in an international culture festival.

The ancient Temple of Ishtar has been rebricked, replastered, and whitewashed. A new 4,000-seat Greek theater is rising on the site of the old.

Workmen on scaffolds are topping the ancient bricks of Nebuchadnezzar's palace with blocks from the government brick works.

One of Babylon's great monuments, the Ishtar Gate, stands today in an East German museum. Only the foundations of the gate, some 120 feet across, are now visible in Babylon.

Carved into the bricks are reliefs of oxen and a mythical beast called the mushrishu, with the head of a serpent, body of a fish, front legs of a lion, and back legs of an eagle.

Surely, these documented accounts are convincing.

Babylon of Mesopotamia (the cradle of civilization) is destined to be the center of man's final effort at human government. Baghdad has already built hundreds of eight to ten-story office building complexes. They are only partially used at present. I rode on an unfinished six-lane superhighway leading from the Persian Gulf toward Babylon and Baghdad. It was lined with many small parks such as we enjoy in the West and it was lighted at the intersections. No one can visit that country as I did and not see their design for something momentous.

No one knows the exact movements of the coming months or years. The Master chess player is the Designer of eternity. Other prophecies will unfold as the events transpire. One thing is certain: He that predicts the future thousands of years in advance will not miss a detail. Babylon and the land of Shinar will be the center of coming events. God will judge her at the appropriate moment and she will sink as did Sodom and Gomorrah. "As God overthrew Sodom and Gomorrah and the neighbour cities thereof, saith the Lord; so shall no man abide there, neither shall any son of man dwell therein" (Jer. 50:40).

The following is a large edited portion of the booklet printed by the Iraqi Ministry of Information and Culture.

Babylon rises again. Glorious in a glorious time. She is the lady of reviving centuries. Rising dignified and holy. Showing the great history of Iraq. Adding to its magnificence. And emphasizing its originality.

The Phoenix of the new time rising alive from the ashes of the past to face the bright present that places it on a golden throne and bringing back to it its charming youth and unique glory.

Babylon was not a city made of rocks and bricks and full of events. It was not a forgotten place of the ancient past. In fact, Babylon is something else. Since its birth Babylon has stretched its arm to the future to be the place of wisdom and to represent the first civilization and to remain as a glittering lighthouse in the dark nights of history. Here is Bab-ilu. . . .

It survived the ages, defied all times and overcame whatever threatened its existence. It won the battles by virtue of its great heritage and the formidable men, who carried that heritage, and defended it throughout the ages that produced unique heroes who know the originality of their city as it rises and revives to add to human civilization something new in writing, law, astronomy, medicine, arts, literature, commerce, agriculture, education, and mathematics. So history can start with it so that it remains the compass throughout the ages.

When Babylon was consisted of small city-states and separate dynasties, Hammurabi waged successive wars to unite these city-states so that Babylon remains as one city, as the bright light of civilization.

However, it suffered more and more from repeated attacks until Nebuchadnezzar came to power and reconstructed. He built temples and high walls as he realized it was the pulpit of the first Iraqi civilization.

Today looks exactly like yesterday.

After long periods of darkness that enveloped the land of Babylon and concealed its characteristics, Saddam Hussein emerges from Mesopotamia, as Hammurabi and Nebuchadnezzar had emerged, at a time to shake the century old dust off its face.

Saddam Hussein, the grandson of the Babylonians, the son of this great land, is leaving his fingerprints everywhere. He directs his attention to the civilization of the ancestors and the historical cities of exceptional significance in the history of Iraq. Thus, Babylon revives everyday and its buried antiquities are revealed by unceasing efforts supervised by president Saddam Hussein who fully realizes Babylon's great landmarks and glory and who reconstructed it after Persian attempts to eliminate it from the face of the earth throughout history.

It is not easy to sum up the history of Babylon since the history of such an ancient city requires many writings reviving throughout the time and since incessant excavation campaigns always reveal exciting aspects of its history.

However, what is available before us is not little because archaeologists and specialists in Iraq's ancient history wrote a great deal about Babylon. Thus old Babylonian periods which lasted for more than five thousand years were full of events, were ruled by many kings and were subject to foreign domination for successive decades. So most of its buildings turned into mere ruins. Yet, from time to time, it came back to the limelight with the emergence of a number of kings who brought it back to its glory, to play its role in human civilisation and to add new pages to the intellectual, national and human history. Therefore, it is difficult to sum up Babylon's eventful history and to give a complete picture of its daily life. However we shall trace the remotest point in the old Babylonian periods and stop at certain dynasties to emphasize the role of the most distinguished kings who ruled, protected and restored the city.

President Saddam Hussein Brings Babylon To Life

Excavations at the archaeological sites in Babylon started in the 1950s. But they were slow and the efforts could not match the greatness of the buried treasures which took the world by surprise when they were dug up.

As soon as President Saddam Hussein assumed responsibility archaeological excavations won the same amount of attention as all aspects of life in Iraq. His Excellency took a direct interest in the excavation operations and paid them a special attention as shown by his regular directives to the supervisors of the archaeological operations, his defining the objectives to be attained, providing the requirements of success to expand the excavation site, and reduce the required time.

Therefore, the new discoveries in Babylon and elsewhere, and the process of restoring Babylon are simply the fruit of the president's directives. Indeed, the president's role went beyond giving directives, to outlining the goals to be achieved such as his orders to restore Babylon, its mountains, lakes, tourist facilities, restaurants, and roads, etc.

The president used to pay regular visits to the work sites to superintend the proper implementation of his directives. His Excellency would discuss them with the engineers and the archaeologists and draw up sketches for carrying out the plans. These visits played a decisive role in ensuring the restoration of Babylon and providing it with better tourist facilities.

President Saddam Hussein was acting in his capacity as heir to this great civilization, and descendant of those Arab dynasties which gave the world a great deal in all walks of life.

His Excellency realized the distinguished role Babylon played, through its patriotic kings, to ward off the successive dangers which threatened its existence. His Excellency was also aware of the great human role which brought forth the greatest human civilization which still illuminates the world and offers it unlimited achievements in various human aspects.

President Saddam Hussein's supervision of Babylon's restoration is a definite proof that the new generations inherit the profound human concepts which revealed and always will, the essential link between a glorious history and a radiant future. Meanwhile, His Excellency draws many and greater lessons from that history to interpret them into rich details which will remain an outstanding lesson for the distant future.

When excavation started in Babylon earlier in this century, archaeologists did not expect to see the ruins of the city in such a deplorable state. The baked bricks from which the city's palaces had been built had disappeared. They had been extracted from within the walls over hundreds of years. Besides, the rest of the city's buildings having been built of mud bricks (especially temples and walls), they were gradually eroded by subterranean water. Moreover, salts, winds, and rains left their marks on this ancient city. Today it is almost lying under palm groves or below the level of salty marshes which appear in Winter and Spring. Or under the sandy hills which cover the important archaeological sites in the city. The ancient Euphrates has changed its course more than once. Nowadays, Shattal Hilla flows far away from its historical course leaving the original riverbed bone dry.

Within the 21-square-mile archaeological city there are several modern villages now such as Sinjar, Al-Jumjuma, and Anana. Babylon revival project aims to rediscover the important parts of the city and restore them. Over the past few years the work concentrated on investigating the damage to the foundations of the walls of the discovered palaces, the gates, and temples, as well as the private houses, the Babylonian amphitheater and its annex, the acting Palace. Most of Nebuchadnezzar II's palace, which covers an area of 52,000 square meters, was discovered and the important parts of its walls were maintained. Restoration and maintenance works also covered three temples: Ishtar, Nabu, and Ninmakh. The recent discovery of a small temple, Nabushakbari, by Iraqi scientists is a unique achievement in the field of archaeology and excavations. Furthermore, most of the Procession Street was also discovered while reconstruction works were carried out on the Babylonian Amphitheater, and the Acting Palace and most of their structures were restored. They have been prepared to host festivals and great festivities. Soon enough Nebuchadnezzar's bridge will be built, and maintenance of the Procession Street will be carried on as far as the bridge gate and work on the city's gates and walls will be finished.

So far, a lot has been achieved to revive Babylon and the restoration works continue in

every part according to stages planned before-
hand.[2]

Reading the above booklet from Iraq is breathtaking.
Saddam Hussein actually believes he is destined to make
Iraq a world class nation. Ancient Babylon is probably a
mystery to him, but somehow this mystery drives him to
dream incredible dreams. How big his part will be in the
New World Order is better left to witness firsthand rather
than to speculation.

Let's look at events that happened relative to Desert
Storm and up to the present. Saddam Hussein has made
himself a man known by the entire world. A sudden meta-
morphosis into a more reasonable president would energize
the world. Even more telling would be for him to make peace
with Israel. Let's look at Saddam Hussein up close.

---

[1]*Prophetic Perspective,* vol. 5, part V, Mahesh Chavda Ministries
International, P.O. Box 472009, Charlotte, NC 28247-2009.

[2]Excerpted from booklet, *From Nebuchadnezzar to Saddam Hussein,
Babylon Rises Again,* printed by Al-Hurriya Press, published
by Ministry of Information and Culture, Department of Information.

Chapter 4

Babylon, Iraq, and Saddam Hussein

Will Saddam Hussein survive to see Babylon and Iraq become an intimate part of the developing New World Order? It would be foolish to speculate, yet, Saddam has survived an incredible length of time and shows no signs of giving up his dream of being the new Nebuchadnezzar. There is clear suggestion that he is still building a grandiose palace and was last reported to be building it in the ancient city of Babylon. Nothing seems to deter him from pressing toward his ultimate plans. A report from the Iraqi News Agency in October of 1994 was reprinted in *The Economist.* The writer stated:

> The Iraqi News Agency last month put out an article praising the "democratic" spirit of Iraq's long-dead kings. In April, on his 57th birthday, Mr. Hussein was shown on television on a gold-coloured throne modeled, it seemed, on that of ancient Babylon. For three hours he sat watching folk dances and receiving tribute."[1]

The statement that his throne was apparently modeled after ancient Babylon would suggest that Saddam Hussein's Babylon dream is still alive. The news is filled with statements demeaning him and describing him as everything but a human being. Yet, the very nature of his dream and the history of others who have had or have the same vision explains his actions. They are only irrational to us because we think in modern terms of human rights and, at least, a minimal belief in democracy. His dream has no such basis of intellectual understanding. He is no more ruthless than hundreds of other similar political leaders over the past several decades or even presently. His dream has simply been magnified in his struggle with the New World Order.

Saddam Hussein represents a small player in the New World Order scheme. Given his likely sense of being, an outsider compared to the president of the United States or the security council member at the United Nations, would serve to make his action more erratic and off the wall. His dream is hardly different than a more civilized member of the Council on Foreign Relations, the Bilderbergers or any other player on the chessboard of World Politics. It just appears more brutal because the game is confined to his small world. War has been the game of those who seek to build a world government since Nebuchadnezzar, Alexander the Great, Napoleon, Hitler, and many others.

Why Saddam Hussein Was Not Killed In Desert Storm

The fact that Saddam Hussein survived was not an accident or the absence of one. It is almost impossible to read anything that discusses him without a statement expressing fear for the Middle East and, especially, Iraq without him. He holds together a country that has little chance of stability for a post-Saddam regime. Another Lebanon is the last thing the Middle East leaders can afford.

It is quite apparent that the coalition, especially the United States, preferred to defeat Saddam, destroy as much as possible of his war machinery, drive him out of Kuwait, but leave him to clean up the mess. *Business Week* discussed Iraq in their "International Outlook" column recently. The following statement echoes the general feeling that appears to reflect strong consensus, both during the war and present.

The real challenge, however, is what to do about Iraq after Saddam. Should he topple, maintaining order in Iraq is likely to be more politically complicated and expensive than even taking on Saddam in battle. Iraq is an odd amalgam of Shiites vs. Sunnis and Kurds vs. Arabs. It has no unifying ethnic thread.

Even imposing a demilitarized zone in the South near Kuwait could trigger an insurrection by the Shiite Muslims who live in the area and who consider themselves distinct from the Sunni-dominated government in Baghdad. Shiite-governed Iran might take advantage of such a move. Kurds in the North also can be expected to make a push for statehood if Saddam is knocked out, raising a tricky set of issues with key U.S. ally Turkey.

Ultimately, if Iraq were to be dismembered or fragmented, it could set off shockwaves that would affect the entire gulf. There almost certainly would be new flows of refugees, for example, exacerbating ethnic and religious tensions. So even if Clinton makes Saddam Hussein blink now, the challenges of maintaining stability in the world's most important oil patch are sure to grow greater.[2]

Many in the political world appear to neither want him alive or dead. Either way he is an undaunting threat to their New World Order and peace in the world's oil patch.

A recent article in *Newsweek*, written by James Baker III, secretary of state during the Gulf War, is quite revealing. It suggests that the survival of Saddam Hussein was tied to his not using biological or chemical agents of warfare during the conflict. Mr. Baker said the following, "The president had decided, at Camp David in December, that the best deterrent of the use of weapons of mass destruction by Iraq would be a threat to go after the Ba'ath regime itself." Baker went further to suggest concerning Saddam, "I purposely left the impression that the use of chemical or biological agents by Iraq could invite tactical nuclear retaliation."

Baker concluded, "But our threat to the regime in Iraq was conditioned on its use of weapons of mass destruction, which we do not believe occurred."[3]

My interpretation is that the president of Iraq was basically promised survival if he did not engage in the use of biological or chemical warfare. When the war was halted, the defeat of Saddam's forces was so complete that the ground forces could have gone straight to Baghdad. The president of the United States, acting in coalition with the world players, was not ready to occupy Iraq or eliminate Saddam Hussein. Can you imagine the world's reaction, especially the Arab world, if the first military adventure of the "New World Order," as it was called, had actually taken control of a country and set up a puppet government to be policed by the U.N. troops? The time was not ripe for such bold action and Hussein was probably part of the future plans. At this writing, Saddam is rattling sabers again, threatening his country's Kurdish population.

The Survival of Saddam Hussein and His Rebuilding Iraq

It is clear that Saddam has survived, and quite well, for the post-war condition of his country. No one doubts that Iraq and its citizens suffered tremendous devastation during the war and much deprivation since it ended. An editorial article in the *Baghdad Observer* quoted a United Nations official as saying:

> The recent conflict has wrought near apoca-
> lyptic results upon the economic infrastructure of

what had been, until January 1991, a rather highly urbanized and mechanized society.

Now, most means of modern life support have been destroyed or rendered tenuous. Iraq, has, for some time to come, been relegated to a pre-industrial age.[4]

This editorial was printed for the Iraqi citizens and certainly represents their own political purpose, but no doubt was an honest picture of a war ravaged nation. The *Baghdad Observer* has constantly reported a terrible picture of the destruction caused by the war. One headline screamed that the "U.S. Killed Iraqis By Random Use Of Cluster Bombs." (January 1, 1995) The following was reported on March 11, 1995:

A research team of experts, scientists, and researchers from University of Baghdad and health institutes conducted visits to the sites of military operations and interviewed many medical specialists to define the impact of the aggression led by the United States on the health of Iraqi citizens. This aggression, which was called as a "Clean War" by the Western mass media, had gone far beyond all international treaties and convention.

The fact that the newspaper is still reporting this kind of war results almost five years after the war would suggest either tremendous suffering or people control or maybe both. Focusing on one's enemy is a powerful psychological tool for uniting the citizens and Saddam has apparently used it to the maximum. It probably represents the constant need of encouraging the citizens and inspiring them by appealing to their hatred for the United States.

The *World Press Review* in June of 1994 had Saddam "Down in Flames?" That was the title of an article showing him on his last leg and ready to commit his last desperate acts. This was clearly more hype than substance. David

Hirst of the liberal *Guardian* of London described a Saddam Hussein that would soon commit a "final act of madness." He added, "If and when he goes down, he will take the world with him or as much of it as he can." An earlier defector from Iraq had told Mr. Hirst that he believed "before long (Saddam) will do something crazy."[5]

I believe that kind of talk is nothing but wishful thinking on the part of avowed detractors. It is amazing how little the world understands the *players* of international politics. It would not surprise me to later learn that the events in Iraq have to some degree been staged to prepare the world for a One World Order. The idea of *"Order out of chaos"* has always preceded great worldwide changes. Most of the players in such world events are certainly unaware of the design and act only as day by day bureaucratic managers.

The Other Side Of The Story

Saddam Hussein is back in business. An extensive report by *Time* magazine of May 1994 documents his progress. The report title was "No Longer Fenced In." It gave excellent details of his ability to wiggle his way around all odds. The article stated:

> Using a clandestine technology-procurement network never fully dismantled, Saddam continues to buy spare parts for T-72 tanks in China and Russia, anti-tank and air-defense missiles from Bulgaria, and may now be turning to West European firms for critical electronics for his air force. At the same time, he has pressed forward with Iraq's ballistic-missile research at newly built laboratories. With a leaner and meaner fighting machine of about 400,000 troops, Iraq still has the largest army in the region.

This article goes much further to describe preparations for extensive trading with a number of nations including several that were partners in the Gulf War. It states:

Anticipating the end of sanctions, Iraq has negotiated a batch of trade agreements with France, Turkey, and Russia, and has even been discussing new contracts with U.S. companies. A loophole in the sanctions allows foreign companies to set up deals with Iraq that will take effect once the U.N. embargo is lifted. The French, Italians, Russians, and Turks have interpreted this to mean they can enter contractual relationships; the U.S. has not. "It would be stupid for us to be the last ones in, when everyone else is lining up to sign contracts for Iraq's reconstruction," says General Jeannou Lacaze, retired chief of staff of the French armed forces.[6]

This article confirms that three of the five permanent members of the U.N. Security Council (France, Russia, and China) want the trade ban eased and appear to be pushing in that direction. France, one of those three security council members, established a diplomatic presence in Baghdad in January of 1995.

The Economist stated in their international section:

Alain Juppe, welcomed Tariq Aziz, Saddam Hussein's deputy as prime minister to Paris. More than that, he then announced that France was about to establish a diplomatic presence in Baghdad by opening an "interests section," manned by French officials, in the Romanian embassy.

Until now, the West has preserved a diplomatic freeze against Iraq.[7]

This move drew sharp criticism from the United States and Britain. The *New York Times* reported:

France has another reason to want normal economic ties with Iraq: Before the gulf war, France was Iraq's main arms supplier and is still owed an estimated $5 billion for various military and civilian contracts. French companies are also eager to take part in the rebuilding of Iraq's oil industry.

France suggested an easing of the oil embargo after Iraq's decision late last year to recognize Kuwait's borders. The timing of the moves today was significant because the Security Council is to meet next week to review Iraq's compliance with resolutions demanding the destruction of facilities that make weapons of mass destruction.

Britain was the first to criticize France. "It is not the moment to relax pressure on Iraq to comply fully with United Nations requirements," a Foreign Office spokesman said, adding that Britain remained "very suspicious" of Iraq since it massed troops on its border with Kuwait last October.

Later in the day a State Department spokeswoman, Christine E. Shelly, said Washington did not consider France's decision to open an interests section to be "helpful or constructive."She added: "We do not believe that now is the appropriate time to make gestures toward Iraq."[8]

Nothing is more important to the New World Order than money, oil, and economic matters. I believe it is just a matter of time before the sanctions will be lifted. Already there appears to be the willingness to look the other way. The New York Times, February 16, 1995, stated clearly that Iraq was now selling its oil on the oil market.

A library abstract of that article stated the following:

Senior oil industry executives and traders said on February 15, 1995, that Iraq has set up a system over the past year to export crude oil and refined products and thus bypass UN sanctions barring such sales. The sales have generated $700 million to $800 million in revenue for the Iraqi economy. The executives also said that Iraq was relying on a growing network of traders motivated to ignore the sanction by big discounts.

A recent report stated that British businessmen are now visiting Iraq for discussions in business matters. The same report stated, "other Western businesses" which probably suggested Americans without naming the country (*World Press Review,* May 1995). While the above report was in the *World Press Review,* the *New York Times* reported:

> In its campaign against crippling economic sanctions imposed by the UN, Iraq on March 16, 1995, won the support of the Vatican, which has long opposed such embargoes because of the harm they inflict on ordinary people.[9]

All of the above is happening while simultaneously the United States is pursuing a "de-stabilize" Iraq policy or at least doing so for public record. Again, the *New York Times,* April 12, 1995, reported that the CIA has asked for $19 million in 1996 to continue covert operations. The stated goal in this report was to de-stabilize Iraq and curb Iran's expansionist ambitions. Politics would be a funny game if it were not so deadly. All of this intrigue and peculiar diplomacy leaves a clear signal that the New World Economy must proceed at any cost. Human rights make good public relations but must not hinder the New World Economy or the rich from getting richer. The truth in Revelation 18:3 is being fulfilled.

> For all nations have drunk of the wine of the wrath of her fornication, and the kings of the earth have committed fornication with her, and the merchants of the earth are waxed rich through the abundance of her delicacies.

Kuwait: Will Saddam Return for the Final Word?

Either Saddam Hussein or his successor will eventually retake Kuwait and probably add it to the Iraqi geography. The Bible is extremely clear that this small nation will be sacked and destroyed during the end times scenario. The act of Saddam Hussein to take Kuwait was a token of this future event, although it was delayed by the success of Desert Storm. Bible prophecy is normally fulfilled in stages with a shadow cast forward in advance of the final act.

The invasion by the Iraqi army appears to have been that shadow which Jeremiah predicted prophetically 2,600 years ago. Join me in looking at this breathtaking prophecy.

> Concerning Kedar, and concerning the kingdoms of Hazor, which Nebuchadnezzar king of Babylon shall smite, thus saith the Lord; Arise ye, go up to Kedar, and spoil the men of the east. Their tents and their flocks shall they take away: they shall take to themselves their curtains, and all their vessels, and their camels; and they shall cry unto them, Fear is on every side. Flee, get you far off, dwell deep, O ye inhabitants of Hazor, saith the Lord; for Nebuchadnezzar king of Babylon hath taken counsel against you, and hath conceived a purpose against you. Arise, get you up unto the wealthy nation, that dwelleth without care, saith the Lord, which have neither gates nor bars, which dwell alone. And their camels shall be a booty, and the multitude of their cattle a spoil: and I will scatter into all winds them that are in the utmost corners; and I will bring their calamity from all sides thereof, saith the Lord. And Hazor shall be a dwelling for dragons, and a desolation for ever: there shall no man abide there, nor any son of man dwell in it (Jer. 49:28-33).

I have documented to my satisfaction that this biblical reference is future and intimately tied to the developing climate in the Middle East. This entire chapter of Jeremiah 49 is a prelude to the tribulation period of seven years and/

or part of its early events and the final Battle of Armageddon. Jordan (Ammonites and Moabites) is mentioned first
(verses 1-6); Saudi Arabia (Edom) is next (verses 7-22);
Damascus, Syria is third (verses 23-27), the small kingdom
of Kuwait is fourth (verses 28-33) with Iran (Elam) last
(verses 34-39). This chapter is a bird's-eye view of these
Middle Eastern countries at the time of the end. Immediately
following this chapter, Jeremiah deals with the city of
Babylon in Iraq for the next two chapters (50 and 51).
Chapter 51 is especially vivid in detailing the final judgment
of Babylon and its complete disappearance into the Euphrates
River. I will deal with the complete destruction of Babylon
in a later chapter.

Kuwait And Prophecy

Saddam Hussein is fond of portraying himself as
Nebuchadnezzar. Throughout Scripture men are given pro-
phetic names because of the nature of their activity. John the
Baptist was called Elijah in prophecy because he came in the
spirit of Elijah. The statement in verse 28, "concerning
Kedar," has reference to 1 of 12 sons of Ishmael born to
Hagar, Sarah's handmaiden. *Zondervan Pictorial Bible
Dictionary*, said of Kedar, "One of the 12 sons of Ishmael,
son of Abraham by Hagar. . . . They helped originate the
Arab peoples. . . . The doom of Kedar as declared in
Jeremiah 49:28-33 tells of something of their desert civili-
zation. . . . Their territory was in the northern part of the
Arabian desert." Three key things noted by Mr. Tenney is
his connection of Kedar to Hazor and to Jeremiah 49:28-33
as well as locating both geographically to the northern area
of Arabia.[10]

The *Britannica Encyclopedia* says, "Archaeological
evidence . . . suggests that Kuwait was part of an early
civilization contemporary with Sumeria (Shinar) and the
Indus Valley (3rd millennium B.C.) . . . Greek colonists
arrived on the island (Faylakah Island in Kuwait Bay)
during the time of Alexander III the Great (323 B.C.)." This

same report notes the arrival of Arabs as follows, "At the beginning of the 18th century A.D., the Amizah tribe of central Arabia began an eastward search for better pasture and water and founded Kuwait city.... The traditional date of founding is 1710.... In 1756 Adb Raham of the Al Sabah became Shikh."[11] There appears to be no doubt that Kuwait is the literal fulfillment of this prophecy as to origin and geographic location.

Kuwait or Hazor

The Bible called this doomed city, "Hazor" which means in the Hebrew, "an enclosed place." The name Kuwait was given to this same area in the early 18th century which comes from the Arabic word, "kut," meaning a "fort" or "fortress." A fort or fortress is indeed an enclosed place. I have a picture of the walls that enclosed this entire city until it was destroyed in 1951 after the discovery of oil and the development of this nation as an oil rich kingdom. In a book, *History of Eastern Arabia,* the following is stated concerning Kuwait: "The name Kuwait is the diminuture of the Arabic 'Kut' or fortress." He further quoted a Father Anistasal-Karmali who stated, "The word 'Kut' in the language of southern Iraq and its neighboring countries of Arabia and parts of Persia is the house that is built in the shape of a fortress or like it so as to be easily defended when attacked."[12]

The *Lange Commentary* on Jeremiah made the following observations. Of Kedar he said, "They lived in the desert between 'Arabia Petraea and Babylonia.' Of Hazor he said, "Hazor is 'the present Hadshar,' a district which occupies the whole northeastern corner of Nedshed, and to which in the wider sense the coastlands of Lachea also belong. This corner is formed by the southern course of the Euphrates and the Persian Gulf." This commentary also stated, "The expression 'some of the East' is the general designation of the Arabs, especially the nomad tribes of Northern Arabia." (Note the last short phrase of verse 28.)[13] It would appear that the evidence is overwhelming for identifying Jeremiah 49:28-33, Kedar and Hazor as a group of Arab people and the country of Kuwait. Finis Dake in his commentary on these verses stated, "Hazor was located near the Euphrates and the Persian Gulf."[14]

Prophetic Fulfillment

This future prophecy must be fulfilled. History provides no possible chance for this to represent a past fact. The efforts of Saddam Hussein were a perfect picture for the wording in this Scripture. Not only the people of Kuwait and their country fit this prophecy, but the prophecy itself fits every event connected with the invasion and its aftermath. Saddam Hussein and his lynchmen methodically dismantled and carried the possession of Kuwait back to Baghdad in exact fulfillment of verse 29:

> Their tents and their flocks shall they take away; they shall take to themselves their curtains, and all their vessels, and their camels; and they shall cry unto them. Fear is on every side (Jer. 49:29).

The following statement appeared in the *Charlotte Observer* on October 26, 1990. "Kuwait's sophisticated oil refineries, extensively damaged after Iraq's invasion, are being dismantled and transported to Iraq piece by piece." Their tactics of fear were apparently elevated to an art form by these brutal soldiers. Numbers of reports describe babies being removed from incubators, children executed in front of their homes and before their parents, pleading women in labor at hospital entrances killed with bayonets and every other imaginable atrocity.

Saudi Arabia

This text reads that Hazor or Kuwait would flee for safety and defense to a country called, "the wealthy nation." This country is described as a country, "that dwelleth without care" (over-confident, at ease) and that "have neither gates nor bars" and "which dwelleth alone." (verse 31). I believe this could be Saudi Arabia. They are certainly a nation that everyone would call wealthy. They are over-confident and their citizens refuse to believe that they could actually experience destruction and judgment.

The judgment in verse 32 could apply to an entire nation or to the troops sent to restore the kingdom of Kuwait. "And their camels shall be a booty, and the multitude of their cattle a spoil; and I will scatter into all winds them that are in the utmost corners; and I will bring their calamity from all sides thereof, saith the Lord" (Jer. 49:32). The possibility of either is awesome to consider.

Kuwait's Future Is Already Set

At the appointed time a nation called by a name that reflects Babylon will take Kuwait again. Will it be Saddam Hussein? The thought is already in the air and Saddam makes all the right moves to indicate his intention. *Business Week* in their "International Outlook" section said:

> Yet, Saddam, the Middle East's great survivor, may also be betting that the writing is on the wall for the pro-Western gulf monarchies. Indeed, since the Gulf War, Kuwait has been convulsed by political squabbling between the ruling Al-Sabah family and the assertive National Assembly. More ominously, chief U.S. ally Saudi Arabia is being buffeted by political stress. An aging King Fahd, an unclear succession, and a sharp rise in religious and political opposition to the ruling Al-Saud clan have been setting nerves on edge. And unlike four years ago, when it bankrolled Desert Storm to the tune of $50 billion, the Saudi Treasury is virtually bankrupt.

The same article spoke of ethnic chaos in Saudi Arabia:

> According to U.S. Treasury estimates, total

debt in Saudi Arabia is $90 billion and rising. A fast-growing population and a political system anchored on buying loyalty through largess have resulted in huge budget deficits. The bottom line: Neither Saudi Arabia nor Kuwait are in a position to bankroll a sustained U.S.-led military presence.[15]

The weaknesses of Kuwait and Saudi Arabia would suggest future trouble in defending themselves against Iraq. If America acts as it did in Desert Storm, the bill will apparently be paid by someone else. At some point Kuwait is just not going to be worth the cost or trouble. When you understand that Iraq, including Kuwait, represents 20 percent of the known world oil deposits and Saudi Arabia represents 20 additional percent of those reserves, it sounds ominous.[16] The present political instability in Russia and their need of trade with Iraq suggests that almost anything could happen to make defending Kuwait or even Saudi Arabia impossible. There is probably no one who dares suggest that the future is secure for the Middle East. Great movements of political, religious, and economic significance must occur to prepare the Middle Eastern countries for their biblical future. Iraq and Israel will be in the very center of these movements.

Saddam Hussein And Israel

A dramatic possibility was just suggested in a recent article in *Newsweek*. Their words were:

> Saddam reportedly has made secret overtures to Israel in hopes of saving his own skin — and Israel is reported to have rejected them because Saddam can't be trusted. But Assad is so preoccupied that his aides have told visitors he is devoting himself to the Iraqi question.[17]

When we consider that a "covenant" must be a part of

the seven-year period called the Great Tribulation, it makes the entire peace process of the Middle East prophetic in nature. Add to this process the entrance of the very man who claims heir to Nebuchadnezzar's throne and the man who is rebuilding the gates of Nimrod (Babylon), and the picture becomes even more prophetic. We must not move beyond what is actually happening, but this does add a very important possibility. I believe that the three main political divisions of the Middle East are Israel, Iraq, and Jordan. Israel's existence will be a matter of dispute until it is settled by the returning Messiah at the end of the Battle of Armageddon. Jordan represents ancient Moab and Ammon and will defend Israel from the Antichrist effort to totally annihilate the Jewish race. Iraq will in some geographical form be a part of the peace process and the final covenant. Iraq and Babylon will later be a part of the breaking of that covenant in connection with the Antichrist. We must always remember that geographical lines may change and political persons may change, but the ultimate facts will be exactly as the Bible has promised.

It would appear that the stage is set. To look at past prophecies thousands of years old being acted out as on a world stage cannot be taken lightly. The very political order of the Middle East nations cannot be less than supernatural. Jesus had stated clearly that not a jot or tittle would pass away.

> Think not that I am come to destroy the law, or the prophets: I am not come to destroy, but to fulfil. For verily I say unto you, Till heaven and earth pass, one jot or one tittle shall in no wise pass from the law, till all be fulfilled (Matt. 5:17-18).

Please notice that this was stated by Jesus Christ to include the prophets and all their prophecies: Daniel, Micah, Jeremiah, Zechariah, etc. These men gave a precise picture of the nations, the events and the final results and we are the privileged guests in the world's theater.

Let us move forward to the city of Jerusalem and its part in the present and future events. To even think of researching Iraq and its future apart from Jerusalem would be impossible. The two cities are eternally opposite and all their inhabitants are mortal enemies. That will not change except temporarily for political purposes and to effect the "covenant of destiny."

[1] *The Economist*, November 12, 1994, p. 59.
[2] *Business Week*, "John Rossant in Rome," October 24, 1994.)
[3] *Newsweek*, October 2, 1995, p. 57.
[4] *Baghdad Observer*, March 3, 1995, p. 1.)
[5] *World Press Review*, Regional Report, the Middle East, June 1994.
[6] *Time*, May 23, 1994, p. 36.
[7] *The Economist*, January 14, 1995, p. 41.
[8] *New York Times*, January 7, 1995, Sec. 1, p. 6.
[9] *New York Times*, March 17, 1995, p. 6.
[10] Merrill C. Tenney, *Zondervan Pictorial Bible Dictionary* (Grand Rapids, MI: Zondervan Publishing House, 1988).
[11] *Britannica Encyclopedia* (1990), p. 7:50 3b.
[12] Ahmad Mustafa Abu-Haninia, History of Eastern Arabia, The Rise of Kuwait (Probsthaine, 1965), p. 47.
[13] John Peter Lange, D.D., *Lange Commentary* (Grand Rapids, MI: Zondervan Publishing House, 1976), p. 399.
[14] Finis Dake, *Dake's Annotated Reference Bible* (Lawrenceville, GA: Dake Bible Sales, Inc., 1963), p. 794, column 1.
[15] *Business Week*, October 24, 1994, p. 59.
[16] *Encyclopedia Britannica*, 15th ed., 1990, p. 592.
[17] *Newsweek*, October 2, 1995, p. 50.

Chapter 5

Jerusalem, Chosen by God

Jerusalem is God's chosen city. From this much loved and much hated city, Jesus Christ will establish His golden kingdom of worldwide glory and righteousness. There are two eternal cities. One will end in glory, and the second will be buried in judgment. One is the capital of all that is righteous, and the other is the stronghold of every unclean spirit. Throughout the Scripture, these cities are seen in contrast. Babylon represents everything that is the opposite of Jerusalem. These two cities must always be seen as antithesis to each other. They are the only two eternal cities on the earth. Everything that is evil must ultimately connect to Babylon, and everything that is holy must always connect to Jerusalem.

One great fact we should always remember — there is only one antidote for error and that is truth. When error arises, we do not just cry out against the error, we re-dedicate ourselves to the wonderful truths of the Holy Scripture. While many are preaching a false utopia kingdom established by men, we who know truth must preach the true millennial kingdom of Jesus Christ. The time of that biblical golden kingdom is at hand. The wild ideals of a utopian world is conclusive proof that God has a true kingdom.

When Melchizedek was still king of Jerusalem and this city was unnamed in the biblical future, Abraham looked for this golden kingdom and a city of eternal abode. The Holy Scripture records:

> By faith he sojourned in the land of promise, as in a strange country, dwelling in tabernacles [a tent or cloth hut] with Isaac and Jacob, the heirs with him of the same promise: For he looked for a city which hath foundations, whose builder and maker is God (Heb. 11:9-10).

His acquaintance with God and the revelations of truths, though much less than the present, assured him that after the present age there was a celestial kingdom and an eternal city. He endured the tents and huts in grand anticipation of the golden future. Faith was his stay.

The first covenant is filled with the hope of the future. Almost every prophet has some revelation of this great reality. Isaiah gave a vivid description in Isaiah 65:17-25:

> For, behold, I create new heavens and a new earth: and the former shall not be remembered, nor come into mind. But be ye glad and rejoice for ever in that which I create: for, behold, I create Jerusalem a rejoicing, and her people a joy. And I will rejoice in Jerusalem, and joy in my people: and the voice of weeping shall be no more heard in her, nor the voice of crying. There shall be no more thence an infant of days, nor an old man that hath not filled his days: for the child shall die an hundred years old; but the sinner being an hundred years old shall be accursed. And they shall build houses, and inhabit them; and they shall plant vineyards, and eat the fruit of them. They shall not build, and another inhabit; they shall not plant, and another eat: for as the days of a tree are the days of my

people, and mine elect shall long enjoy the work of their hands. They shall not labor in vain, nor bring forth for trouble; for they are the seed of the blessed of the Lord, and their offspring with them. And it shall come to pass, that before they call, I will answer; and while they are yet speaking, I will hear. The wolf and the lamb shall feed together, and the lion shall eat straw like the bullock: and dust shall be the serpent's meat. They shall not hurt nor destroy in all my holy mountain, saith the Lord.

Zechariah clearly placed this day as the day (revelation) of the Lord (Jesus Christ) when He would descend from the Father's right hand to take possession from our enemies.

Then shall the Lord go forth, and fight against those nations, as when he fought in the day of battle (Zech. 14:3).

And the Lord shall be king over all the earth: in that day shall there be one Lord, and his name one (Zech. 14:9).

In that day shall there be upon the bells of the horses, HOLINESS UNTO THE LORD; and the pots in the Lord's house shall be like the bowls before the altar. Yea, every pot in Jerusalem and in Judah shall be holiness unto the Lord of hosts: and all they that sacrifice shall come and take of them, and seethe therein: and in that day there shall be no more the Canaanite in the house of the Lord of hosts (Zech. 14:20-21).

They shall beat their swords into plowshares, and their spears into pruninghooks: nation shall not lift up sword against nation, neither shall they learn war any more (Isa. 2:4).

The wolf also shall dwell with the lamb, and

the leopard shall lie down with the kid; and the calf
and the young lion and the fatling together; and a
little child shall lead them (Isa. 11:6).

The earth shall be full of the knowledge of the
Lord, as the waters cover the sea (Isa. 11:9).

The first covenant literally abounds with these kinds of
expressions as these Holy Ghost inspired servants labored
under pressure but lived with spiritual eyes trained on the
golden kingdom. They knew better than to even suggest this
kingdom would be of their own doing. It was the payday
someday that they lived to enjoy. Paul said, "Of whom the
world was not worthy: they wandered in deserts, and in
mountains, and in dens and caves of the earth . . . having
obtained a good report through faith, received not the
promise" (Heb. 11:38-39). Believe me, they will yet receive
the promise!

This hope of a golden age was so embedded in the
Jewish mindset that the disciples of Jesus could not grasp
His kingdom concepts. They wanted an earthly kingdom
but, He was establishing a spiritual one. Even at His ascension in the Book of Acts, they were still asking the question,
"Wilt thou at this time restore again the kingdom to Israel?"
(Acts 1:6). The Messiah, as they supposed, was to fulfill all
those golden promises. They finally saw the *Church Age* or
dispensation as the interlude between Christ's death and the
golden future. After they were filled with the Holy Spirit
they labored untiringly, always watching for Jesus to return
to receive them. The time of His coming was their biblical
signal that it was time for judgment followed by the golden
kingdom. We are still watching as they did for that event (the
Rapture) and the beginning of the consummation of all
things.

The Time Is at Hand

Every biblical sign points to the completing of the
church age. Israel is in place in Palestine. Babylon is being

readied for the Antichrist. A world religious alliance never before considered by religious leaders is almost complete. World government is being either demanded or considered by almost every leader of the world. The only group of people in all the societies of the world that are losing their rights are Bible-believing fundamental Christians and Orthodox Jews. We are becoming more than ever a despised minority.

Before the final judgment of the wicked called the wrath of the Lamb, Jesus will come for His *bride*. Satan hates this great biblical truth, but he cannot stop Him or us. We will rise.

> Let not your heart be troubled: ye believe in God, believe also in me. In my Father's house are many mansions: if it were not so, I would have told you. I go to prepare a place for you. And if I go and prepare a place for you, I will come again, and receive you unto myself; that where I am, there ye may be also (John 14:1-3).

Following the seven years of the Great Tribulation, Jesus and His raptured saints will return to the earth to establish the golden kingdom. Jesus Christ clearly stated that this dark day of Tribulation would precede this kingdom of righteousness.

> For then shall be great tribulation, such as was not since the beginning of the world to this time, no, nor ever shall be. And except those days should be shortened, there should no flesh be saved: but for the elect's sake those days shall be shortened (Matt. 24:21-22).

Theologically, this golden kingdom has been called the Millennium which means, one thousand years. John spoke as the Holy Ghost gave him the utterance:

> And I saw thrones, and they sat upon them,

and judgment was given unto them: and I saw the souls of them that were beheaded for the witness of Jesus, and for the word of God, and which had not worshipped the beast, neither his image, neither had received his mark upon their foreheads, or in their hands; and they lived and reigned with Christ a thousand years (Rev. 20:4-6).

These words are very clear and they are to be interpreted literally. Jesus alone can defeat the armies of Satan and He will do so with His raptured saints joining Him in victory.

Both the first covenant and the second covenant give great support to the role of the Messiah in His personal victory over our enemies. Daniel saw all of the man-made empires as a great image made of divers metals with a mixture of clay in her last stage. Then he saw the victor as following:

> Thou sawest till that a stone was cut out without hands, which smote the image upon his feet that were of iron and clay, and brake them to pieces. Then was the iron, the clay, the brass, the silver, and the gold, broken to pieces together, and became like the chaff of the summer threshing-floors; and the wind carried them away, that no place was found for them: and the stone that smote the image became a great mountain, and filled the whole earth (Dan. 2:34-35).

The little stone (our crucified Saviour) became a great mountain and filled the whole earth. This great kingdom will be a one world government with Jesus Christ as the King of kings and Lord of lords. Always remember that Satan's efforts are an imitation of the Father's plan. Lucifer's one world government headed by the Antichrist is an ill-conceived effort to pre-empt the kingdom of Jesus Christ. It will fail miserably.

The Celestial Kingdom

The glory of the Garden of Eden presents a foretaste of this grand time. Every distasteful result of human sin that has spoiled our planet will be removed. Vicious earthly creatures will become as tame as a house kitten. The harsh atmospheric conditions will be changed to that which enhances our pleasure and comfort. From east to west and north to south, our world will be free of the curse. The only reminder of our former state will be the death of natural men who survived the tribulation and a withholding of earthly blessing from those of this same group who refuse the worship of the true creator God and His Son Jesus Christ.

Human government has been a dismal failure. Our nation of America has probably been the greatest success of all efforts to govern society. Even this nation will continue to disintegrate as we approach the end. Most governments have made life unbearable for their subjects. Babylon under Nebuchadnezzar elevated human control over the masses to an art form. Bureaucracies were established to create a system of domination. You should notice how the churches have become an extension of this same design. The *shepherding/discipleship* disaster (still strong) was a striking example. (Shepherding/discipleship teaching: Complete control by pastor and elders over the life decisions of the church membership.) Jesus will set up a government that is righteous and just.

The bride of Christ that was raptured before the Tribulation and other orders of resurrected saints will reign with Christ over this golden kingdom. As soon as the Bride arrives in heaven a celebration commences.

> And they sung a new song, saying, Thou art worthy to take the book, and to open the seals thereof: for thou wast slain, and hast redeemed us to God by thy blood out of every kindred, and tongue, and people, and nation: And hast made us unto our God kings and priests: and we shall

reign on the earth (Rev. 5:9-10).

This heavenly event will end in the coronation of the King himself and will then proceed to leave the heavenly city for the inauguration of the new King in the world capital — "Jerusalem."

> And I saw heaven opened, and behold a white horse; and he that sat upon him was called Faithful and True, and in righteousness he doth judge and make war. His eyes were as a flame of fire, and on his head were many crowns; and he had a name written, that no man knew, but he himself. And he was clothed with a vesture dipped in blood: and his name is called the Word of God. And the armies which were in heaven followed him upon white horses, clothed in fine linen, white and clean. And out of his mouth goeth a sharp sword, that with it he should smite the nations: and he shall rule them with a rod of iron: and he treadeth the winepress of the fierceness and wrath of Almighty God. And he hath on his vesture and on his thigh a name written, KING OF KINGS, AND LORD OF LORDS (Rev. 19:11-16).

Isaiah the prophet spoke of this glorious day. Obedient believers living by faith and reveling in their love for Jesus, have tasted a little of this joy as we await the grand finale. That foretaste of our future has given us hope to endure.

> The wilderness and the solitary place shall be glad for them; and the desert shall rejoice, and blossom as the rose. It shall blossom abundantly, and rejoice even with joy and singing: the glory of Lebanon shall be given unto it, the excellency of Carmel and Sharon, they shall see the glory of the Lord, and the excellency of our God. Strengthen ye the weak hands, and confirm the feeble knees. Say

to them that are of a fearful heart, Be strong, fear not: behold, your God will come with vengeance, even God with a recompence; he will come and save you. Then the eyes of the blind shall be opened, and the ears of the deaf shall be unstopped. Then shall the lame man leap as an hart, and the tongue of the dumb sing: for in the wilderness shall waters break out, and streams in the desert. And the parched ground shall become a pool, and the thirsty land springs of water: in the habitation of dragons, where each lay, shall be grass with reeds and rushes. And an highway shall be there, and a way, and it shall be called The way of holiness; the unclean shall not pass over it; but it shall be for those: the wayfaring men, though fools, shall not err therein. No lion shall be there, nor any ravenous beast shall go up thereon, it shall not be found there: but the redeemed shall walk there: And the ransomed of the Lord shall return, and come to Zion with songs and everlasting joy upon their heads: they shall obtain joy and gladness, and sorrow and sighing shall flee away (Isa. 35:1-10).

The center of this stream of earthly prosperity and sanctified government shall be Jerusalem and the throne of David. Righteousness will literally fill the earth.

The animal kingdom will become a joy to all mankind (read Isa. 11:6-9). Everything that our Father created was for His and our pleasures. It will be a worldwide zoo of uncaged creatures in their natural habitats. It will be a delight to experience their beauty. No animal slaughter will ever occur again.

And in that day will I make a covenant for them with the beasts of the field, and with the fowls of heaven, and with the creeping things of the ground: and I will break the bow and the sword and the battle out of the earth, and will make them to lie down safely (Hos. 2:18).

Glorified saints of the nations of the world will be His ruling elite. Governors, princes, mayors, and all governing individuals will be His faithful servants who have earned the right to rule by virtue of obedience to Him. It will be a world of justice, mercy, equality, and compassion. Every saint will be rewarded according to what they have done in the flesh. It will be a merit system instead of a caste system. We will have equal rights but individual rewards.

Multiple scriptural details describe the grandness of this hour. The return of this triumphant redeemer riding His great white stallion will be too glorious to describe. His appearing in the air above the marching hordes of the Antichrist's army will strike paralyzing fear. The sword of His mouth is but His piercing Words of judgment. The entire army of millions will be instantly defeated. The Battle of Armageddon will be months in organizing and moments in finalizing. The Word of God will take flaming vengeance on this diabolical mob.

With the same expression of eternal glory He will turn to the establishment of His earthly kingdom after the enemy is vanquished. This entire planet will become His parish and the object of His kingly favor. Not a detail will be forgotten. Every member of His bride will be placed in proper authority. The resurrected saints who were guests of the Bride or the Groom will be given places of service. He will quickly establish a worldwide theocracy based on the holiness of His person. With sin judged and adjudicated, the earth will be free of its curse. Even the beauty of a sunrise will be enhanced by the absence of a poisoned atmosphere. Every expression of our natural world will be a testimony of the Redeemer's created glory.

Every believer should live in grand anticipation of this golden kingdom. It is hard to imagine, but after this one thousand years of righteousness, an even greater period will follow. The New Jerusalem will descend from God out of heaven to be fixed over this planet Earth. Only then will Abraham enter into that city with foundation suspended in the mid-air above the earthly kingdom. John described this city as a bride adorned for her husband (Rev. 21 and 22). It is the final glory of His kingdom and eternity will begin. This glorious Kingdom will be the everlasting abode of our eternal God and His glorified family. Every believer should learn to live daily in expectation of this triumphant future.

Before this glorious future can be inherited, the world must be the scene of final events. The one world religion is a dark picture and every biblical believer must prepare to discern this false copy of truth. Let us look at a one world religion right now developing on the world's horizon.

Chapter 6

A One World Religion

The prophetic picture in Holy Scripture is absolutely clear: There must be a new world religion, a spiritual Babylon to help present to the world the Antichrist-controlled New World Order. No political entity has ever succeeded without a form of religion to give it inspiration and purpose. Nazism was a child of eugenics (a system of human improvement by genetic means rooted in evolution) in which Hitler convinced the German people that they were a master race. It became a religion of satanism ready to destroy six million Jews and as many Christians. By eliminating inferior persons, they were convinced they would produce a master race of Germans to control the world. Only God kept them from succeeding.

Communism was a religion of Karl Marx, another madman who had rejected Jesus Christ and became possessed by demons. It was only slightly different from Nazism in that the emphasis was on the class struggle. They were committed to the elimination of all forms of capitalism so that the elite Communists could then control a world without competition where all men lived equal under totalitarian control except the master controllers at the top. Only the idiot god named Lucifer could conceive a plot so barbarous and cruel. During 70 years of this mindless idea they murdered millions of innocent lives.

Our political leaders have chosen the United Nations as the primary political entity to head their much heralded New World Order. It is not hard to discover the basic philosophy that underlines this organization. Almost from its inception, the rhetoric and action of the U.N. has been anti-American, anti-Christian, anti-Israel, and anti all the values that lay at the heart of Judeo-Christian traditions. They could not have made a worse choice if they had chosen the KGB of the Soviet Union. The United Nations has been busy promoting religious heathenism in its many forms for decades. It is a New Age organization at best. Read the following poem that was aired internationally from the U.N. building on the anniversary of John Lennon's death.

> Imagine there's no heaven, It's easy if you try. No hell below us, Above us only sky. Imagine all the people living for today.
>
> Imagine there's no country, It isn't hard to do. Nothing to kill or die for, and no religion, too. Imagine all the people living in peace.
>
> Imagine no possessions, I wonder if you can. No need for greed or hunger, a brotherhood of man. Imagine all the people sharing all the world.
>
> You may say I'm a dreamer, But I'm not the only one. I hope some day you'll join us, And the world will be as one.

New World Religious Order

The Holy Scripture has perfectly foretold of this one world religious order that would give credibility and power to the one world political system. This religious system, or its primary leader, is called a beast and/or a false prophet. (This system is called Spiritual Babylon in Rev. 17.) Here is John the Revelator's first description:

And I beheld another beast coming up out of the earth; and he had two horns like a lamb, and he spake as a dragon. And he exerciseth all the power of the first beast before him, and causeth the earth and them which dwell therein to worship the first beast, whose deadly wound was healed. And he doeth great wonders, so that he maketh fire come down from heaven on the earth in the sight of men, And deceiveth them that dwell on the earth by the means of those miracles which he had power to do in the sight of the beast; saying to them that dwell on the earth, that they should make an image to the beast, which had the wound by a sword, and did live. And he had power to give life unto the image of the beast, that the image of the beast should both speak, and cause that as many as would not worship the image of the beast should be killed. And he causeth all, both small and great, rich and poor, free and bond, to receive a mark in their right hand, or in their foreheads: And that no man might buy or sell, save he that had the mark, or the name of the beast, or the number of his name. Here is wisdom. Let him that hath understanding count the number of the beast: for it is the number of a man; and his number is Six hundred threescore and six (Rev. 13:11-18).

Several functions of this religious order are clearly described in the above quotation. Please note carefully how important these actions are in promoting this new world political system or New World Order as our leaders are calling it.

    1. The one world religion has the same power and standing as the new world political order and is the authority that requires the people to worship the Antichrist (verse 12).

    2. The head of this religious order will resur-

rect the false christ after he is slain with a sword. This will be a kind of mimic of the resurrection of Jesus Christ (verse 14).

3. This religious giant will also have power to animate a statue of the false christ and cause the statue to speak and pronounce judgment (verse 15). There are reports of weeping statues of the Madonna preparing people for this kind of phenomenon. This statue of the Antichrist is called by Jesus in Matthew 24:15, "The Abomination of Desolation," and will be installed in the Jewish temple in Jerusalem.

4. The new world religious order will be the force behind the mark of the beast. This will be a religious mark, not just an economic number like our social security identification. To receive this mark requires obedience to the New Religion. People cannot be identified until they are initiated into the religion of the unholy trinity: Satan (anti-God), first beast (Antichrist), second beast or false prophet (anti-Holy Spirit) (verse 16).

Since the mark of the beast (666) is a religious mark identifying the person as a worshipper of the new godhead, no person can be redeemed or saved after receiving this mark. They are lost forever.

> And the beast was taken, and with him the false prophet that wrought miracles before him, and with which he deceived them that had received the mark of the beast, and them that worshipped his image. These both were cast alive into a lake of fire burning with brimstone (Rev. 19:20).

New World Religion Called The Great Whore

The description of this false religion becomes even more graphic as the picture unfolds. It is called a beast or false prophet in the previous explanation, but after receiving power from the Antichrist and great acceptance and worship from the world population, this new world religion becomes a mammoth force. It is now called The Great Whore and is seen "riding a scarlet-coloured beast, full of names of blasphemy" (Rev. 17:3). Let us look carefully at John's description:

> Come hither; I will show unto thee the judgment of the great whore that sitteth upon many waters. With whom the kings of the earth have committed fornication, and the inhabitants of the earth have been made drunk with the wine of her fornication. So he carried me away in the spirit into the wilderness: and I saw a woman sit upon a scarlet-coloured beast, full of names of blasphemy, having seven heads and ten horns. And the woman was arrayed in purple and scarlet colour, and decked with gold and precious stones and pearls, having a golden cup in her hand full of abominations and filthiness of her fornication: And upon her forehead was a name written, MYSTERY, BABYLON THE GREAT, THE MOTHER OF HARLOTS AND ABOMINATIONS OF THE EARTH. And I saw the woman drunken with the blood of the saints, and with the blood of the martyrs of Jesus: and when I saw her, I wondered with great admiration (Rev. 17:1-6).

Please note her characteristics and vileness.

1. This religious whore is a great fornicator and is guilty of changing, twisting, and debauching the Word of God. God has pronounced judgment on anyone who adds to or subtracts from the Word of God. "For I testify unto every man that heareth the words of the prophecy of this book, If any many shall add unto these things, God shall add unto him the plagues that are written in this book: And if any

man shall take away from the words of the book of
this prophecy, God shall take away his part out of
the book of life, and out of the holy city, and from
the things which are written in this book" (Rev.
22:18-19).

2. She is rich, but spends her riches on herself.
She is proud and worldly and decks herself with
costly jewels. She drank from a golden cup in
which the content has become vileness and abomination.

3. She is a mother of harlots and all her
offspring are as wicked as herself.

4. Her greatest hatred is for the true believers
who hold to the Holy Bible and its infallible truths.
She is drunk with the blood of murdered saints.

Nothing is as vile as religion that has lost its way and
departed from purity and holiness. There have been many
dark moments in the past when this has happened. Jesus
came in a time when the Jewish religion was a botched form
of greed and selfishness. He walked into the temple with a
whip and drove out the temple evangelists. The Reformation
came after a thousand years of Madonna-worship, indul-
gences (buying sin rights from the priest in advance), and
distorted communion called Mass. Again, the Holy Spirit
drove out the priest and pope, and the gospel was heard by
millions. Very soon religion will be more vicious and vile
than ever before, and multitudes will either worship a false
god or will be tortured and slain. The Son of God will arrive
on schedule to cleanse this earth of the last religious deception and He will be installed as King, Prophet, and Priest.

This New World Religion Is at Hand

We have passed the day of the old ecumenicalism;
churches working together under the name of Jesus Christ as
Lord, the new ecumenical force is at least two steps removed. The second step of the ecumenical world included

a working relationship between Protestants, Catholics, and Jewish individuals or groups. The new ecumenical movement has embraced all religious expression and is clearly setting sights on a return to the Catholic fold. Listen to these expressions:

Dr. Robert Schuller: It's time for Protestants to go to the shepherd (the pope) and say "What do we have to do to come home?" (*Los Angeles Herald Examiner*, September 19, 1987)

USA Ministers: Heads of the American Protestant and Eastern Orthodox churches who were meeting with Pope John Paul II on Friday hailed their first, broadly representative discussion as a landmark on the road to greater unity. . . . The Reverend Donald Jones, a United Methodist and chairman of the University of South Carolina religious studies department, termed it "the most important ecumenical meeting of the century." . . . The Reverend Paul A. Crow Jr., of Indianapolis, ecumenical officer of the Christian Church (Disciples of Christ), called it a "new day in ecumenism" opening a future in which God "is drawing us together." (*The Montgomery Advertiser*, September 12, 1987)

Anglican Leader: Anglican leader Archbishop Robert Runcie called Saturday for all Christians to accept the Roman Catholic Pope as a common leader "presiding in love." "For the universal church, I renew the plea," he said. "Could not all Christians come to reconsider the kind of primacy the bishop of Rome (the pope) exercised within the early church?" (*The Dallas Morning News*, October 1, 1989, *Associated Press*)

Baptist & Catholic Theologians: Southern Baptists and Roman Catholics, the nation's two largest denominations, generally have been regarded as doctrinally far apart, but their scholars find they basically agree. . . . The 163-page report is seen as the most full-scale, mutual examination of respective positions of the two traditions. Achieving it was an unprecedented experience for Southern Baptists, commonly averse to ecumenical affairs. . . . The talks, sponsored by the Catholic Bishops' Committee on Ecumenical and Inter-religious Affairs and the Southern Baptist Department of Interfaith Witness, involved 18 meetings between 1978 and 1988. (*The Bakersfield Californian*, August 27, 1989, *Associated Press*)

Never before have church leaders been so intent on unifying all varying expressions of religion. It is like a mad dash into the very spirit of Babylonian confusion. The World Council of Churches recently met in Australia. A leader, Nicholas Lossky, was asked by a television journalist, "How close are we to church unity?" His answer was:

"Only God can answer that, we must do whatever we can for unity: but only God can decide to produce the event." The same article that recounted this exchange stated, "Church unity is listed first among the WCC's functions and purposes in its constitution." The same article then mentioned a session on unity which included Deegalle Mahinda, a Buddhist monk from Sri Lanka.[1]

Pagans At World Council of Churches Assembly — 1991

The World Council of Churches chose to open its seventh assembly with a ceremonial welcome from pagans of Australia. Aboriginal witch doctors performed animalistic ceremonies to welcome the Catholics, Presbyterians, Methodists, Disciples of Christ, Evangelical Lutherans,

American Baptists, and others to this event. The religion of these pagans is animalistic and does not differ at all from African heathenism. Not only did they perform, but all the worshippers at the Assembly opening session were forced, if they attended, to enter the Assembly Hall through a pagan cleansing ritual. Here is the description of that ritual from their publication:

> The worship began with an Australian Aboriginal ritual. Participants entered the tent through the smoke of burning branches, a traditional aboriginal cleansing ritual.[2]

The blood of Jesus Christ was blasphemed as they dared claim cleansing through a pagan and heathen ceremony.

It is hard to believe such mindless activities could be tolerated by an organization claiming to represent the major Christian churches of the world, much less force all who attend to blaspheme God. You cannot call this action anything but a direct act of pagan worship in defiance of the first commandment, "Thou shalt have no other gods before me" (Exod. 20:3).

An article in the same edition as listed above described the religious belief of the Aborigines. Note how carefully the speakers blended paganism with Christianity.

> "The spirituality of the Aboriginal women keeps them going. The power of the Spirit enables each person to have strength," said Agnes Palmer of Alice Springs. "This is the power we have through our dreaming and the power of Jesus, who came not to destroy our culture [pagan] but to fulfill it." She used water as an example of the oneness between Aboriginal spirituality and Christian faith. "In our spirituality, water is a sign of life, a source of life, just as, in Christianity, baptism with water gives new life."[3]

New World Religion Fads

The Islamic Faith. Every religious entity of significance seems to have some form of expectancy toward a new world religious order. The Islamic (Moslems or Muslims) faith is promoting a World Constitution that is rooted in the Quran theology. This is probably the fastest growing religion in the world and now claims over one billion adherents. The very spirit of Islam is especially similar to the stated actions and attitude of the Antichrist in Scripture.

Charismatics/Pentecostals. A large portion of the Charismatic/Pentecostal world is going crazy over Kingdom Dominion theology. This is best described as a revived form of post-millenniumism, although differing on many major theological points. The bottom line is that we are to become an army of saints (called Joel's Army) to beat back all forces and to establish the kingdom of Christ on earth. It is said to be, to those who buy this deception, a world ruled by the church and ready to bring Christ back to earth.

The Catholic Church. The Catholic church authorities have worked toward and have expected a new world religious system for many years. They expect to be at the helm to rule this new temporal religious kingdom. Note these two quotes of 50 years ago and 114 years ago, respectively:

> They (Protestants) conveniently forget that they separated from us, not we from them; and that it is for them to return to unity on Catholic terms, not for us to seek union with them, or to accept it, on their terms. . . . Protestantism is rebellion against the authority of Christ vested in His Church. It neither possesses authority, or has any desire to submit to authority. . . . Protestantism has really proved to be the ally of paganism. . . . All forms of Protestantism are unjustified. They should not exist.[4]

We believe in the triumph of the Catholic Church over infidelity, heresy, schism, revolution, and despotism; over Judaism, Mohammedanism, and heathenism. The restoration of the Pope's temporal kingdom is necessary to this triumph, and therefore we believe it will be restored.[5]

New Agers. No religious entity is expecting or progressing toward a new world religion more devotedly than the New Agers. While they represent many strains of thought they are bound together as a network of loosely connected organizations. There are a few key spokespersons who certainly speak with some degree of unity. Benjamin Creme is one of those key voices. He has continued to suggest since early in the eighties that the *christ* is here and ready to be revealed. His latest claims say that *he* has appeared on several occasions. His christ is clearly a false prophet.

Bible Believers. True believers who are willing to endure unto the end will be hated by this religious crowd. If Jesus does not return before this religious order is united, we will be in for dark days of persecution. Faith in the infallible Word of God and the saturation of its wonderful doctrines is imperative. **We must know the truth to be free.** Do not fill your mind with any thoughts or ideas except the liberating truths of Scripture. They will prepare you for anything that Satan can cast in your direction.

There will be a new world religion. Its ultimate position of power will not be realized until the rapture of the Bride. The new world religion will ride as a great whore upon the back of a New World Order. "So he carried me away in the spirit into the wilderness: and I saw a woman sit upon a scarlet-coloured beast, full of names of blasphemy, having seven heads and ten horns" (Rev. 17:3).

While she will reach great heights of world glory and power with the false political systems of Antichrist, when he has used her to gain the hearts of the world population, he will then burn her with fire. "And the ten horns which thou sawest upon the beast, these shall hate the whore, and shall make her desolate and naked, and shall eat her flesh, and burn her with fire" (Rev. 17:16).

Religion is never more than a tool to the great political empires. When President George Bush called a world renowned religious leader to the White House the night our military forces invaded Iraq, we should have read the handwriting on the wall. I do not suggest he was being crafty, but I do suggest that biblical prophecy was being fulfilled. Religious leaders who allow themselves to be tools in building a New World Order are certainly careless in discerning biblical events.

The most appropriate instruction for this hour is to "look up, our redemption draweth nigh." We are waiting in the foyer for the king. Do not be lazy or slothful. It is an hour for biblical diligence, fasting and intercession, soul winning and alms giving. It is time to be holy. The King is coming!

Let us proceed to see the mark or identification by which the Babylonian or Assyrian Antichrist will control his vast kingdom. The world is already prepared for this fateful hour.

[1] *Assembly Line*, World Council of Churches, Seventh Assembly, February 13, 1991.
[2] Ibid., February 7, 1991, no. 1, page 1.
[3] Ibid., February 8, 1991.
[4] *American Catholic* periodical, January 4, 1941.
[5] *The Catholic World*, August 1877, Vol. XXV, page 620.

Chapter 7

The MARK of
the Beast

More Scripture is being fulfilled right now in one generation than ever before in human history. On the surface, the secular news is horrifying, but coupled with biblical prophecy, it invokes the promise, "Look up, and lift up your heads for your redemption draweth nigh" (Luke 21:28).

The shadow of the wrath of the Lamb is clearly in view. Signs of the end have been visible in previous generations, but never have so many signs converged at one time. Many of these signs have never been seen before. While previous individuals or nations have aspired to a one world government, the means to control the world have not existed. Technology now makes it possible to issue a mark (may be spelled marc) to every living individual within a matter of months and to tabulate and control every monetary action of each individual. Incredible, possible, and already being discussed by both the media and big government.

The Biblical Facts, Revealed In Advance

The Book of Revelation records this kind of future history in advance. No wonder liberal preachers deny the biblical value of this prophetic book. It leaves no doubt about what is going to happen. There is going to be a great deception ending in an effort to force everyone to worship the false christ. This false christ (Antichrist) will be an almost perfect imitation of the Lord Jesus Christ. Remember, Satan is the master imitator.

Please read these words carefully:

> And I beheld another beast coming up out of the earth; and he had two horns like a lamb, and he spake as a dragon. And he exerciseth all the power of the first beast before him, and causeth the earth and them which dwell therein to worship the first beast, whose deadly wound was healed. And he doeth great wonders, so that he maketh fire come down from heaven on the earth in the sight of men, And deceiveth them that dwell on the earth by the means of those miracles which he had power to do in the sight of the beast; saying to them that dwell on the earth, that they should make an image to the beast, which had the wound by a sword, and did live. And he had power to give life unto the image of the beast, that the image of the beast should both speak, and cause that as many as would not worship the image of the beast should be killed. And he causeth all, both small and great, rich and poor, free and bond, to receive a mark in their right hand, or in their foreheads: And that no man might buy or sell, save he that had the mark, or the name of the beast, or the number of his name. Here is wisdom. Let him that hath understanding count the number of the beast: for it is the number of a man; and his number is Six hundred threescore and six (Rev. 13:11-18).

A verse by verse look at this biblical revelation reveals many details of the coming deception. This beast has two horns like a lamb (remember that lambs don't have horns) and speaks as a dragon. This reveals the false religious quality of his character. It is a picture of beastly piety or arrogant sacredness; religion with a political agenda and a sword instead of a cross.

The duty of this beast, which is the third member of the unholy trinity, is to lead or deceive the world into the worship and service of the false christ. He will be the charismatic leader of the one world religious system. That system is being developed as you read this chapter.

Recently, leading evangelicals signed an agreement with the Catholic church to work together as fellow Christians and to refrain from proselytizing each other. The leaders that signed this agreement read like a Who's Who of the evangelical world. The Pope has clearly welcomed heathens into fellowship with the Catholic church. This places heathen witch doctors and numerous pagan religions, etc. in union with Pentecostal, Evangelical, and many other mainline Christian organizations. A one world religion is at the door.

Pope John Paul II, while addressing Brazilians during his 1991 meeting to that country, warned them about the evangelical sects. In March 1994 the Bishops of Brazil declared his threat against those same evangelicals:

> We will declare a holy war; don't doubt it. . . .
> The Catholic church has a ponderous structure, but when we move, we'll smash anyone beneath us."[1]

A report on this event recorded the following comment:

> According to Bohn (Catholic bishop of Brazil), an all-out holy war can't be avoided unless the 13 largest Protestant churches and denominations sign a treaty — similar to treaties signed by nations to end wars. He said it would require Protestants to stop all evangelism efforts in Brazil. In exchange, he said, Catholics would agree to stop all persecution directed toward Protestants. Bohn called his

proposal an "ultimatum," and he said it would leave no room for discussion.[2]

The Associated Press stated the following in a recent news article:

> A new Vatican document on how to interpret the Bible condemns the fundamentalist approach as distorting, dangerous, and possibly leading to racism. . . . The . . . harsh language reflects the challenge that fundamentalism poses to the church . . . fundamentalism actually invites people to a kind of "intellectual suicide," said the document, written by the Pontifical Biblical Commission. . . . The authors saved their harshest language for Christian fundamentalist denominations. . . . The fundamentalist approach is dangerous, for it is attractive to people who look to the Bible for ready answers to the problems of life. (This came from a 130-page Vatican document entitled "The Interpretation of the Bible in the Church.")[3]

A Lamb With Horns

Does this not sound like a lamb with horns that speaks as a dragon? It is amazing that world religion leaders could be so deceived as to believe such an agreement holds water, much less spiritual credibility. We will continue to see religious leaders who appear to know nothing about Jesus Christ and biblical prophecy involved in the new world religion.

The Mark Will Be Enforced By the One World Religion

Many Bible students have not realized that it will be the religious arm of the one world government that enforces the mark (read verses 14-16 again). There will be miracles and all manner of supernatural happenings. (Holy laughter is a current deception that is sweeping Charismatics.) Paul the

Apostle described it as the following:

> For the mystery of iniquity doth already work:
> only he who now letteth will let, until he be taken
> out of the way. And then shall that Wicked be
> revealed, whom the Lord shall consume with the
> spirit of his mouth, and shall destroy with the
> brightness of his coming: Even him, whose com-
> ing is after the working of Satan with all power and
> signs and lying wonders, And with all
> deceivableness of unrighteousness in them that
> perish; because they received not the love of the
> truth, that they might be saved (2 Thess. 2:7-10).

People, especially religious people, are highly suscep-
tible to emotional events. If you will give the majority of our
present day church members a religious high they will
accept anything you tell them. Look at the crowds that
follow one religious guru after another. Thousands are
traveling for many hours and spending thousands of dollars
to be excited by their favorite guru. All of this is in preparation for the ultimate deceiver. The church world is being
conditioned for deception. Biblical ignorance has never
been greater in the church. The Bible calls it a famine for
hearing the Word of God.

> Behold, the days come, saith the Lord God,
> that I will send a famine in the land, not a famine
> of bread, nor a thirst for water, but of hearing the
> words of the Lord (Amos 8:11).

Constantly, I get calls from individuals who are experiencing visions, dreams, revelations, and prophecies. There
are genuine experiences in all of these categories but always
in perfect harmony with the Word of God. Those whom God
uses in spiritual revelations are mature Christians that have
a firm footing in Holy Scripture and who have established
credibility in their church body by a Holy lifestyle. Most of
what we are hearing today is juvenile humbug. God does not

excite flesh to make known His Words. He reveals himself through our spirit and by His Word and His revelations are always given in decency and in order.

The Mark Is Almost Ready

I truly believe (no one can set dates) the mark is as ready as it needs to be before Jesus appears for the chosen betrothed. No sign is ever needed for Jesus to come and we should not look for such. His coming will be unannounced and sudden. The signs we are witnessing are signs of the things that will happen after the Rapture of the blood-washed church.

A Cashless Society

The world planners, including our president and many of our national leaders, have already envisioned America under the control of the United Nations and completely eliminating the need for cash in pocket. Here is a quote from Don McAlvany, editor of *The McAlvany Intelligence Advisor.*

> The U.S. Commission on Immigration Reform, the Clinton INS, and liberal Establishment types such as California Republican Governor Pete Wilson are pushing hard for a single, tamper-resistant INS card for all Americans (including your social security number, photo, fingerprint, and bar code) to verify employment eligibility. This card would be linked to a nationwide government database and would allegedly solve the problem of illegal aliens getting jobs.
>
> Marc Rotenberg, director of the Electronic Privacy Information Center, said in *USA Today* (7/14/94), "It will become a way to monitor people, like an internal passport."
>
> This Orwellian nightmare will, like the government's privacy/bank/cash reporting laws,

allow the government to monitor 260 million Americans who are *not* illegal aliens, just as they monitor the cash transactions of 260 million Americans who are *not* drug dealers.

Lucas Guttentage, of the ACLU (with whom this writer seldom agrees) said in the same USA Today article, "It won't work, it will cost billions, it won't solve the problems, and it will cause new forms of discrimination."

And Steve Moore of the Cato Institute points out that just as the government has abused the once private social security number and now uses it as a national ID number which ties together dozens of U.S. databases on each U.S. citizen, so it will abuse this card. Moore observed: "Look at history and see the abuses — they used social security numbers to round up and incarcerate the Japanese-Americans during World War II."

Mr. McAlvany, the editor, added: And look how government has violated its promises and abused gun owners in New York and California who were stupid enough to register their guns. In New York City they have confiscated many of those guns, and in California the 43,000 who registered 60 different firearms were computerized and are now closely monitored by numerous local, state, and federal agencies.

Later in the same article, Mr. McAlvany said:

The Clinton Administration is no longer debating *if*, but *how* they can create and introduce this smartcard (which will interact with any and all government agencies) to *all* Americans.

A further comment stated:

The Postal Service has acknowledged that it is prepared to put more than 100 million of the cards in citizens' pockets within months of Administration approval. This means that this project for the computerized control of all Americans is not only on the fast track, but is much further advanced than most people would suppose. And it is not being done with Congressional approval but rather through a series of presidential executive orders. [**Editor's Note:** Do we already have a dictatorship and just do not know it?]

President Clinton is close to signing two executive orders that would greatly expand the government's access to personal records, including an order that would allow the IRS to monitor individual bank accounts and automatically collect taxes on the results. Chamberlain said the IRS is aggressively pursuing plans for an identity card for taxpayers.

"There would be *one U.S. Card for every member of your family*. In the not-too-distant future, you are likely to find harmless looking SmartCards in the mail in an official envelope. *Without the U.S. Card (or whatever the SmartCard is ultimately called) you won't be able to own property, receive government benefits, get medical attention, conduct bank or credit card transactions, etc.* Without it, you can't do anything! Your life will be completely controlled by the device if the Clinton administration adopts the Postal Service proposal. Executive orders have already been drafted to adopt the cards and force them on the American people without congressional approval!"[4]

A recent article in the *Digital Media* (5/94), which was entitled "Ever Feel You're Being Watched? You Will," stated:

"There won't be anything you do in business that won't be collected and analyzed by the government. This National Information infrastructure is a better surveillance mechanism than Orwell or the government could have imagined. This (blank blank) thing is so pervasive and the propensity to connect it is so great that it is unstoppable." Murray continued: "Most of this shift in privacy policy is apparently being done by executive order at the initiative of the bureaucracy and without any congressional oversight or concurrence. They are not likely to fail. You know, Orwell said that bureaucrats, simply doing what bureaucrats do, without motive or intent, will use technology to enslave the people."

The writer was William Murray, an information system security consultant to Deloitte and Touche (May 1994).

Already the U.S. military is issuing a card reported to be a national ID prototype. Of all possible names to use, the military chose a biblical one: Marc (Multi-Technology Automated Reader Card). Mr. McAlvany described this card, "The MARC Card and its ID chip will be used by DOD to manage *all* medical information on *all* U.S. military personnel worldwide (i.e., it will store all medical information on each card carrier in its IC chip). It will store *all* personal information on each carrier, *all* legal information, *all* family information, and *all* personal data (i.e., educational background, police record, religious background — everything you would expect to be on a highly detailed job resume.)"

Beyond The Card: A Biochip

The card was just the beginning. The new idea is a biochip implant. It is already highly developed and being used in animals and humans. A type of this biochip has been used as an animal identification for a number of years. When an animal is lost, it can be located by the proper homing device and retrieved.

Now the biochip is being used for humans. An article in the *Los Angeles Times* Business Section (August 17, 1994) recently reported this with the following headline, "Giving Surgical Implants IDs." It stated that, "At least 6 million medical devices a year worldwide are surgically implanted in people — everything from breast implants to chin implants, vascular grafts and penile implants."

It further stated, "The information on the chip would also be recorded on a computer-linked global registry." Does this mean that a global registry is already in operation and recording the implant's number and information? It certainly would appear so.

An article appeared in *The Washington Times* (October 11, 1993) that was entitled, "High-Tech National Tattoo." This article discussed the SmartCard held by President Clinton when he spoke to the nation early in the year. After the author in the *Washington Times* discussed the card, he stated:

> You see, there is an identification system made by Hughes Aircraft Company that you can't lose. It's the syringe implantable transponder. According to promotional literature it is an "ingenious, safe, inexpensive, foolproof and permanent method of . . . identification using radio waves. A tiny microchip, the size of a grain of rice, is simply placed under the skin. It is so designed as to be injected simultaneously with a vaccination or alone."
>
> How does it work? Well, the "chip contains a 10-character alphanumeric identification code that is never duplicated. When a scanner is passed over the chip, the scanner emits a 'beep' and your . . . number flashes in the scanner's digital display."
>
> Sort of like a technological tattoo, and far more efficacious than the numbers that the Nazis marked indelibly on the inner forearms of concentration camp prisoners.

True, an implanted transponder can't yet hold anywhere near as much material as a smartcard. But if the desire is there, larger size implants and tiny microchips could soon increase its data storage capacity.

Tim Willard, managing editor of a bi-monthly magazine *Futurist* and, also executive officer of Washington, DC, based World Future Society (claiming 27,000 members) gave some incredible information. He spoke of a biochip with these words:

> The technology behind such a biochip implant is fairly uncomplicated and with a little refinement, could be used in a variety of human applications.

> Conceivably, a number could be assigned at birth and follow that person throughout life. Most likely, it would be implanted on the back of right or left hand so that it would be easy to scan at stores. Then you would simply scan your hand to automatically debit your banking account.

> The biochip implant could also be used as a universal type of identification card that would replace all credit cards, passports and that sort of thing. It could also become our medical care ID chip. It could even replace house and car keys someday.[5]

One company, Sematech, claims it has invented a biochip that is 1/200th the size of a strand of hair. This company is the largest employer in the nation and a maker of the components for advanced weapon systems used in the Gulf War. This 1993 article stated:

> The consortium announced that it had demonstrated the ability to manufacture integrated circuits with electronic device widths of 0.35 microns. And it did so using only American-made

tools. To reach this achievement, Sematech has spent $1 billion since its inception five years ago. Half was invested by a handful of private corporations that represent 75 percent of semiconductor manufacturing in the US. The other half was paid by the federal government through the Defense Advanced Research Projects Agency, which has a $1.5 billion budget to sponsor research by universities and national laboratories.[6]

Technology: Ready For World Control

This has never been possible before. Only the incredible capacities of computers, integrated circuits, scanners, satellites circling the earth with minute reading abilities, and other advanced technologies could render this operational. It is now practically ready and waiting for government bureaucrats to take control.

The present administration is anxious to set us up for the one world government. Almost all of our leaders are committed one-worlders. They envision in their mind a world where a nation making war on another nation is impossible. They have been sold the lie that peace is possible and a New World Order will achieve a wonderful world. There is no doubt but that Satan is the author of this bold lie.

The Countdown Is On

As we countdown to this New World Order, a spirit of genocide is gripping the world. A recent world leader demanded, in a report entitled "Global 2000," "that by the year 2000 the world population be reduced to two billion people." Look at what is being done to accomplish the reduction of population:

- In America alone, 37 million babies have been aborted since 1973.
- Communism has killed 130 million people since 1917.

- Two million people were allowed to die in Somalia before intervention.
- Five hundred thousand people died in Rwanda.
- There is incredible speculation (maybe facts) that AIDS was started by the medical arm of the U.N. They inoculated Africans almost 20 years ago with a smallpox vaccine.

According to the belief of Dr. William Campbell Douglass (editor of *The Second Opinion*), it all started with that inoculation. He says that AIDS broke out wherever that vaccine was administered. Presently, AIDS threatens half of Africa's population (almost 250,000,000 people). He further states that 10,000 Haitians were working in Belgian Congo and received this inoculation. They then took it back to Haiti where American homosexuals would go to fun and frolic in the sun. The homosexuals picked it up and brought it to America. He believes this is why it started with homosexuals in America and heterosexuals in Africa.

The United Nations is clearly a false religious organization. It has always been an enemy on our shores and a supporter of *one world government, one world religion, and one world economics.* President Bush said in a speech presented on September 17, 1990, "The Persian Gulf crisis is a rare opportunity to forge new bonds with old enemies . . . a unique and extraordinary moment. . . . Out of these troubled times a new world order can emerge under a United Nations that performs as envisioned by its founders."

World Identification, Not the Final Mark

I believe it is possible that world identification could begin before the Rapture. The final mark of the Antichrist includes more than a SmartCard or a biochip implant. I do not want either of these, but the final mark includes the worship of the Antichrist himself. It is a mark that includes world identification technology, but is also tied to the one world religion. Every person who takes this mark is committing themselves to the worship of a world messiah. They are selling him their soul for the right to do business in his world government. The Bible does not say which comes first.

Any person who is dependent on government welfare, food stamps, subsidies, etc. will probably be the first to be targeted. It is extremely important that you learn to trust in the Lord with all of your heart. He will supply all your needs. If socialized medicine comes to America with the proposed SmartCard supervision, you had better learn that Jesus is the Master Physician. In fact, you would be much better off if you learned that under any circumstance.

The Rapture: Any Day Now!

Before the Antichrist can be revealed and the mark initiated, the restrainer must be removed. The restrainer is the Holy Ghost and He cannot be removed until the betrothed of the Lord is raptured. His removal and our rapture will happen simultaneously. The Lord Jesus said that the Holy Ghost would be present in His church until the end of the church dispensation. Paul recounted His words: "For he hath said, I will never leave thee, nor forsake thee" (Heb. 13:5).

The Antichrist will be unhindered and open-throttled just as soon as the restrainer and the chosen Bride are removed to heaven. Unless you can survive in a world without God, you had better be ready to leave with the Holy Spirit and meet the Lord Jesus Christ in midair. Any moment now!

To view this beast of a man is a heart-rending experience. Saddam Hussein is nothing but a flash in the pan compared to this evil genius. The Antichrist is called an Assyrian because he will arise from the ancient empire of which Babylon was an intimate part. When an Assyrian was in great power he ruled Babylon and when Babylon was in great power they ruled Assyria. Just as Nineveh, the former capital of Assyria, is presently a province of Iraq, so these two areas are biblical ones. To call the Antichrist an Assyrian is but to speak of Babylon in its wider application of the former glory in Nebuchadnezzar's era. The term Assyrian suggests he will be a descendant from within the ancient boundaries of the Assyrian nation, but not particularly from Iraq. The Bible never misses these minute details. Let us look further at this evil genius.

[1] *Evangelicals and Catholics Together: The Christian Mission in the Third Millennium*, fifth draft, February 28, 1994, p. 1.

[2] *Charisma*, May 1994, p. 74.

[3] Associated Press, quoting *Evangelicals and Catholics Together: The Christian Mission in the Third Millennium*, fifth draft, February 28, 1994, p. 2.

[4] The McAlvany Intelligence Advisor, August 1994, p. 8-9

[5] *The Marin Independent Journal* (April 2, 1989), reprinted from *The Mark of the New World Order* by Terry Cook (Indianapolis, IN: Virtue International Publishing, 1996), p. 600.

[6] *The Electronic News*, January 25, 1993.

Chapter 8

The Assyrian and the Middle East

The most vicious beast ever known to man; diverse from all others; described in Scripture as the lion, bear, or leopard; or all three simultaneously, ". . . dreadful and terrible, and strong exceedingly . . . great iron teeth; it devoured and brake in pieces . . ." (Dan. 7:7), such is the biblical description of the Antichrist. This portrait is not of his appearance but of his character. No man in the Holy Bible has ever been described as this man. He is the greatest divulgence of evil and viciousness ever expressed in human flesh. In fact, empowering the Antichrist is one of the final expressions of Lucifer, ". . . and the dragon gave him his power, and his seat, and great authority" (Rev. 13:2). Satan, who has controlled all evil since he rebelled against the Creator, now will vest a portion of his authority to this final and extreme expression of himself. He (Satan) will still be playing God as he seeks to produce a counter-person to God's Son.

Everything that Jesus Christ loves, died for, and represents will be opposed by this Antichrist. Jesus was born of Jewish lineage near Jerusalem and died outside the city wall. Every Jew is still beloved of the Father. "As concerning the gospel they are enemies for your sakes: but as touching the election, they are beloved for the Father's sake" (Rom. 11:28). The city of Jerusalem is soon to be the center of the whole earth. "Beautiful for situation, the joy of the whole earth, is Mount Zion, on the sides of the North, the city of the great king" (Ps. 48:2). The Antichrist will hate the Jews and seek their complete annihilation. He will set his sight on Jerusalem in order to first control it, then he will later seek to destroy it.

He will also oppose true biblical Christianity. While he will use the mystery religions, which will include apostate Christians, he will hate every Bible-believing and Bible-obeying person. The bride of Christ will have escaped by the Rapture but millions of lukewarm professors and sinners who miss the Rapture will become radical servants of God by washing their garments in the blood of the Lamb. "They that are with him are called, and chosen, and faithful" (Rev. 7:14). These are hated by the Antichrist with a diabolical hatred. Thousands or even millions will be killed. "I beheld, and the same horn made war with the saints, and prevailed against them; until the Ancient of Days came" (Dan. 7:21-22). This clearly states that Christians will be slain right up to the point that Jesus appears in triumph and victory to establish His earthly kingdom.

The Seat Of The Antichrist

The Middle East is the center of the whole earth; Babylon is the seat of Satan; Jerusalem is the spiritual center of the Judeo-Christian revelation and soon to be the seat of Christ's kingdom. Iraq is rightly called the Cradle of Civilization because the Garden of Eden was in its southern tip where the Tigris and Euphrates Rivers meet just before entering the Persian Gulf. To look for Satan's final activities in any other area than the Middle East is to look in vain and in error.

It is very important to establish the geographical location for the Antichrist's appearance and the Holy Scripture has done so very carefully. Daniel's vision of the four wild beasts (Dan. 7:1-28) gives a clear picture of the last four World Empires. All four are seen to appear from the geographical area of the Mediterranean Sea. "Daniel spake and said, I saw in my vision by night, and, behold, the four winds of the heaven strove upon the great sea. And the four great beasts came up from the sea, diverse one from another." The scholar G.H. Lang said, "In Hebrew usage 'the great sea' is a proper noun and means invariably the Mediterranean." Every political power in the world is at this moment focusing on the Middle East. It has been utterly confirmed that control of the Middle East is the key to world influence. America and Russia have both positioned for this privilege for many years. Our military might and government are constantly seeking to influence the activities of this region.

Antichrist to Be an Assyrian

The Scripture has left no doubt that this beast of a man will be from Assyrian nationality. Three times Isaiah called him by this name. "O, Assyrian, the rod of mine anger, and the staff in their hand is mine indignation" (Isa. 10:5). This clearly suggests that he will attack Israel while they are still in unbelief. Isaiah further states: "I will break the Assyrian in my land, and upon my mountains tread him under foot: then shall his yoke depart from off them, and his burden depart from off their shoulders" (Isa. 14:25). In this prophecy, God's prophet declares that the Antichrist/the Assyrian will be broken upon the mountains of Israel which God calls *my mountains.*

Now note the third reference:

Behold, the name of the Lord cometh from far, burning with his anger, and the burden thereof is heavy: his lips are full of indignation, and his tongue as a devouring fire: And his breath, as an overflowing stream, shall reach to the midst of the neck, to sift the nations with the sieve of vanity:

and there shall be a bridle in the jaws of the people, causing them to err. Ye shall have a song, as in the night when a holy solemnity is kept; and gladness of heart, as when one goeth with a pipe to come into the mountain of the Lord, to the mighty One of Israel. And the Lord shall cause his glorious voice to be heard, and shall shew the lighting down of his arm, with the indignation of his anger, and with the flame of a devouring fire, with scattering, and tempest, and hailstones. For through the voice of the Lord shall the "Assyrian" be beaten down, which smote with a rod (Isa. 30:27-31).

This reference places his judgment in the final act of God's wrath at Armageddon. "His tongue (Jesus Christ) as a devouring fire" is almost the same statement as John the Revelator states: "Out of his mouth goeth a sharp sword that with it he should smite the nations" (Rev. 19:15). The statement, "For through the voice of the Lord shall the 'Assyrian' be beaten down," suggests the very same reality. "And there shall be a bridle in the jaw of the people causing them to err," is also a picture of the mindless unity with which the Antichrist gathers his army to march against Jerusalem in his last act of desperation.

Antichrist to Be from Seleucia Kingdom (Eastern Division of Grecian Empire)

Further support for the Middle East connection to the Antichrist is found in Daniel's vision of Daniel 8. This vision brings a scene of the Medes Persian conquest of Babylon followed by the armies of Grecia (Alexander the Great) which soon broke up into four regional kingdoms. The four regions were as follows: Gassander (Macedonia and Western part), Lysimachus (Thrace and the northern part), Seleucia (Syria and Eastern part), and Ptolemy (Egypt and southern part). Then Daniel said:

And in the latter time of their kingdom, when

the transgressors are come to the full, a king of fierce countenance, and understanding dark sentences, shall stand up. And his power shall be mighty, but not by his own power: and he shall destroy wonderfully, and shall prosper, and practice, and shall destroy the mighty and the holy people (Dan. 8:24-25).

Two things connect this passage to the Middle East. Isaiah said he would be an Assyrian which places his origination from the Seleucid Kingdom, presently Syria, including the eastern area of the old Assyrian Kingdom. (This included Northern Iraq, Northern Iran, and Southern Turkey.) Second, a great, great, great grandson of Seleucus was Antiochus IV (Epiphanes) who ruled from 175 to 163 B.C. He was a clear forerunner of the Antichrist. He actually slew a hog on the altar in the temple at Jerusalem. His anti-Jewish sentiments pre-date and provide a historical and prophetic picture of the coming Beast.

Jesus Christ Returns to Defeat the Assyrian

Micah may have seemed to be a minor prophet, but his presentation of the Messiah's first coming and rejection, and then His second coming to establish the long expected kingdom, is nothing short of eloquent. This prophet also named the Antichrist as the *Assyrian* and proclaims his defeat by the returning Christ.

Now gather thyself in troops, O daughter of troops: he hath laid siege against us: they shall smite the judge of Israel with a rod upon the cheek. But thou, Bethlehem Ephratah, though thou be little among the thousands of Judah, yet out of thee shall he come forth unto me that is to be ruler in Israel; whose goings forth have been from of old, from everlasting. Therefore will he give them up, until the time that she which travaileth hath brought forth: then the remnant of his brethren shall return unto the children of Israel. And he shall stand and feed in the strength of the Lord, in the majesty of the name of the Lord his God; and they shall abide: for now shall he be great unto the ends of the earth. And this man shall be the peace, when the Assyrian shall come into our land: and when he shall tread in our palaces, then shall we raise against him seven shepherds, and eight principal men. And they shall waste the land of Assyria with the sword, and the land of Nimrod in the entrances thereof: thus shall he deliver us from the Assyrian, when he cometh into our land, and when he treadeth within our borders (Mic. 5:1-6).

This breathtaking prophecy connects the Land of Assyria with the Land of Nimrod (Babylon and Iraq). The Assyrian capital was Nineveh or modern Mosul which is now in northern Iraq. It is clear that this event is the end of the Gentile kingdoms and the Battle of Armageddon. There is no historic event that could fulfill this prophetic truth. Also the victor is proclaimed to be the God/man born in Bethlehem and declared by Micah, "Yet out of thee shall he come forth unto me that is to be the ruler in Israel; whose goings forth have been from of old, from everlasting" (Mic. 5:2). Again Micah speaks with precision, "And this man shall be the peace, when the Assyrian shall come into our land . . . thus shall he deliver us from the Assyrian when he cometh into our land, and when he treadeth within our borders" (Mic. 5:5-6). Such eloquent prophecy gives powerful proof to the infallible Scripture and hope to the waiting bride of Jesus Christ.

Islam Religion and Mystery Babylon

The Islam or Moslem religion provides an excellent covering for the rise of the Antichrist. This false religion is nothing but a propaganda tool for anti-Jewish and anti-Christian sentiment. No one can question that the Moslem faith denies the right for the Jew even to exist much less possess a homeland in their midst. It is a crime worthy of capital punishment for a Saudi Arabian Moslem to convert to Christianity. Although some Arab countries treat a Moslem conversion to Christianity differently, all see the Jews and Christians as heathens. The root of this religion is pantheism which basically means that "God is all and all is God." It is the same as our modern New Agers have introduced into the West.

Prophetic writers have been warning of this for decades. G.H. Lang said, "And in practice, hero worship has never been more loudly exhibited than in the flaming devotion of his satanically blinded followers to Mohammed (founder of Moslem religion). Thus the system may be expected to blend easily into that of the Antichrist when he arises in its own native region, the Middle East."

Dr. Lang continued to describe this comparison between the founder of Islam and the final ruler of the Middle East, the Antichrist. He said, "His early career of wide and ruthless desolation will resemble closely that of Mohammed, and his fierce alternative, "Submit or perish!" will be precisely that of Islam, which very word itself means *submission*".[1]

A recognized intelligence specialist in England made the following statement, "The old communist Russia is becoming merely incidental to the main course of events which is going to be Islamic vs. Zionist. . . . The force of Islam will inevitably destroy Israel unless America intervenes at some stage."[2] This vicious philosophy of anti-Jewish/anti-Christian propaganda (Islam) will soon be fully united with the bankrupt religion of Rome and the West as well as numerous heathen religions of many other nations.

Every major church denomination is deeply involved in compromise and unity movements to show how broad-minded they can be. This provides Satan with the very best possible human soil to spread his hellish doctrines. Be wary of the very word *unity*. To real Christians unity already exists, so watch those who proclaim loudly such unity as must be achieved by human effort and compromise.

The Middle East Possesses All Elements of Antichrist Preparation

There is no other geographical area on planet Earth where the Antichrist could appear but the Middle East. Those who continue to look only toward the European Common Market as the primary movement toward the Antichrist will soon be disappointed. These nations will certainly come under the sway of his ruthless carnage and become a part of his vast Empire. The Antichrist will first appear, and then he will consolidate his kingdom. John stated, "And the ten horns which thou sawest are ten kings which have received no kingdom as yet; but receive power as kings one hour with the beast. These have one mind and shall give their power and strength unto the beast" (Rev. 17:13-13). This cannot be anything other than Daniel's ten toe image (Dan. 2:41-44) or his ten horns (Dan. 7:20). They cannot unite into the last great world empire until the Antichrist is on the scene. Any political coalition presently in effect may or may not have significance. The political powers and armies of Europe will come under his power only after he establishes himself.

While Europe, the Common Market, and Rome will be a part of this end-time kingdom, the center stage will be the Middle East. It is significant to see Yasir Arafat and other PLO leaders meeting with representatives from the Vatican. Two bishops that recently met were Hillarlon Capucci and Sergio Goretti. Capucci was condemned to 53 years in prison after being found guilty of assisting terrorists in Israel. They released him to the custody of the Vatican. Arafat was granted an audience with the Pope in 1982, 1988, and again in late 1990.

The pendulum has shifted from the West to the East. The satanic New Agers controlled by deceiving spirits are touting this change of consciousness from a western mindset to an eastern one. They speak of a paradigm shift to global consciousness. They are busy preparing multitudes for the Antichrist's appearance. They, along with the religious and political world, will follow blindly as he leads them to hell.

Nothing is so prophetic as the new spirit within the Christian world. The spirit of the goddesses in the church is proof beyond question that this generation is living in end-time fulfillment. Let us look at this goddess mood so prevalent in today's culture and religious institutions.

[1] G.H. Lang, *The Histories and Prophecies of Daniel* (Hayesville, NC: Schoettle Publishing Co., 1940), p. 78.

[2] Ibid., p. 105.

[3] Special Office Brief, October 16, 1990, Longborough, Moreton-in-Marsh, Glos., England.

[4] *News from Israel*, Wlm. Margo, December 1990.

Chapter 9

The Spirit of the Goddess Feminism

Nothing happening in the present day church is more diabolical and evident of the developing Antichrist kingdom than the feminization of the church. Two thousand years of church history have never witnessed anything of this magnitude. The only possible past competition comes from the introduction of the mother goddess Madonna to the church many centuries ago. It is now perfectly clear that this was a compromise between the church and the pagan culture directly influenced by the Babylonian cult of Nimrod and his mother Semiramis. I have personal pictures of mother-child figurines dating back to approximately 3000 B.C. that I took in the Baghdad, Iraq, museum. These had been located in the ruins of southern Mesopotamia (Sumer or Shinar) where Babylon and the earliest city-state were developed.

Radical feminism is intimately tied to the different streams of the rising Antichrist spirit. Satan and his diabolical agents or evil spirits are affecting every expression of our present world. All that is happening is in preparation for the

final onslaught of Satan and his hordes. Homosexual prolif-
eration, a one world government, the rebuilding of ancient
Babylon, the ecumenical movement and radical feminism
are probably five of the most graphic illustrations of Revelation 17, visible to the true child of God that the final
consummation is at hand.

Biblical Perspective

In order to more clearly identify the rising Antichrist
spirit, it is important to emphasize again the distinction
between Revelation 17 and 18. One is mystery Babylon,
while the second is political Babylon. The first is seen as a
mystery (to be understood and revealed at the proper time
which I believe has arrived) while the latter is literal and has
been a city in evidence ever since the Holy Spirit inspired
these words. The city of Babylon has never ceased to exist.
Although its name was changed on two occasions (Two
Mosques and Al-Hillah), it has never been totally unpopulated.
Hillah presently has over 250,000 citizens and was built
almost completely of bricks from parts of the old city of
Babylon. Peter wrote his first letter from the city of Babylon
and sent greetings from the church located in this ancient
wicked city. "The church that is at Babylon, elected together
with you, saluteth you" (1 Pet. 5:13). One of the most popular
Jewish documents, called the "Babylonian Talmud," was
written in Babylon in the sixth century after Christ.

Most important to this chapter is Revelation 17, or
Mystery Babylon. There is little debate among Bible scholars but that this represents apostate religion whether it be
apostate Catholicism, Protestantism, or the many streams of
false religions. Babylon, built by Nimrod, grandson of
Noah, was the location where the ultimate false religion
found its foundation. The Tower of Babel was built to
express this new and foreign approach to divine power. The
city's legendary god, Marduk, was believed to have been
named after its founder, Nimrod. Also, there is strong
connection between Gilgamesh of the Babylonian epic of

creation and the epic of the Flood and biblical Nimrod. There is considerable documentation that they were the same individual.

Two Historical Women

The two streams of feminine strength and character flow directly from two different ancient women. The first was Semiramis, the mother of Nimrod, and the second was Sarah, the wife of Abraham. Semiramis popularized everything that is vile to womanhood — rebellion, loudness, and dominance. Her attire was of gaudy gold, silver, and jewels, plus a painted face. She could not be represented better than as the harlot woman of Revelation 17.

> Come hither; I will shew unto thee the judgment of the great whore that sitteth upon many waters: With whom the kings of the earth have committed fornication, and the inhabitants of the earth have been made drunk with the wine of her fornication. So he carried me away in the spirit into the wilderness: and I saw a woman sit upon a scarlet coloured beast, full of names of blasphemy, having seven heads and ten horns. And the woman was arrayed in purple and scarlet colour, and decked with gold and precious stones and pearls, having a golden cup in her hand full of abominations and filthiness of her fornication (Rev. 17:1-4).

This woman is the final expression of sin and paganism prior to the judgment of God.

Sarah, the wife of Abraham, epitomized the biblical example of a godly lady. She was happy to fulfill her lofty role as helpmeet to the father of faith. She called him lord and believed with him for the son of promise. Apostle Peter clearly identifies her as the example of the New Testament woman.

> Whose adorning let it not be that outward adorning of plaiting the hair, and of wearing of

gold, or of putting on of apparel; But let it be the hidden man of the heart, in that which is not corruptible, even the ornament of a meek and quiet spirit, which is in the sight of God of great price. For after this manner in the old time the holy women also, who trusted in God, adorned themselves, being in subjection unto their own husbands: Even as *Sara obeyed Abraham, calling him lord:* whose daughters ye are, as long as ye do well, and are not afraid with any amazement (1 Pet. 3:3-6, emphasis added).

Every expression of modern, secular, radical feminism is a departure from the infallible Word of God and is only a few steps ahead of secular feminism. Here are four expressions of the modern feminist:

1. "The simple fact is that every woman must be willing to be identified as a lesbian to be fully feminist." (*National NOW Times,* January 1988)

2. "Since marriage constitutes slavery for women, it is clear that the women's movement must concentrate on attacking this institution. Freedom for women cannot be won without the abolition of marriage." (Radical feminist leader Shelia Cronan)

3 "Overthrowing capitalism is too small for us. We must overthrow the whole #@*!ing patriarch!" (Gloria Steinem, radical feminist leader, editor of *MS* magazine)

4 "Marriage has existed for the benefit of men; and has been a legally sanctioned method of control over women. . . . We must work to destroy it. The end of the institution of marriage is a necessary condition for the liberation of women. Therefore, it is important for us to encourage women to leave their husbands and not to live individually with men. . . . All of history must be re-

written in terms of oppression of women. We must go back to ancient female religions like witchcraft." (From "The Declaration of Feminism," November 1971)

Religious Feminism

In a new book entitled *What Will Happen To God?* William Oddie examines *feminism and the reconstruction of Christian belief.* The following statement fully expresses what he sees as the goal of so-called Christian feminists.

> It is clear that for the Christian women's movement it is secular feminism which provides the initial impetus and, to some extent, the ideological nurture for its own revolutionary objective: the substantial reconstruction of the Christian religion itself.
>
> The year after Kate Millet's *Sexual Politics* (1970) "rocketed her," in Mary Daly's words, "into the role of American counterpart to Simone de Beauvoir," Daly was writing (in an essay significantly entitled "After the Death of God and the Father") that "As the woman's revolution begins to have its effect upon the fabric of society, transforming it from patriarchy into something that never existed before — into a diarchal situation that is radically new — it will, I believe, become the greatest potential challenge to Christianity to rid itself of its oppressive tendencies or go out of business. Beliefs and values that have held sway for thousands of years will be questioned as never before."[1]

Their entrance point may be the full rights of women in business, church leadership, and administrative functions, but their ultimate goal is to replace God the Father with God the Mother.

The Presbyterian Church, USA, just voted to remove

language barriers to allow them to address God either as a Father or a Mother. Recently a Catholic priest speaking to a Charismatic ladies group spoke of God as possessing both a feminine and masculine nature. His twisted theology brought God down to the level of the Chinese pagan religion Tai Chi, in which the yen and yang express the two natures (male and female) of all ultimate reality. We have barely seen the beginning of this mindless perversion.

New Age Jewelry

The gold, silver, and jewels worn by women today are no longer innocent worldliness. As is all compromise with the world, the wearing of jewelry seems so insignificant at the start. However, Satan always tricks and snares godly individuals by slow intoxication. His approach is deadly and the churches of America are prime examples. Although we have accomplished much for God in America's 200-year history, our greatest missions and endeavors can be credited only to our past surrender to godly living. Today, we are hardly a song compared to our past as the world has moved in and the power has moved out. And although it goes much deeper than our externals, we must recognize that our external appearance reflects our internal character.

Recently, I have seen three examples of paganistic jewelry. One lady came for counseling wearing large yen and yang earrings. Second, a student attended school wearing ankh earrings. Third, a lady came to purchase materials with moon and star combination earrings. None of the three claimed knowledge of their pagan artifacts. The yen and yang is the symbol of Tai Chi Chinese paganism. The ankh is the artifact of the Egyptian goddess of fertility. The moon and star is representative of Diana (Scriptures call her Diana of the Ephesians). Each of these symbols carry the spirit of demons which they represent. It is impossible to wear such and not be affected. Ignorance is absolutely no excuse. A godly saint would immediately be troubled in spirit by such an attachment to demons.

Feminism and Church

The ultimate purpose of Mystery Babylon is the impact the feminists are making in our churches. The feminist and diabolical spirit has invaded every major Christian movement. Their goal is to place women right beside men in administration, decisions of doctrine, and practice and superintendent responsibilities. They would rather the church cease to exist than to fail their goal, and, in fact, the church will cease to be a part of Christ's body if they succeed. His church will either conduct His affairs by His divine mandate or He will have no part. The Holy Scripture leaves no room for compromise on the roles of men and women in the church or the home. God is the head of Christ, Christ is the head of man, and man is the head of woman (1 Cor. 11:3).

A noted religious leader recently commented on the matter of sexism terminology in the evangelical world. The pressure is apparently on by key feminists (some being men) to demand allegiance to their radical ideas. This writer said:

> I suspect that for some the primary concern is another agenda altogether. For them, nonsexist language is an ideological test to distinguish the "sensitive" sheep from the "reactionary" goats. The linguistic case matters little: the real object is to determine who will salute when the radical feminist flag is raised.

He continued with the following:

> First, it would threaten the division of roles essential to Christian conceptions of the family and the church. For believers there is no moral or spiritual superiority of one sex above another. But there is a biblical division of responsibilities in both the family and the church. To question these is not a revolt against unwarranted prejudice but a revolt against the order of the universe itself. Second, blurring gender distinctions would not

only disrupt order in church and family, but could eventually blur our understanding of who God is" (*Christianity Today*, December 9, 1988, page 80).

The Price of Feminism

When a woman rebels against God and His designated role for her, she always misses His will. Not only does she miss His will, but she causes indescribable damage. Eve was first deceived in the garden because she took a matter into her own hands. If she had submitted to the headship of man, she would not have been close to the forbidden fruit much less defeated by Satan regarding its meats. Because Adam was weak and effeminate toward Eve's sin against God and her dominance of Adam, he became the guilty transmitter of sin to all humankind. What devastation was wrought!

Jezebel wrought the same havoc among the ten northern tribes of Israel when Ahab made her his queen. She introduced the Babylonian goddesses and the wicked Jezebel lifestyle into the chosen family and Israel has yet to recover. Their true nationality and their proper promised land has never been completely reclaimed; although, they will be restored by the Messiah shortly. Revelation 2 tells of her spirit at work in the Church doing the same filthy damage.

It is fitting that the last rampage of confused religionists will be symbolized by a harlot woman. Not only will the symbol be a woman, but loud and dominating women will help lead the charge. It is happening at this moment. Many of the leading pastors and ministers of our day are married to Jezebel-appearing and Jezebel-acting women. In fact, most young ministers trained in our institutions are not looking for a godly wife, they are looking for a *tippy* doll. Such women have immeasurable power over their husbands. They control their husbands as the spirit of Babylon controls them. How could such men dare preach a biblical standard of godliness? (If a pastor or wife reads this message who is guilty, please don't get angry, but fall on your knees in repentance and help turn the church back to God and the Holy Bible.)

This harlot church is gathering worldwide power. She hates true biblical righteousness and fundamentalist Christians and will stop at nothing to wipe out their testimony. Any denominational leader, publisher, writer, or pastor who falls prey to her influence will slide right into the mindset that exalts this feminist spirit. While there are many other characteristics of this harlot church, feminism and an effeminate nature are her true personality. Homosexual men and lesbian women will find a growing acceptance in this multi-faceted religious institution. The music will be both loud and *silly-sweet*. Its theme will be love but a kind of love that makes the harlot woman *giddy*. A true child of God will be repulsed.

She is coming like a storm and riding the crest of worldly acceptance and support. Her riches will buy much favor and she will boast of her great accomplishments. The poor and persecuted remnant will wonder with amazement. Many who have weathered the storms of past trials will buy her lie and sell their birthright for a mess of pottage. However, the holy bride of Christ will settle for a tent while they await the city with foundation whose builder and maker is God.

Never has it required so much true biblical discernment to rightly understand churchwide developments. Jesus said, "For many shall come in my name (His name, the name of Jesus), saying, I am Christ; and shall deceive many" (Matt. 24:5). Multitudes are being told to free their minds, forget all past teachings, just let your emotions be in control and receive the new experiences. Believing the Bible is called legalism. Only those who are absolutely committed to Holy Scripture and its literal interpretation will maintain a balanced spiritual life.

Our hope is His triumphant return. Let us look at the grand fact of His promised Rapture.

Chapter 10

The Triumphant Day of Jesus Christ

There is a worldwide yearning for a christ; someone to save us from our own hands of destruction; someone to answer the call of spiritual hunger in our hearts. In 1982 the Tara Center in California produced a full-page ad in major newspapers proclaiming, "The Christ is Here." The writer described their Christ in ecumenical terms. Such a universal expectation cannot be taken lightly.

The enemy of righteousness and of the kingdom of God has never failed to produce a counterfeit. At every biblical junction there has been a barrage of false signs and signals produced by the idiot god Satan. The design is obviously calculated to frustrate the biblical prophecies and to confuse the unsuspecting. There continues to be someone or some group who constantly sets a date when Jesus Christ is to appear. The growing frequency of this hyper group and the gullibility of many to believe their predictions indicates a growing sense of urgency.

The apostle Paul described this universal hunger for redemption.

For the earnest expectation of the creature waiteth for the manifestation of the sons of God. For the creature was made subject to vanity, not willingly, but by reason of him who hath subjected the same in hope. Because the creature itself also shall be delivered from the bondage of corruption into the glorious liberty of the children of God. For we know that the whole creation groaneth and travaileth in pain together until now. And not only they, but ourselves also, which have the firstfruits of the Spirit, even we ourselves groan within ourselves, waiting for the adoption, to wit, the redemption of our body (Rom. 8:19-23).

He clearly shows that this hope is expressed in all human hearts. Deep in the human spirit is a God-given call for the Creator. He said, "The whole creation groaneth and travaileth in pain," for this manifestation of redemption. He adds, ". . . not only they [the unredeemed world], but ourselves (the body of Christ) also, which have the firstfruits of the Spirit, even we ourselves groan within ourselves, waiting for the adoption, to wit, the redemption of our body." This universal call for a Christ was clearly prophesied by the apostle Paul and appears to have reached an unparalleled fulfillment. The day of the Lord is at hand.

The Day of Christ

In Paul's second letter to the Thessalonian church he dealt with this idea of the day of Christ.

Now we beseech you, brethren, by the coming of our Lord Jesus Christ, and by our gathering together unto him, That ye be not soon shaken in mind, or be troubled, neither by spirit, nor by word, nor by letter as from us, as that the day of Christ is at hand. Let no man deceive you by any means: for that day shall not come, except there come a falling away first, and that man of sin be revealed, the son of perdition; Who opposeth and exalteth himself above all that is called God, or that is worshipped; so that he as God sitteth in the temple of God, shewing himself that he is God. Remember ye not, that, when I was yet with you, I told you these things? And now ye know what withholdeth that he might be revealed in his time. For the mystery of iniquity doth already work: only he who now letteth will let, until he be taken out of the way. And then shall that Wicked be revealed, whom the Lord shall consume with the spirit of his mouth, and shall destroy with the brightness of his coming (2 Thess. 2:1-8).

What does the Bible writer mean by the day of Christ or the day of the Lord? The context will show that they were not speaking of one event or a one-day affair, but of a period in which Jesus Christ would be revealed in all His redemption. Just as we see the church period as a dispensation that has now covered almost 2,000 years, so the day of Christ will cover a minimum of 1,007 years. It is the time of His judgment, glory, and revelation.

The day of Christ can be easily divided into three sections. The first is the day of His lordship, in which He will rapture the Bride and reward her for her faithful service and celebrate with her at the Marriage Supper. The second section is the day of His judgeship, which we call the Tribulation or the wrath of the Lamb. It covers a minimum of seven years. The last is the day of His kingship. He will sit on the throne of David governing Israel and will reign as the King of kings over the entire universe for a millennium (1,000 years).

The Day of His Lordship (When He Is Manifest to His Church)

It is easy to see some overlap between the church dispensation and the day of His Lordship. Only those who surrender to His redeeming grace and allow Him to rule their lives are truly His disciples. He said, "And whosoever doth not bear his cross, and come after me, cannot be my disciple" (Luke 14:27). He must be Lord of all or He will not be Lord at all. We cannot serve God and mammon. At the present, His lordship is spiritual and His kingdom is in our heart. When He appears in the clouds, suddenly and without warning, He will resurrect the dead and transform the living. That will be the triumphant day of His lordship.

This glorious event that the apostle Paul called the Rapture (caught up) will signal the beginning of the day of the Lord. His lordship over the saints that has existed in a spiritual relationship for the duration of the church universal will now become an intrinsic and personal union. Each saint will have a new name written in a white stone known only to Him and the individual. The seven promises to the seven churches in Revelation 2 and 3 show the extent of His personal commitment to those saved and made overcomers by His grace.

> He that hath an ear, let him hear what the Spirit saith unto the churches; To him that overcometh will I give to eat of the tree of life, which is in the midst of the paradise of God (Rev. 2:7).

> He that overcometh shall not be hurt of the second death (Rev. 2:11).

> To him that overcometh will I give to eat of the hidden manna, and will give him a white stone, and in the stone a new name written, which no man knoweth saving he that receiveth it (Rev. 2:17).

> And he that overcometh, and keepeth my works unto the end, to him will I give power over the nations: And he shall rule them with a rod of iron; as the vessels of a potter shall they be broken to shivers: even as I received of my Father. And I will give him the morning star (Rev. 2:26-28).

He that overcometh, the same shall be clothed in white raiment; and I will not blot out his name out of the book of life, but I will confess his name before my Father, and before his angels (Rev. 3:5).

Because thou hast kept the word of my patience, I also will keep thee from the hour of temptation, which shall come upon all the world, to try them that dwell upon the earth (Rev. 3:10).

Him that overcometh will I make a pillar in the temple of my God, and he shall go no more out: and I will write upon him the name of my God, and the name of the city of my God, which is new Jerusalem, which cometh down out of heaven from my God: and I will write upon him my new name (Rev. 3:12).

To him that overcometh will I grant to sit with me in my throne, even as I also overcame, and am set down with my Father in his throne. (Rev. 3:21).

This is His revelation of completed redemption to the called and chosen Bride. The apostle Paul revealed this as a mystery to the Corinthian saints.

Behold, I shew you a mystery; We shall not all sleep, but we shall all be changed, In a moment, in the twinkling of an eye, at the last trump: for the trumpet shall sound, and the dead shall be raised incorruptible, and we shall be changed. For this corruptible must put on incorruption, and this mortal must put on immortality. So when this corruptible shall have put on incorruption, and this mortal shall have put on immortality, then shall be brought to pass the saying that is written, Death is swallowed up in victory (1 Cor. 15:51-54).

The day of Christ begins with this glorious revelation of our resurrected and raptured bodies to begin our reign with Jesus Christ. Jesus said, "That where I am there ye may be also" (John 14:3). His lordship over the Church will now be revealed in the glory that the Father has desired for His creation. We will receive our reward at the Judgment Seat of Christ, revel in the banquet and Marriage Supper of the Lamb, and then mount our white horses, dressed in sparkling white to return with Christ from Heaven to finish the Battle of Armageddon and set up a righteous government on the earth.

The Day of Christ's Judgment

The second aspect of the day of Christ is a judicial and legal act of cleansing. The earth is under the curse of sin and is controlled, governmentally, by the god of this world. He is also the prince of the power of the air so that he rules in both the physical and mental sphere. Any talk about a righteous kingdom or dominion by godly people over this earth is just plain unbiblical foolishness until the day of His judgment has occurred. His judicial cleansing will purify this earth by fiery indignation. The moral condition of our world's cultures would certainly suggest that His cup of wrath is nigh full.

A breathtaking picture of this impending judgment was revealed to Saint John in the panorama of the Revelation.

> And I saw in the right hand of him that sat on the throne a book written within and on the backside, sealed with seven seals. And I saw a strong angel proclaiming with a loud voice, Who is worthy to open the book, and to loose the seals thereof? And no man in heaven, nor in earth, neither under the earth, was able to open the book, neither to look thereon. And I wept much, because no man was found worthy to open and to read the book, neither to look thereon. And one of the elders saith unto me, Weep not: behold, the Lion of the tribe of Juda, the Root of David, hath prevailed to open the book, and to loose

the seven seals thereof. And I beheld, and, lo, in the midst of the throne and of the four beasts, and in the midst of the elders, stood a Lamb as it had been slain, having seven horns and seven eyes, which are the seven Spirits of God sent forth into all the earth. And he came and took the book out of the right hand of him that sat upon the throne. And when he had taken the book, the four beasts and four and twenty elders fell down before the Lamb, having every one of them harps, and golden vials full of odours, which are the prayers of saints. And they sung a new song, saying, Thou art worthy to take the book, and to open the seals thereof: for thou wast slain, and hast redeemed us to God by thy blood out of every kindred, and tongue, and people, and nation; And hast made us unto our God kings and priests: and we shall reign on the earth (Rev. 5:1-10).

This little book was more than a casual scroll of insignificance. It represented the title deed of a lost possession and the judicial acts for its repossession. Its importance was revealed in the search for someone worthy to take it from the eternal Father's hand and to transact its processes. Again, the great importance of its content was visible in the weeping of the aged Saint John because no one was found. Even greater in significance was the vision of a worthy personage to take this book. John then saw "a lamb as it had been slain," while a redeemed elder spoke to John, "Weep not, the Lion of the Tribe of Judah, the root of David hath prevailed to open the book."

Every act and victory from this scene in Revelation 5 until the earth is a planet of righteousness was written in this seven-sealed book. It was the document that the apostle Paul called the purchased possession. "Which is the earnest of our inheritance until the redemption of the purchased possession, unto the praise of his glory" (Eph. 1:14).

Only Jesus Christ (the Lamb of God) had paid the

ransom price which was written in blood at Calvary. He could take this Book and open its seal because He had been slain as a vicarious offering unto God. This prophetic scene will be transacted in full view of the raptured saints as the seven-year period of wrath begins. Every picture of carnage and distortion during the seven years (70th week of Daniel) will follow the opening of this sealed book. It is the going forth of righteous judgment to cast out the dispossessed and clean up the dung of sin's foolishness.

So often the Book of Revelation is viewed as the revelation of Lucifer, the Antichrist, and the false prophet. They play a significant role, but only because their grand finale is allowed by God. Satan is given a last chance to show an unbelieving world the folly of rebellion against the Creator.

Jesus Christ is the centrality of this closing book of the biblical Revelation. He will judge the earth in righteousness and make a crooked world straight and ready for possession by the rightful heirs. All preparation for this event was secured at His cross of redemption. The Father has spoken, "Sit on My right hand, until I make thine enemies thy footstool" (Heb. 1:13). This is an extremely important part of the day of Christ. His holiness demands justice. Whatever part of this world's system that is not redeemed by His grace in the church dispensation will be judged by His grace in the period of His day of wrath. Then He can reign in righteousness. He cannot set His feet on this earth until His judicial process of redemption and renewal is complete.

The Day of His Kingship

As Jesus Christ the Lamb takes the little book from the Father's right hand, the redeemed saints break forth in worship and godly celebration. It is the day they, we, have been waiting for so long. Their song is of great significance. After singing of their redemption and His worthiness, they then sing, "And hast made us unto our God kings and priests, and we shall reign on the earth" (Rev. 5:10).

Probably the most important message of the Book of Revelation is the fact that the kingship of Jesus Christ will be established on this earth. The entire Bible pictures the fall of man from the Garden of Eden into a garden of slime and crookedness. The best efforts of both the secular and religious worlds have been clouded with the wicked inclinations of human flesh. Man is desperately wicked and has no hope apart from the Saviour. Yet, he longs for a world in control.

We were created to rule under the theocracy of our Creator. Man is a lofty creature and has an innate ability to take dominion. Present efforts in this direction almost always end in greed and personal aggrandizements because of our fallen nature. Redeemed and glorified flesh with Jesus Christ as King of kings will accomplish God's intended earthly dominion. It will be a world of breathtaking beauty and holiness unto the Lord.

The nation of Israel and the capital city of Jerusalem will finally witness the glory prophesied by the First Testament prophets. Zechariah spoke of this day:

> In that day shall there be upon the bells of the horses, HOLINESS UNTO THE LORD; and the pots in the Lord's house shall be like the bowls before the altar. Yea, every pot in Jerusalem and in Judah shall be holiness unto the Lord of hosts: and all they that sacrifice shall come and take of them, and seethe therein: and in that day there shall be no more the Canaanite in the house of the Lord of hosts (Zech. 14:20-21).

Malachi added to this:

> But unto you that fear my name shall the Sun of righteousness arise with healing in his wings; and ye shall go forth, and grow up as calves of the stall. And ye shall tread down the wicked; for they shall be ashes under the soles of your feet in the day that

I shall do this, saith the Lord of hosts (Mal. 4:2-3).

Isaiah made a crowning description of the glory of Christ's kingship over His chosen people and their future under His righteous reign.

> For Zion's sake will I not hold my peace, and for Jerusalem's sake I will not rest, until the righteousness thereof go forth as brightness, and the salvation thereof as a lamp that burneth. And the Gentiles shall see thy righteousness, and all kings thy glory: and thou shalt be called by a new name, which the mouth of the Lord shall name. Thou shalt also be a crown of glory in the hand of the Lord, and a royal diadem in the hand of thy God. Thou shalt no more be termed Forsaken; neither shall thy land any more be termed Desolate: but thou shalt be called Hephzibah, and thy land Beulah: for the Lord delighteth in thee, and thy land shall be married. For as a young man marrieth a virgin, so shall thy sons marry thee: and as the bridegroom rejoiceth over the bride, so shall thy God rejoice over thee (Isa. 62:1-5).

While the nation of Israel, with Jesus Christ on the throne of David, experiences unparalleled prosperity, the Gentile Bride will rule the kingdoms of the world. Glorified saints will be kings and priests and a garden-like atmosphere will develop on a worldwide scale. Seasons and climates will be altered as the pristine purity of early creation returns to crown the reclaimed world for its Creator. John made several prophetic statements to our future expectation.

> But the rest of the dead lived not again until the thousand years were finished. This is the first resurrection. Blessed and holy is he that hath part in the first resurrection: on such the second death hath no power, but they shall be priests of God and of Christ, and shall reign with him a

thousand years (Rev. 20:5-6).

> And I saw a new heaven and a new earth: for the first heaven and the first earth were passed away; and there was no more sea (Rev. 21:1).

It is very important to understand that Israel's blessings during the Millennium will be larger than just the one nation. It is a worldwide prosperity of abundance, peace, and righteousness. One of God's specific promises to Abraham and Israel was to make them a blessing to all mankind. Here is God's promise:

> And I will make of thee a great nation, and I will bless thee, and make thy name great; and thou shalt be a blessing: and I will bless them that bless thee, and curse him that curseth thee: and in thee shall all families of the earth be blessed (Gen. 12:2-3).

The Church may have special promises as the Gentile Bride of Jesus Christ, but we also share every promise to Abraham because in Christ we are sons of Abraham.

A New Heaven and a New Earth

Heaven is already the place of indescribable beauty. When Paul was caught up to the third heaven (the first is the atmospheric heaven, the second is the celestial heaven, and the third is the heavenly Jerusalem) he called it paradise.

> I knew a man in Christ about fourteen years ago, (whether in the body, I cannot tell; or whether out of the body, I cannot tell: God knoweth;) such an one caught up to the third heaven. And I knew such a man, (whether in the body, or out of the body, I cannot tell: God knoweth;) How that he was caught up into paradise, and heard unspeakable words, which it is not lawful for a man to utter (2 Cor. 12:2-4).

His testimony was indicative of a mental eclipse. He was so overwhelmed by the splendor (paradise means Eden or a place of great, unspoiled beauty) that he sounded unsure of how to explain what had transpired. The words he heard were unspeakable. There was no language this educated man knew to describe what he had seen.

Regardless of the beauty of heaven, God the Creator is going to make it new. The new beauty and glory will be such that no celestial being or living creature will ever invade with another rebellion. There will be no more Lucifers.

It is difficult for us to imagine a new heaven, but no such problem exists as to the earth. It is now groaning and travailing for such a day when everything old becomes new again. "For we know that the whole creation groaneth and travaileth in pain together until now" (Rom. 8:22).

Every natural disaster is an expression of earth's travail. It seems strange to us that the very earth we stand on, the air we breathe, and the environment we inhabit, is in bondage to sin and its results. Sin and unjudged rebellion have become an intimate part of nature itself. "The whole world lieth in wickedness" (1 John 5:19).

There have been 6,000 years of human rebellion, shedding of innocent blood, and disobedience to sacred laws. One can understand why the world is in such complete turmoil. But this earth will be new and free from every mark of sin. All the expressions of eternal life that were evident in the Garden of Eden will be present and accelerated. We shall see an incredible display of creation and a beautiful world full of everything that suggests life at its supernatural best.

Present Jerusalem will be the earth's capital city forever. The beauty of this re-created jewel will shine with splendor. Israel, as a nation, will inhabit the original, promised Palestine.

Not only will the present land be a mass Garden of Eden, but the contour of the land and sea will be altered. There will be no more seas occupying two-thirds of the earth's surface. Yes, there will be rivers, streams, and adequate water supply, but they will be available to serve the land, not just to cover it.

It will be a world filled with every imaginable fruit, vegetable, and delightful food. The animals will be present to enhance and beautify, not to kill or be killed.

The Creator can again look at His creation and say, "It is very, very good."

The Day of Christ Completed

The Messiah (Jesus Christ) is coming! This time He will come not as an infant sharing the likeness of sinful men, but as the glorified and exalted kinsman Redeemer. He will take possession of His rightful throne and will be magnified in His redeemed family and creation. When the Millennium of peace is concluded, Satan has been cast into the Lake of Fire, and the New Jerusalem is the dwelling place of His Bride; then the Day of the Lord or the Day of Christ will be finished.

His last act as Redeemer and finisher will be to deliver the new creation to God, the Father.

> Then cometh the end, when he shall have delivered up the kingdom to God, even the Father; when he shall have put down all rule and all authority and power. For he must reign, till he hath put all enemies under his feet. The last enemy that shall be destroyed is death. For he hath put all things under his feet. But when he saith all things are put under him, it is manifest that he is excepted, which did put all things under him. And when all things shall be subdued unto him, then shall the Son also himself be subject unto him that put all things under him, that God may be all in all (1 Cor. 15:24-28).

The Day of Jesus Christ is a certainty. While the time is unannounced, our duty is to watch and be ready. Three things Jesus told us to do: Keep your loins girded (ready to run the race of faith), your lights burning (filled with the Holy Spirit), and yourself as men/women that wait for their Lord.

> Let your loins be girded about, and your lights burning; And ye yourselves like unto men that wait for their lord, when he will return from the wedding; that when he cometh and knocketh, they may open unto him immediately. Blessed are those servants, whom the lord when he cometh shall find watching: verily I say unto you, that he shall gird himself, and make them to sit down to meat, and will come forth and serve them (Luke 12:35-37).

At any moment, He cometh!

One of the greatest hopes of man is the promise of Jesus that we are not appointed unto wrath. Never has God judged the righteous with the wicked. Yes, the righteous have suffered tribulation with the wicked, but not the wrath of God himself. Noah built an ark for the righteous in his day. Angels led Lot out of Sodom and Gomorrah, and the Rapture will deliver us to the bridal chamber before the wrath of seven fateful years.

> Thy dead men shall live, together with my dead body shall they arise. Awake and sing, ye that dwell in dust: for thy dew is as the dew of herbs, and the earth shall cast out the dead. Come, my people, enter thou into thy chambers, and shut thy doors about thee: hide thyself as it were for a little moment, until the indignation be overpast. For, behold, the Lord cometh out of his place to punish the inhabitants of the earth for their iniquity: the earth also shall disclose her blood, and shall no more cover her slain (Isa. 26:19-21).

Let us look at why the Rapture must occur before the seven years of the wrath of the Lamb begins.

There is never any doubt as to who rules Iraq. Saddam Hussein's picture is displayed prominently and often.

Saddam likes photo opportunities. Here he is pictured inspecting the rebuilding of Babylon. This picture appears in the booklet, *From Nebuchadnezzar to Saddam Hussein: Babylon Rises Again.*
(Courtesy of Iraqi Ministry of Information and Culture)

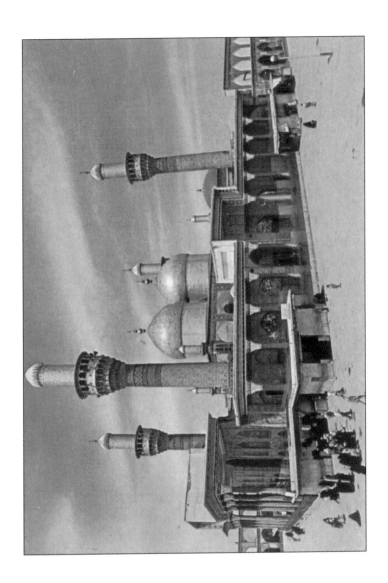

The Mosque of Iman
Moussa Al Kadhem
in Baghdad.

An Iraqi war memorial, containing the remains of an Israeli plane. Israel's very existence is the major source of frustration for regimes like the one in Iraq.

Another war memorial, this one commemorating the conflict with Iran, which ended in 1988. Of course, during the Gulf War, Saddam sent 177 of his best fighter planes to Iran for safekeeping. Even enemies can find common ground when looking west to Jerusalem.

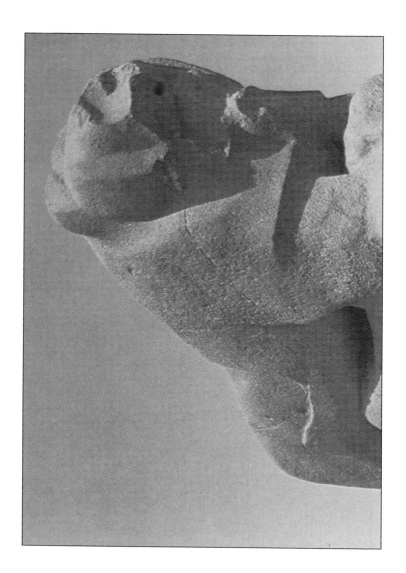

"The Lion of Babylon," ancient symbol of that wicked city and culture, is now Iraq's symbol.

The author on top of the ruins of the Temple of Inanna, at Uruk. Inanna was the Sumerian name for Ishtar, the Babylonian goddess. The goddess is making a comeback, even in the United States.

The famed Ishtar Gate of Babylon, now reconstructed.
The blue-colored brick is quite striking.

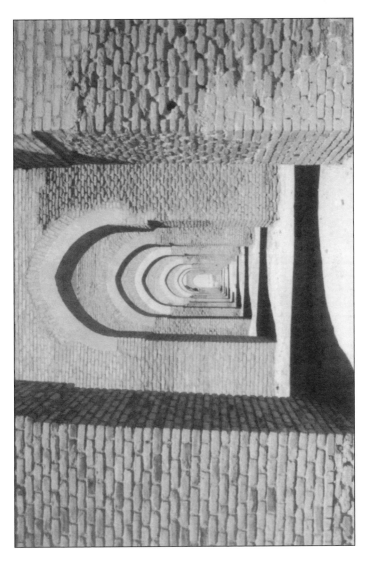

An imposing view of some of the restored walls of ancient Babylon.

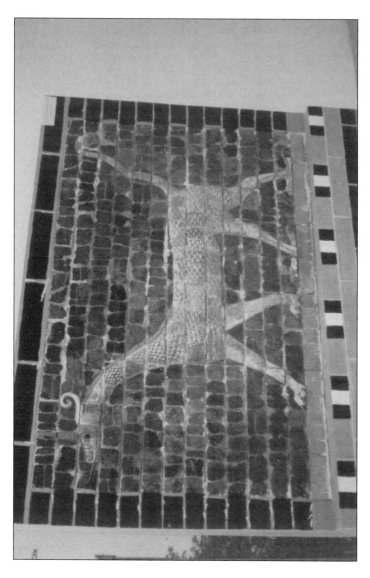

A dragon of glazed, enameled brick, located in an Iraqi museum. This figure symbolizes the god Marduk, and dates to the time of Nebuchadnezzar (605-568 B.C.)

Another example of the god Marduk, this one in the bright sunshine of ancient Babylon.

In the heart of old Babylon, new brick added to ancient foundations (see Zech. 5:1-11).

Another view of the foundation restoration, this from outside the city's walls.

A section of the old Ishtar gate, as it was in
the days of Nebuchadnezzar.

An inside look at
the city of
prophecy,
Babylon.

The
reconstructed
throne room of
Nebuchadnezzar.

Notice the fine brick work of these walls of Babylon; ancient skills manifested in our present day.

From the Iraq Museum, this hideous figurine depicts the Mother-goddess, from Ur (3000 B.C.) Upon close inspection, this should have relevance for churches today.

A harp
from Ur.

Jewelry from
Ninevah,
looking
remarkably
modern.

Statue of Nimurta, god of thunder-showers
and floods of spring (3000 B.C.)

This photo, and the one that follows, show the pageantry of the Second Annual International Babylonian Festival.

Note the solemn expression. The author did not hear the name Jesus once during his two-week stay in Iraq.

The city walls of an ancient city, standing guard over the tents of present-day shepherds.

The remains of an ancient gate from the city of Baghdad.
(Courtesy of Press Office, Embassy of the Republic of Iraq)

A winged god at the entrance of the Nimrud Palace in Ninevah.

Some of the ruins of Uruk (Erech, mentioned in Genesis 10:10).

Slanted pillars from the temple dedicated to the goddess Inanna, at Uruk (biblical Erech).

A spiral ziggurat at Samarra. This is the style preferred by illustrators of the Tower of Babel, but the real one probably resembled a block-style.

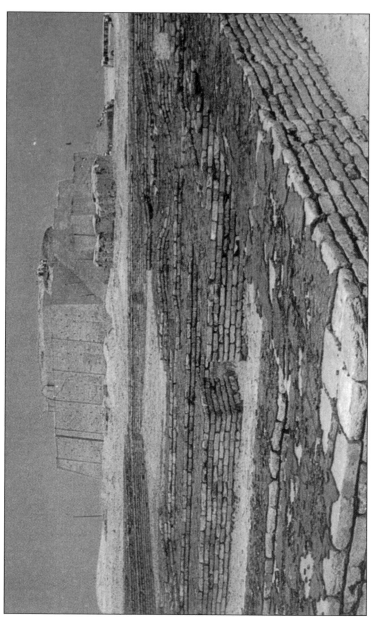

Possibly the ziggurat that Abraham refused to worship at, in Ur. This preceded his journey to the Promised Land.

A view of the ziggurat steps at Ur.

Holy place in a pagan temple, at Nimrud Palace.

Chapter 11

Why the Rapture before the Tribulation?

One of the greatest promises in Holy Scripture is the blessed hope of a miraculous Rapture of the saints. It is seen throughout the First and Second Testaments. The raptures of Enoch and Elijah are perfect examples. The Psalmist spoke of it in glowing terms as follows:

> All thy garments smell of myrrh, and aloes, and cassia, out of the ivory palaces, whereby they have made thee glad. Kings' daughters were among thy honourable women: upon thy right hand did stand the queen in gold of Ophir (Ps. 45:8-9).

> So shall the king greatly desire thy beauty: for he is thy Lord; and worship thou him. And the daughter of Tyre shall be there with a gift; even the rich among the people shall intreat thy favour. The king's daughter is all glorious within: her clothing is of wrought gold (Ps. 45:11-13).

Isaiah described it in these words:

Thy dead men shall live, together with my dead body shall they arise. Awake and sing, ye that dwell in dust: for thy dew is as the dew of herbs, and the earth shall cast out the dead. Come, my people, enter thou into thy chambers, and shut thy doors about thee: hide thyself as it were for a little moment, until the indignation be overpast. For, behold, the Lord cometh out of his place to punish the inhabitants of the earth for their iniquity: the earth also shall disclose her blood, and shall no more cover her slain (Isa. 26:19-21).

We should not expect this rapturous event to be announced by any particular sign or warning. It is to be an unannounced removal of the prepared Bride just like a thief in the night. The many signs we see speak of judgment to follow and Christ's return to set up His kingdom on earth, but the Rapture is that secret event that only the watching shall experience.

Jesus, himself, announced:

Let not your heart be troubled: ye believe in God, believe also in me. In my Father's house are many mansions: if it were not so, I would have told you. I go to prepare a place for you. And if I go and prepare a place for you, I will come again, and receive you unto myself; that where I am, there ye may be also (John 14:1-3).

I love those words, "that where I am there ye may be also." The chosen Bride will never be separated from her Bridegroom again. The apostle Paul added this explanation to the simple announcement above. He said:

For the Lord himself shall descend from heaven with a shout, with the voice of the archangel, and with the trump of God: and the dead in Christ shall rise first: Then we which are alive and remain shall be caught up together with them in the

clouds, to meet the Lord in the air: and so shall we
ever be with the Lord (1 Thess. 4:16-17).

It would be difficult to confuse such clarity unless there
is an evil design. We are to watch for His return to translate
us up into His presence. It is clear that we meet Him in the
air and that we will forevermore be with Him. In Saint John,
Jesus said that He was preparing the place so that this
wedding might be at His house and not at our house.

The final coronation of the wedding is called the
"Marriage Supper of the Lamb" and is clearly in Heaven
right before we return with Christ to set up the earthly
Millennium.

Let us be glad and rejoice, and give honour to
him: for the marriage of the Lamb is come, and his
wife hath made herself ready. And to her was
granted that she should be arrayed in fine linen,
clean and white: for the fine linen is the righteousness of saints. And he saith unto me, Write, Blessed
are they which are called unto the marriage supper
of the Lamb. And he saith unto me, These are the
true sayings of God (Rev. 19:7-9).

The biblical support for a pre-Tribulation Rapture is
indeed overwhelming. Let me share nine reasons why I
believe the Rapture must occur before the seven-year tribulation period or the wrath of the Lamb can begin.

It Fits Biblical Precedence of God's
Judgment for the Wicked

David was bold in his proclamation, "I have been
young, and now am old; yet have I not seen the righteous
forsaken, nor his seed begging bread" (Ps. 37:25). To
suggest that God the Father will deny 6,000 years of history
and judge the church in the same horrible hour as the wicked
doesn't fit His character. The nature of the tribulation period
as the wrath of the Lamb (the final judgment of man's

rebellion against God) makes that suggestion totally impossible.

When the antediluvian world reached its zenith of debauchery and the Father was ready to pour out His wrath, Noah found grace (unmerited favor) in His eyes. Noah's family was saved while the rest of mankind was completely obliterated. (The law of first mention makes this event a powerful factor).

Sodom and Gomorrah had descended into the mire of sexual perversion. There is a good possibility that a disease like AIDS was proliferating and God acted to stop the plague. The very geography of the landscape had to be cleansed by fire and destruction. Homosexuality was the prevailing life style. Yet the angel said to Lot, "Haste thee, escape thither; for I cannot do any thing until thou be come thither" (Gen.19:22).

When judgment reached Jerusalem in A.D. 70, a prophetic word had already warned the young Christian church and they had fled the city. The Lord Jesus had spoken, as recorded in Luke 21:20-24, of the signal for which they were to watch. This judgment was for Israel who had rejected their own flesh and blood, Jesus Christ. The believing church was miraculously delivered. Yes, both the church and the world do experience God's judgment, but always on a clearly different level.

The Church Is to Be Judged before the Wicked World Is Judged

Rather than positioning the church in the tribulation judgment, the biblical warning is that judgment begins first at the house of God. Privilege is always a factor in determining God's judgment. He said, "For unto whomsoever much is given, of him shall much be required: and to whom men have committed much, of him they will ask the more" (Luke 12:48).

The apostle Peter, clearly distinguishing himself as a New Testament leader, warned, "For the time has come that judgment must begin at the house of God: [Remember it was the Jewish nation who was first to be judged in the First Testament] and if it first begin at us [the Second Testament believers], what shall the end be of them that obey not the gospel of God?" (Peter 4:17). There is no excuse for anti-Semitism in the Christian church. Our judgment as the church is of a different nature but clearly precedes that of both the Jewish people and the God-denying and blaspheming world.

Also, remember that the bride of Christ will share with her Bridegroom (Jesus Christ) in this final judgment of wickedness. After we are judged and receive His promise of positions of authority, we will join in judging the world. Paul, speaking to the church at Corinth made this fact very clear: "Do ye not know that the saints shall judge the world? and if the world shall be judged by you, are you unworthy to judge the smallest matters?" (1 Cor. 6:2). You will find glorified saints sharing in the horrible hour of tribulation as acted out in the Book of Revelation.

> And I fell at his feet to worship him. And he said unto me, See thou do it not: I am thy fellow-servant, and of thy brethren that have the testimony of Jesus: worship God: for the testimony of Jesus is the Spirit of prophecy (Rev. 19:10).

The Bride of Christ Is to Be Presented Unto Himself in an Exclusive Ceremony

Redemption is much, much more than fire insurance. The root and foundation of God's love for the world and the sending of His only begotten Son was His desire to redeem man to be His family. The family unit is the closest thing on earth to the heart of God. The invitation to salvation is an invitation to a marriage feast and our salvation establishes us in a family relationship in preparation for that time. Worship, in its purest sense, is a celebration of that family relationship with our spiritual priest; we celebrate His love until we can celebrate His presence.

This marvelous salvation is a betrothing experience that lives everyday in expectation of the wedding celebration. We are like young virgins worshipping at His unseen presence, as we anxiously anticipate His coming for the wedding. Jesus gave a parable that shows these awaiting virgins (Matt. 25:11-13). Ten virgins took their lamps and went forth to meet the bridegroom. Five had come under the intoxicating influence of worldliness and had let their lamps go out. Five had brightly glowing lights in their lamps. The second group of virgins went to the marriage and the door was shut. Remember, God also shut the door of the ark in Noah's day.

John the Revelator describes this honorable event as it transpires in heaven before Christ and His bride return to establish the Millennium on earth. The Bride has been judged and rewards have been given. The victorious tribulation saints have been added as the guests of the Bride. Wickedness is in its final moments of fiery judgment on earth; and now, the Bride rejoices with the Bridegroom. Listen!

> Let us be glad and rejoice, and give honour to him: for the marriage of the Lamb is come, and his wife hath made herself ready. And to her was granted that she should be arrayed in fine linen, clean and white: for the fine linen is the righteousness of saints. And he saith unto me, Write, Blessed are they which are called unto the marriage supper of the Lamb. And he saith unto me, These are the true sayings of God (Rev. 19:7-9).

His Absolute Promise to Keep His Faithful Bride from the Hour of Tribulation

The Holy Scripture deals effectively with His assurance that this awful hour is not designed for His chosen. The prophet Isaiah described the final episodes with minute detail. Let us look at this passage again.

> Thy dead men shall live, together with my dead body shall they arise. Awake and sing, ye that dwell in dust: for thy dew is as the dew of herbs, and the earth shall cast out the dead. Come, my people, enter thou into thy chambers, and shut thy doors about thee: hide thyself as it were for a little moment, until the indignation be overpast. For, behold, the Lord cometh out of his place to punish the inhabitants of the earth for their iniquity: the earth shall no more cover her slain (Isa. 26:19-21).

In the first verse of this quote He identified the Resurrection. Next, He calls for the chosen Bride to enter with Him into her chambers (an appropriate nuptial place as she prepares for her presentation to the Groom) to be securely hidden away for a short moment until the wrath or rage of God is finished. The third verse of this text pictures the going forth of God's righteous judgment to finish sin, to disclose hidden life styles, and to give an equal response from God's holiness to man's evil actions.

The minor prophet Malachi is no less descriptive while he added the thought of a special *Book of Remembrance* that I believe deserves the label as the *Bride of Christ roll-call*. Note the two key verses that describe this future event we call the Rapture.

> Then they that feared the Lord spake often one to another: and the Lord hearkened, and heard it, and a book of remembrance was written before him for them that feared the Lord, and that thought upon his name. And they shall be mine, saith the Lord of hosts, and in that day when I make up my jewels; and I will spare them, as man spareth his own son that serveth him (Mal. 3:16-17).

As in the Isaiah text, all three components: the Resurrection, the Rapture, followed by the Judgment, are presented in the same order.

When these two Old (First) Testament texts are harmonized with Revelation 3:10, the picture presented is a strong endorsement for pre-Tribulation theology. The message to the Philadelphia church was clear: "Because thou has kept the word of my patience, I also will keep thee from the hour of temptation which shall come upon all the world, to try them that dwell upon the earth" (Rev. 3:10).

The Pre-Tribulation Rapture Is the Only Reasonable Explanation of a Time When Some Are Taken and Some Left

No sensible explanation can be given of Matthew 24 that excludes the warning of a sudden Rapture that catches men unprepared. Jesus warned of the suddenness of that day, that only the Father knows the time and that the day was as Noah's day, where men were eating, drinking, and giving in marriage. Then He said, "Then shall two be in the field: the one shall be taken, and the other left. Two women shall be grinding at the mill; the one shall be taken, and the other left" (Matt. 24:40-41). He concluded the warning by saying: "Watch therefore: for ye know not what hour your Lord doth come" (Matt. 24:42).

To try to rearrange the Lord's teachings and explain away this great truth borders on arrogance. When we suggest that the one being taken away is the wicked and the believer is left, where is the wicked taken, and for what is the believer left? Any such explanation will be hard put to fit into the pattern of events.

The word for "coming" as used in this context is the Greek *"parousia"* not *"apokalupsis."* When *"parousia"* is used, it means a coming to a specific place at a specific time for a specific meeting. It is personal. When *"apokalupsis"* is used, as in verses 30 and 31 of this same chapter, it means the unveiling of His awesome holiness and glory. It is general rather than personal and relates to His return to fight the battle of Armageddon and to establish His kingdom.

Then He Warns of a Specific Day Coming Unawares of Which Only Those Watching Shall Escape

These verses are so crucial for establishing this great "Hope of the Church" that we must analyze them closely.

> And take heed to yourselves, lest at any time your hearts be overcharged with surfeiting, and drunkenness, and cares of this life, and so that day come upon you unawares. For as a snare shall it come upon them that dwell on the face of the whole earth. Watch ye therefore, and pray always, that ye may be accounted worthy to escape all these things that shall come to pass, and to stand before the Son of man (Luke 21:34-36).

Christians are so casual today about what constitutes readiness for the Rapture they make me tremble. Ask a given Sunday morning crowd: "How many are ready to go?" and you will find it hard to see the unlifted hands. Many have not been to church in weeks, maybe never tithe, do not read the Bible more than sporadically; and yet, they feel secure and ready. The only explanation is that we are living in the great apostasy.

Please note Jesus' warning: "take heed to yourselves." He warned of an overcharged heart; surfeiting (reveling and rioting), drunkenness (giving opportunity to drunkenness), and the cares of this life. He said the day would come as a snare (trap) and catch men unaware. Satan is right now springing his carefully devised trap to keep the Bride from her readiness for her Groom. Satan is furious with the thought of you and I in the nuptial chamber with our redeeming Prince.

Jesus is jealous over you, His betrothed. He will not share your love with an uncircumcised world. That is why He said: "Watch ye therefore, and pray always, that ye may be accounted worthy to escape all these things that shall come to pass, and to stand before the Son of man" (Luke

21:36). The very language is pregnant with the hope of our rapture before the awful hour of hellishness soon to come upon our unbelieving world.

The Law of the Farmer Demands That the Harvest Be Gathered before the Winter Begins

No vineyard dresser or tiller of the ground would think of laboring through the spring and summer only to leave the ripened harvest in the field as the winter arrives. A wise proverb of Solomon says, "He that gathereth in summer is a wise son: but he that sleepeth in harvest is a son that causeth shame" (Prov. 10:5). It contradicts everything my Father has provided and promised, to suggest that He won't gather His harvest of the world until the winter of divine retribution is in full swing.

Isaiah is prolific in describing this harvest out of an impending winter of evil. He prophesied, "The righteous perisheth (escape), and no man layeth it to heart: and merciful men are taken away (removed), none considering that the righteous is taken away from the evil to come" (Isa. 57:1). The words "taken away" literally mean to "collect as in harvest."

The next verse is a perfect picture of this harvest, safely cradled in her haven of rest, as evil spreads itself in defiance of the gathering storm. "He [bridegroom] shall enter into peace: they shall rest in their beds, each one walking in his uprightness" (Isa. 57:2). That storm of evil is clearly described in the next three verses.

> But draw near hither, ye sons of the sorceress, the seed of the adulterer and the whore. Against whom do ye sport yourselves? Against whom make ye a wide mouth, and draw out the tongue? Are ye not children of transgression, a seed of falsehood, Enflaming yourselves with idols under every green tree, slaying the children in the valleys under the clifts of the rocks? (Isa. 57:3-5).

The Holy Scripture Affirms Emphatically That the Antichrist Cannot Be Revealed Until a Restraining Force Is Removed

The church at Thessalonica received this word from the apostle Paul:

> And now ye know what withholdeth that he might be revealed in his time. For the mystery of iniquity doth already work: only he who now letteth will let, until he be taken out of the way. And then shall that Wicked be revealed, whom the Lord shall consume with the spirit of his mouth, and shall destroy with the brightness of his coming (2 Thess. 2:6-8).

The word "withholdeth" in verse six and "letteth" in verse seven are identical and mean to restrain or hold back. A picture emerges of this great and overwhelming force of evil that is ever ready to spread across God's creation but is restrained because of an even greater power. It is like a reservoir of water held in check by a dam. If the dam is suddenly removed, the waters will flood the valley with great destruction.

Whatever the weakness of the church, she is still a mighty force. Socialist Russia murdered a multitude of her citizens for 70 years, but the underground church never died, and still lives in the power of Jesus' Resurrection. No state power ever represented the Antichrist more than the Soviet state; and yet, the church of Jesus Christ survived and grew. Until this masculine man-child from the bosom of the sun clothed woman is caught up to God and His throne, the Antichrist must operate behind this dam of restraining force (Rev. 12).

Do not ever forget that there is an invisible church within the bosom of the visible church that will not bow to the Antichrist spirit. This sanctified company has no other love but the one King. She cannot be purchased by another for she has no price. She has found the pearl of great price and forfeited all other wealth. As long as His chosen are here, the Antichrist cannot be revealed.

Even the New Agers are saying that their "Age of Aquarius" cannot be realized as long as the defective seeds (Christians) are filling the world with negative thought patterns (the gospel of Jesus Christ). They have suggested in their literature that we must be removed to a non-physical plane (their words) before the New Age can arrive. That is one message they got right.

The Lord's Absolute Promise to Catch Away His Chosen to Meet Him in the Air

> For the Lord himself shall descend from heaven with a shout, with the voice of the archangel, and with the trump of God: and the dead in Christ shall rise first: Then we which are alive and remain shall be caught up together with them in the clouds, to meet the Lord in the air: and so shall we ever be with the Lord. Wherefore comfort one another with these words (1 Thess. 4:16-18).

What a climatic finish to an exciting search of Holy Scripture. The Lord isn't sending Gabriel or Michael, He is coming himself.

You hear people say the word "rapture" is not in our Bible. To begin with, the Bible wasn't written in English, so we must look for the equivalent word from the language in which it was written. (As with many other words, its exact equivalent is in the Bible and is included in the above three verses.)

The two words "caught up" are derived from a Greek word "harpazo" which means "snatched up." My Webster's dictionary gives the meaning for rapture as "transported or to snatch away." The original Greek goes much further than the simple but powerful meaning "snatched up." It means "to steal openly with no thought of hiding." It includes a removal by force in expectation of a hindering power. It also expresses the personal expression of taking for one's self. The Holy Ghost chose the perfect word to describe the rapture of the church.

Satan is marshaling his forces in heaven (he is the prince of the power of the air) and on earth in his effort to stop the greatest exodus of human history. The exodus from Egypt was a biblical foreshadow, but it pales in comparison, even as the animal sacrifice fails to rightly compare to Calvary. Jesus actually descends into the atmospheric heaven below the reigning powers of Lucifer. He then leads His resurrected and glorified army back through the evil dominion to the throne of God himself. The triumph of that event leaves Satan weakened, and Michael with his armies then casts him out and down to the earth. He will never leave the earth again until he is judged and cast into the bottomless pit (Rev. 12).

Watch and Be Ready

The nine biblical reasons for the Rapture before the wrath of the Lamb or the Great Tribulation should convince each of us to *watch*. The commandment to watch is really evidence itself. Over and over the Holy Scripture warns us to watch or to watch and pray. The many clear expressions for the need to watch for His coming, that it would be sudden, that the enemy would try to put us to sleep, that the Day would come unawares, all express that this event would be unannounced. The Holy Spirit emphatically states, "Unto them that look for him shall he appear the second time without sin unto salvation" (Heb. 9:28).

I believe in honoring all men as commanded by the Word. Those who know and serve Jesus Christ are my brothers and sisters, even though they may disagree on this great truth. While we fulfill the above in Christian love, I contend that the Rapture must transpire before the tribulation can begin. The gathering storm has shaken the faith of many. The fire of expectancy, of watching and waiting, of looking for His appearing, has gone out of many lives.

Some are looking to build a kingdom here, while others are looking for great tribulations and planning how not to take the mark. I believe that the Bride should look for His appearing, occupy His spiritual and invisible kingdom, and expect to be gone when the great "deceiver" is having one final fling. "Look up and lift up your heads; for your redemption draweth nigh" (Jesus: Luke 21:28).

The First Fruits of Harvest Time Begin Here

The highest honor possible to a redeemed man is to share in the bridal glories of Jesus Christ and to reign with Him in His millennial kingdom. This honor does not end with the wedding celebration and the one thousand years of righteous government. It carries this same honored company into the New Jerusalem built foursquare where they will share the golden city and live with the Creator God forever. The Bride will behold the Son of God, her Bridegroom, as He presents her, His glorified jewels to the Father and the Father receives the redeemed creation.

A question then to be asked of all believers: Can this highest of all honors be forfeited or lost? Two things are very important. Not to remember either of them is serious to a proper understanding of Scripture. One: We are saved by the free gift of God.

> For by grace (unmerited favor) are ye saved through faith; and that not of yourselves: it is the gift of God: Not of works, lest any man should boast. For we are his workmanship created in Christ Jesus unto good works which God hath before ordained that we should walk in them (Eph. 2:8-10).

Salvation is the gift of God. To suggest the need of anything on our part prior to receiving this gift is to reduce and cheapen grace. Grace needs no support except that given it by the redeeming life and blood of Jesus Christ. Two: When we are saved or redeemed into the family of God we are a new creature (creation) with a new nature. "Therefore if any man be in Christ, he is a new creature: old things are passed away; behold, all things are become new" (2 Cor. 5:17). To then suggest that this born-again-from-above believer will continue in willful transgression is to blaspheme that same grace that saves without merits. This same apostle who speaks of this new creation also forbids any consideration of a sinning (practicing sin) Christian.

> What shall we say then? Shall we continue in sin, that grace may abound? God forbid. How shall we that are dead to sin, live any longer therein? Know ye not, that so many of us as were baptized into Jesus Christ were baptized into his death? Therefore we are buried with him by baptism into death: that like as Christ was raised up from the dead by the glory of the Father, even so we also should walk in newness of life. For if we have been planted together in the likeness of his death, we shall be also in the likeness of his resurrection: Knowing this, that our old man is crucified with him, that the body of sin might be destroyed, that henceforth we should not serve sin. For he that is dead is freed from sin (Rom. 6:1-7).

It is important to know that He does make provision for the believer who falls into unplanned sin. None of us have grown from a baby in Christ to a mature saint without human errors and failures. The Holy Spirit gave us a powerful provision for this trail to sainthood.

> My little children, these things write I unto you, that ye sin not. And if any man sin, we have an advocate with the Father, Jesus Christ the righteous: And he is the propitiation for our sins: and not for ours only, but also for the sins of the whole world (1 John 2:1-2)

The fallen Christian repents, confesses, makes restitution to man and God, and then proceeds to His lofty destination; Holy Spirit filled living.

The Highest Honor: Reigning with Christ

Now, can this highest of all honors be forfeited or lost? If this honor of actually reigning with Jesus Christ as kings and priests and spending eternity in the New Jerusalem cannot be lost, then any discussion of rewards or honors is empty talk. Holy Scripture is emphatic, we are saved by grace, but once saved we will be rewarded by our obedience to God's will.

> Now if any man build upon this foundation gold, silver, precious stones, wood, hay, stubble; every man's work shall be made manifest: for the day shall declare it, because it shall be revealed by fire: and the fire shall try every man's work of what sort it is. If any man's work abide which he hath built thereupon, he shall receive a reward. If any man's work shall be burned, he shall suffer loss: but he himself shall be saved; yet so as by fire (1 Cor. 3:12-15).

A great prophetic writer, G. H. Lang, said:

> We heard it boldly stated from a platform that the sharing in the bridal glories of the wife of the Lamb is guaranteed absolutely no matter what our practical life may or may not have been. But obviously if the very highest of all honors cannot possibly be forfeited plainly nothing is forfeitable, and the whole notion of reward for effort, so heavily emphasized in Holy Scripture is swept away.

Hudson Taylor, the great missionary, said:

> We wish to place on record our solemn conviction that not all who are Christians, or think

themselves to be such, will attain to that resurrection of which Saint Paul speaks in Philippians 3:11, or will thus meet the Lord in the air. Unto those who by lives of consecration manifest that they are not of the world, but are looking for Him, 'He will appear without sin unto salvation'."[1]

The apostle Peter seemed to scream out in his written prophecy.

Wherefore the rather, brethren, give diligence to make your calling and election sure: for if ye do these things, ye shall never fall: For so an entrance shall be ministered unto you abundantly into the everlasting kingdom of our Lord and Saviour Jesus Christ (2 Pet. 1:10-11).

To proclaim obtaining such a part in Christ's future Millennium by tying it to diligence to our calling, is powerful theology. Anything else as a preparation to be kings and governors in a Kingdom of justice, mercy and holiness is unthinkable and cheap. Even angels were cast out of Heaven for disobedience, and forfeited their reward.

These following words by the Lord Jesus need no interpretation.

Let your loins be girded about, and your lights burning; And ye yourselves like unto men that wait for their lord, when he will return from the wedding; that when he cometh and knocketh, they may open unto him immediately. Blessed are those servants, whom the lord when he cometh shall find watching: verily I say unto you, that he shall gird himself, and make them to sit down to meat, and will come forth and serve them (Luke 12:35-37).

And the Lord said, Who then is that faithful and wise steward, whom his lord shall make ruler over his household, to give them their portion of meat in due season? Blessed is that servant, whom his lord when he cometh shall find so doing. Of a truth I say unto you, that he will make him ruler over all that he hath. But and if that servant say in his heart, My lord delayeth his coming; and shall begin to beat the menservants and maidens, and to eat and drink, and to be drunken; The lord of that servant will come in a day when he looketh not for him, and at an hour when he is not aware, and will cut him in sunder, and will appoint him his portion with the unbelievers. And that servant, which knew his lord's will, and prepared not himself, neither did according to his will, shall be beaten with many stripes. But he that knew not, and did commit things worthy of stripes, shall be beaten with few stripes. For unto whomsoever much is given, of him shall be much required: and to whom men have committed much, of him they will ask the more" (Luke 12:42-48).

An Orderly Resurrection

The Resurrection is an orderly series of events. The Apocalypse (Book of Revelation) is the book of unveiling. Its purpose is to unveil future events for spiritual edification. While the whole Bible supports the doctrine of a resurrection and clearly distinguishes between the resurrection of the just and the unjust, Revelation gives details of seven different resurrections or rapture-type events.

The seven distinct resurrections and raptures in Revelation are as follows:

1) **First fruits**: (Rev. 4:1-11; 5:1-14) This privileged company are around the throne before the Tribulation period of seven years begins.

2) **The Tribulation Saints**: (Rev. 7:9-17) This group either missed the Rapture because of a lukewarm condition or were saved during the first

3-1/2 years of the Great Tribulation. Many of these will be martyrs and will have to be resurrected at this time. I believe there will be others resurrected from the dead who were not worthy to be a part of the Bride. This company will be guests at the Wedding Feast.

3) **The Two Witnesses**: (Rev. 11:11-13) These two witnesses are slain after ministering for 1,260 days of the Great Tribulation. They will be resurrected and raptured right before the eyes of their enemies.

4) **First Fruits of the Jewish Nation**: (Rev. 14:1-5) These Jewish witnesses are sealed and protected while they evangelize the Jewish nation worldwide. Near the middle of the Tribulation, they are raptured to the throne of God. They are a distinct and honored company and will certainly share in the Jewish government under the reigning Christ.

5) **Jewish Remnant:** (Rev. 15:1-4) This group is the Jewish remnant that rejects the Antichrist and are probably slain by him. They refuse his mark and number and are now resurrected and/or raptured to the throne of God. This event will transpire near the end of the seven years.

6) **Conclusion of the First Resurrection**: (Rev. 20:4-5) These are resurrected individuals from the Gentile nations. There are persons in this company who were killed in the last 3-1/2 years of the Tribulation as well as additional individuals resurrected from their graves. Those in this company missed the honour of the wedding feast and the coronation of the King of kings. They do, however, share the kingdom of Christ for one thousand years.

7) **White Throne Judgment**: (Rev. 20:11-15) This is the final judgment of man and is the

judgment of the wicked dead. There will also be saved persons at this judgment. Righteous persons who died during the millennium will be judged at this time. I believe there will be individuals who were saved so as by fire (1 Cor. 3:12-15), but received no reward, who will not be resurrected until after the millennium. This is the only judgment mentioned in Scripture which occurs after the same. If there were not saved persons, the Scripture would not have said, "And whosoever was 'not' found written in the book of life was cast into the lake of fire" (Rev. 20:15).

The following Scripture shows clearly that the first Resurrection is not considered complete until the end of the seven year wrath of the Lamb. Consequently, every part of the first six events must constitute a part of the whole. The inclusion of the Resurrection of Jesus Christ, our first fruits, would make this a sevenfold or completed Resurrection.

> And I saw thrones, and they sat upon them, and judgment was given unto them: and I saw the souls of them that were beheaded for the witness of Jesus, and for the word of God, and which had not worshipped the beast, neither his image, neither had received his mark upon their foreheads, or in their hands; and they lived and reigned with Christ a thousand years. But the rest of the dead lived not again until the thousand years were finished. This is the first resurrection (Rev. 20:4-5).

The White Throne Judgment of the wicked is identified as the final resurrection.

> And I saw a great white throne, and him that sat on it, from whose face the earth and the heaven fled away; and there was found no place for them. And I saw the dead, small and great, stand before God; and the books were opened: and another book

was opened, which is the book of life: and the dead were judged out of those things which were written in the books, according to their works. And the sea gave up the dead which were in it; and death and hell delivered up the dead which were in them: and they were judged every man according to their works. And death and hell were cast into the lake of fire. This is the second death. And whosoever was not found written in the book of life was cast into the lake of fire (Rev. 20:11-15).

The apostle Paul laid the foundation for this orderly series in 1 Corinthians 15:35-42:

But some man will say, How are the dead raised up? and with what body do they come? Thou fool, that which thou sowest is not quickened, except it die: And that which thou sowest, thou sowest not that body that shall be, but bare grain, it may chance of wheat, or of some other grain: But God giveth it a body as it hath pleased him, and to every seed his own body. All flesh is not the same flesh: but there is one kind of flesh of men, another flesh of beasts, and another of fishes, and another of birds. There are also celestial bodies, and bodies terrestrial: but the glory of the celestial is one, and the glory of the terrestrial is another. There is only one glory of the sun, and another glory of the moon, and another glory of the stars: for one star differeth from another star in glory. So also is the resurrection of the dead.

This great apostle made several things clear. Each of us are sowing seed for our future rewards and God himself will place our resurrection in the order of deserved justice. "That which thou sowest . . . but bare grain it may chance of wheat or of some other grain: But God giveth it a body as it hath pleased Him." Then this apostle added, "There are also celestial bodies . . . terrestrial . . . but the glory of the celestial is one . . . terrestrial is another. . . . one glory of the sun . . . another glory of the moon . . . stars . . . one star differeth from another star in glory. . . . So also is the resurrection of the dead." The word distinguishing different degrees of honor is the word "glory." It suggests individual reputation or appearance. (Glory: *doxa*, refers to the recognition belonging to a person, honor, renown.)[2]

The Millennium, the new heaven and earth, and the New Jerusalem, is not a place of copycat saints in glorified splendor. It is a place of individual glory, rewards, and honor for our eternal enjoyment. The church at Pergamos was promised, "To him that overcometh will I give to eat of the hidden manna, and will give him a white stone, and in the stone a new name written which no man knoweth saving he that receiveth it" (Rev. 2:17). Here is a picture of an individual relationship with the Bridegroom including a personal name known only to the person and their Lord. We will share an intimate personal fellowship with our Lord Jesus Christ and the Heavenly Father forever.

First Fruits of Harvest

The event we have called the Rapture, which indeed it is, must be understood as a gathering of the first fruits of the Resurrection harvest. It is not the completed first Resurrection or a general removal of all the believers from either the grave or the church. To suggest the same is to deny a great portion of Scripture, including the teachings of Jesus Christ himself. He said:

> And take heed to yourselves, lest at any time your hearts be overcharged with surfeiting, and drunkenness, and cares of this life, and so that day come upon you unawares. For as a snare shall it come on all them that dwell on the face of the whole earth. Watch ye therefore, and pray always, that ye may be accounted worthy to escape all

these things that shall come to pass, and to stand before the Son of man (Luke 21:34-36).

The Rapture of the bride of Christ is no casual affair. Our soft 20th century church has reduced theology to the wild imagination of soft men and women. Apostle Paul expressed the tension of his longing when he said, "That I may know Him, and the power of His resurrection, and the fellowship of His sufferings, being made conformable unto his death, if by any means I might attain unto the resurrection of the dead" (Phil. 3:10-11). An excellent rendering of this last passage is this:

> If by any means I may arrive at the resurrection which is out from among the dead. If by any means I may — "if" with the subjunctive of the verb — cannot but declare a condition; and so on this particle in this place, Alford says, "It is used when an end is proposed, but failure is presumed to be possible" and so lightfoot: "The Apostle states not a positive assurance but a modest hope."[3]

Jesus made it plain in His description of the ten virgins (Matt. 25:1-13) which of the ten would go in the first fruits harvest. Foolish virgins who had left their first love, and consequently the fire of the Holy Ghost, were not prepared to escape. The apostle Paul speaks of the Rapture of the first fruits in writing to the Thessalonians.

> For the Lord himself shall descend from heaven with a shout, with the voice of the archangel, and with the trump of God: and the dead in Christ shall rise first: Then we which are alive and remain shall be caught up together with them in the clouds, to meet the Lord in the air: and so shall we ever be with the Lord (1 Thess. 4:16-17).

Since the above passage of Scripture does not draw any distinctions between the first fruits, the Tribulation saints in the middle of the seven years, or the resurrection of additional dead in Revelation 20:4-5 at the end of the seven years of Tribulation; many have concluded that everyone is resurrected or raptured at one time. The resurrected saints around the throne in Revelation 4 and 5, were distinctly different than the group in Revelation 7 or Revelation 20. The first fruits (1 Thess. 4:16-17; Rev. 4 and 5) were seated on thrones, clothed in white raiment, and had crowns of gold. They also sang of their redemption saying He "hast made us kings and priests and we shall reign on earth." The Tribulation saints have white robes and palms in their hands. "These are they which came out of great tribulation and have washed their robes and made them white in the blood of the Lamb" (Rev. 7:14). These are standing not seated, have no crowns on their heads and do not speak of reigning with Christ, but rather serving Him.

Conclusion

Jesus Christ was the first fruits of our resurrection. The Bride is His first fruits of His resurrection. Please note that there are six stated resurrection events as relating to the first Resurrection in the order given in the Book of Revelation. Jesus Christ and His resurrection coupled with these six create the completed number of seven. The white throne is separate and following the one thousand years of Christ's earthly kingdom.

No one need be excluded from the first fruits harvest. Jesus Christ has made ample provision for your perfection and unquestioned obedience. We do not follow Him by our own wisdom or power. Our security is in understanding the bankruptcy of the flesh and the crucifying of our nature every day. Carnal flesh cannot inherit the kingdom of God. The blood of Jesus and the authority of Holy Scripture made manifest by the Holy Ghost in our lives will purify us unto holiness of heart and soul. "Follow peace with all men, and holiness, without which no man shall see the Lord" (Heb. 12:14).

He is coming for His bride any minute! Are you truly ready or have you been intoxicated by modern theology? It could be too late to get oil any minute.

Every believer that has forsaken all to follow Jesus has a promise of deliverance before the Wrath of the Lamb. Next, I want to establish this fact beyond question.

[1] G.H. Lang, *First Fruits and Harvest* (Hayesville, NC: Schoettle Publishing Co., Inc., 1985), p. 17.

[2] Ibid., copied from Hudson Taylor, *Union and Communion* (Minneapolis, MN: Bethany House Publishers, 1971), p. 83.

[3] James Strong, *Strong's Exhaustive Concordance* (Grand Rapids, MI: Baker Book House, 1979).

[4] Lang, *First Fruits and Harvest*, p. 13.

Chapter 12

Delivered from the Wrath of the Lamb

The Tribulation period of seven years is deeply misunderstood by many Bible students. The distinction between tribulation in general and what Jesus calls the Great Tribulation is extremely important. Much of the confusion about the Rapture of Christ's Church (or Bride) and when it occurs could easily be solved if we clarify what actually happens during this seven-year period. It is not just tribulation as the church has experienced during the past 2,000 years. Saints have been martyred by the thousands, sawn asunder, fed to the lions, had their own children slaughtered before their eyes, and suffered untold deprivations. The gates of hell have beat the church with indescribable vengeance, but has not prevailed to eliminate her testimony. The true Church of Jesus Christ lives on as a remnant of blood-washed saints who still love holiness and who fear the Lord with great joy.

To think of the Great Tribulation as simply more of the above is to totally miss the truth of Holy Scripture. The devil has beat up on God's saints with indescribable hatred and that hatred will grow as the end approaches. Satan will continue to hate anyone who confesses Jesus Christ after the seven years begin. The Jewish nation will reap their last great sorrows during this period as Satan and his cohorts, the Antichrist and the false prophet, unleash vengeance against the chosen nation through which Christ came 2,000 years ago. Satan's primary hatred has always been the Jews first and then the followers of Jesus Christ.

The Wrath of the Lamb

But the Great Tribulation will be more, much more, than Satan's anger against the Jews and those who confess Christ after the Rapture. This period is the time of God's wrath or to use another biblical term, the wrath of the Lamb (Rev. 6:17). The only precedents in history to this time are the worldwide flood of Noah's generation and the destruction of the cities of Sodom and Gomorrah. Of course, this event of the Lamb's wrath will be the ultimate judgment of wickedness and will certainly surpass those two prior events as named above. Jesus made it clear in Matthew 24 that this is the finale of earthly judgment against the vileness of human sin.

> For then shall be great tribulation, such as was not since the beginning of the world to this time, no, nor ever shall be. And except those days should be shortened, there should no flesh be saved: but for the elect's sake those days shall be shortened (Matt. 24:21-22).

The First Testament prophets gave a clear description of this time. Isaiah prophesied,

> Behold, the name of the Lord cometh from far, burning with his anger, and the burden thereof is heavy: his lips are full of indignation, and his tongue as a devouring fire: And his breath, as an overflowing stream, shall reach to the midst of the neck, to sift the nations with the sieve of vanity:

and there shall be a bridle in the jaws of the people, causing them to err. Ye shall have a song, as in the night when a holy solemnity is kept; and gladness of heart, as when one goeth with a pipe to come into the mountain of the Lord, to the mighty One of Israel. And the Lord shall cause his glorious voice to be heard, and shall show the lighting down of his arm, with the indignation of his anger, and with the flame of a devouring fire, with scattering, and tempest, and hailstones. For through the voice of the Lord shall the Assyrian (the Antichrist) be beaten down, which smote with a rod (Isa. 30:27-31).

Again he prophesied,

Who is this that cometh from Edom, with dyed garments from Bozrah? This that is glorious in his apparel, traveling in the greatness of his strength? I that speak in righteousness, mighty to save. Wherefore art thou red in thine apparel, and thy garments like him that treadeth in the winefat? I have trodden the winepress alone; and of the people there was none with me: for I will tread them in mine anger, and trample them in my fury; and their blood shall be sprinkled upon my garments, and I will stain all my raiment. For the day of vengeance is in mine heart, and the year of my redeemed is come. And I looked, and there was none to help; and I wondered that there was none to uphold: therefore mine own arm brought salvation unto me; and my fury, it upheld me. And I will tread down the people in mine anger, and make them drunk in my fury, and I will bring down their strength to the earth (Isa. 63:1-6).

Such language has no kinship to what we understand as tribulation. This is the kindled fury of a Holy God who has given perfect judicial opportunity for man's redemption. Now His spurned holiness has become a full cup and He will march through His creation to cleanse it of every defilement. It is indeed a beautiful sight to see the glory of God in holiness as He goes forth to punish sin and purify His earth.

Imagine a courtroom scene as a white-haired judge listens to the cry of a mother whose daughter has been ravaged by a maniacal man until her life was snuffed out. The mother is absolutely devastated. Her beautiful daughter is gone. Her young pure life has been needlessly destroyed. This mother keeps asking if there is any justice in the world. Finally, the evidence is complete. He is guilty beyond question. Hell has spurred its fire on another home, but the judge sees the truth. His verdict is finally stated. Death by hanging at sunrise the next morning. A grieving mother arises from her seat and with strong determination leaves the courtroom. Her entire person finally feels relief. Justice has won the day. Her daughter did not die in vain. A serial killer will never kill again. She sleeps after months of torment.

That is the beauty of this day of God's vengeance. Evil has stalked the land like a thousand rapists. Dark deeds of the night have filled the world with sorrows. Good people have had to endure endless attacks because they chose to be different. Sin has no satisfaction except in destruction, but now the Judge of all the world will put this beast out of business. It is a beautiful sight indeed to see the Light of the World coming with justice to put out the *darkness* and bring the world back to sanity.

Judgment Because They Rejected His Son

This terrible day of Tribulation has an ultimate purpose beyond the previous description. Yes, our Holy God does hate sin. In fact, He hates it so much that He gave His only Son to save the world from sin and its consequences. But, now, most of the world has rejected that only begotten Son and has chosen a thousand paths other than the one that streams from Calvary. God will judge the world because they rejected His Son and His ultimate love to man. Jesus describes this judgment.

> And Jesus answered and spake unto them again by parables, and said, the kingdom of heaven is like unto a certain king, which made a marriage for his son, and sent forth his servants to call them that were bidden to the wedding: and they would not come. Again, he sent forth other servants, saying, Tell them which are bidden, Behold, I have prepared my dinner: my oxen and my fatlings are killed, and all things are ready: come unto the marriage. But they made light of it, and went their ways, one to his farm, another to his merchandise: And the remnant took his servants, and entreated them spitefully, and slew them. But when the king heard thereof, he was wroth: and he sent forth his armies, and destroyed those murderers, and burned up their city (Matt. 22:1-7).

When the picture of this event Jesus called the Great Tribulation is understood biblically, then it bears no resemblance to the present tribulation that all believers endure to some degree. The gas chambers of Hitler were hell on earth and snuffed out millions of lives. At least six million Christians died along with six million Jews. But this judgment to come is not just the death of men and women yet to be raised in resurrection and to face God for vindication and justice. This Tribulation is the wrath of the Lamb himself to which there are no claims of higher appeal.

This Wrath Is toward Wicked and Ungodly Men

There is no place in Scripture that this day can be identified to affect the godly servants of the Lord. Whenever the First Testament prophets spoke of judgment, they always showed that God provided a haven for the righteous. Isaiah spoke of a day of indignation, but clearly revealed the provision of the Lord for the saints to be hid in a secret chamber (wedding chamber). Let us look at this powerful Scripture again.

> Thy dead men shall live, together with my dead body shall they arise. Awake and sing, ye that dwell in dust: for thy dew is as the dew of herbs, and the earth shall cast out the dead. Come, my people, enter thou into thy chambers, and shut thy doors about thee: hide thyself as it were for a little moment, until the indignation be overpast. For, behold, the Lord cometh out of his place to punish the inhabitants of the earth for their iniquity: the earth also shall disclose her blood, and shall no more cover her slain (Isa. 26:19-21).

Such language leaves no question but that our God never, never judges the righteous with the wicked. Malachi spoke of this care which the Father provides for His own.

> Then they that feared the Lord spake often one to another: and the Lord hearkened, and heard it, and a book of remembrance was written before him for them that feared the Lord, and that thought upon his name. And they shall be mine, saith the Lord of hosts, in that day when I make up my jewels; and I will spare them, as a man spareth his own son that serveth him. Then shall ye return, and discern between the righteous and the wicked, between him that serveth God and him that serveth him not (Mal. 3:16-18).

The Holy Scripture is filled with this evident difference that the God of this earth makes between the holy and the unholy. "Noah found grace in the eyes of the Lord" (Gen. 6:8). God would vent His wrath on the antediluvian world. The ark became his haven above the storm. Lot was told by angels, "Haste thee, escape thither; for I cannot do any thing till thou be come thither" (Gen. 19:22). Can you imagine the angels saying, "I cannot do any thing till thou be come thither"? It is impossible in God's kingdom of judicial perfection for a righteous person to be treated as an unrighteous individual. The God of this earth will do it right. His justice is perfect.

The Day of Wrath

The apostle Paul identifies the wrath of God in his inspired writings. This wrath is a specific action by the Creator and is always directed in a very narrow frame. Paul stated, "For the wrath of God is revealed from heaven against all ungodliness and unrighteousness of men, who hold the truth in unrighteousness" (Rom. 1:18).

Paul then speaks of a specific day, a day of wrath that was to be manifest at a future time. "But after thy hardness and impenitent heart treasurest up unto thyself wrath against the day of wrath and revelation of the righteous judgment of God; Who will render to every man according to his deeds" (Rom. 2:5-6).

An important statement in verse 6 clearly reveals that this day will be just and it will be rendered to each person according to his deeds. The righteous will be rewarded as they have lived and the wicked will be judged as they have lived. The apostle Paul also stated to the church at Colosse, "For which things sake the wrath of God cometh on the children of disobedience" (Col. 3:6).

The biblical record is clear that the Great Tribulation Jesus spoke of is identical to the period which commences in chapter six of Revelation. This period is called the day of His wrath by the apostle John. "And said to the mountains and rocks, Fall on us, and hide us from the face of him that sitteth on the throne, and from the wrath of the Lamb: For the great day of his wrath is come; and who shall be able to stand?" (Rev. 6:16-17).

The Scripture is abundantly clear. The day of the wrath of the Lamb and the Great Tribulation are the same event in God's economy. God will judge wickedness and a day has been established for that to transpire.

One of the final reasons for this day of wrath is to teach the inhabitants of the earth righteousness. This awesome day will instill the fear of God in mankind. The prophet Isaiah said, "With my soul have I desired thee in the night; yea, with my spirit within me will I seek thee early: for when thy judgments are in the earth, the inhabitants of the world will learn righteousness" (Isa. 26:9).

The Righteous Will Escape This Day

It has never been the plan of God to pour out His wrath on His obedient children. While there is always a community effect of evil and judgment and the lives of everyone in any culture is affected by wickedness, that is distinctly different from a direct act of God's wrath. The apostle Paul wrote to the church these words, "And to wait for his Son from heaven, whom he raised from the dead, even Jesus, which delivered us from the wrath to come" (1 Thess. 1:10). We have been delivered from the wrath to come.

Paul adds, "For God hath not appointed us to wrath, but to obtain salvation by our Lord Jesus Christ" (1 Thess. 5:9).

If the Great Tribulation is the day of His wrath, and it certainly appears clear in Scripture, then the saints cannot be on earth during that period. To speak of Christ's very Bride on earth during any portion of the seven years of wrath is to defy every principle of biblical harmony.

God hath delivered us "from the wrath to come" (1 Thess. 1:10). "We are not appointed unto wrath" is boldly spoken by the spirit of prophecy (1 Thess. 5:9). The blood of Jesus was shed because Christ took upon himself our wrath by a breathless act of substitution. It is impossible for us to identify with Jesus Christ in His redemption and still be subject unto God's wrath.

Paul said, "Much more then, being now justified by his blood, we shall be saved from wrath through him. For if, when we were enemies, we were reconciled to God by the death of his Son, much more, being reconciled, we shall be saved by his life" (Rom. 5:9-10).

The Rapture before the Wrath of God

There will be a blessed day of escape for the righteous servants of our Holy God. Before the Son of God sends His angels to judge wickedness and right the multiple wrongs of this world, He will come himself to get His bride. John the Revelator spoke as the Holy Ghost gave him his vision. He promised, "Because thou hast kept the word of my patience, I also will keep thee from the hour of temptation, which shall come upon all the world, to try them that dwell upon the earth" (Rev. 3:10).

This is only one of many promises, but it is sufficient for the conclusion of this article. Before the hour of temptation which shall come can begin, the faithful will be removed. This hour of temptation is synonymous with the Great Tribulation and the day of wrath. This world is about to see the cup of God's wrath. When it is concluded after seven years, there will be no doubters. All Israel will be saved in one day as the Scripture promises. The inhabitants of this earth will learn righteousness. The holy Bride will be with her Bridegroom as this earth sees a picture of God's holiness that no man will ever forget.

The time of seven years clearly established by Daniel in the 70 weeks of his revelation is identified to this period called the wrath of the Lamb. During that period the earth will be a spiritual wilderness. Following are results of the Rapture. "When The Restrainer Is Gone" is a picture of unhindered wickedness. Read the next chapter carefully.

Chapter 13

When the Restrainer Is Gone

The Bible describes a future day when this world as we know it will be totally free of the Creator's restraining power. As God himself has maintained evil on a leash, that leash will be removed and Satan will be free to manifest his vilest nature. Can you imagine our present society suddenly free of all moral restraints? Everything that now represents purity and the high and holy will be absolutely removed and non-existing, allowing unfettered evil to completely baptize the world. It will be a dark and filthy place. Satan will realize his long held dream of world control and will turn this globe into hell on earth.

Before that can occur, God's restraining powers must be removed. For the entire period of man's earthly existence, the Holy Spirit of God has been the restrainer. Most of us have never realized the wonderful activity of the Holy Spirit's restraining power, holding evil at bay. This future period in God's economy will end this action of God's Spirit and the results will be terrifying. The Church has never developed the truth of this area of Holy Ghost activity, or at least I have not seen it.

From the very dawn of creation as God the Father acted to call forth order and create beauty, the Holy Ghost has been the agent of restraint. The nothingness out of which God created the worlds and all manner of creatures was a chasm of emptiness. Why that was true the Bible does not explain. The first act we see of the Holy Spirit was at this moment. "And the world was without form, and void and darkness was upon the face of the deep. And the 'Spirit of God' moved upon the face of the waters, and God said, Let there be light and there was light" (Gen. 1:2-3).

Out of nothing but a void and formless chasm, the Father called forth light and order while the Holy Spirit pushed back the darkness. The second person of the triune godhead was also actively present as the eternal Word of God and Light of all creation. You can see the Son of God's presence in these words, "And God said," and in the glory of light that followed that creative statement. The Son of God is the Word of God and that means every word God speaks. It was a display of God's entire personhood and reveals that our God is beyond all human explanation. The Holy Spirit's unique place in the godhead is as the Father's and the Son's right arm of power and authority. All hell is held at bay by the Holy Spirit.

The Holy Spirit Came upon Men/First Testament

Many times you read in the First Testament where the Holy Ghost came upon men to give them powers above the human.

> And thou shalt speak unto all that are wise hearted, whom I have filled with the spirit of wisdom, that they may make Aaron's garments to consecrate him, that he may minister unto me in the priest's office (Exod. 28:3).
>
> And Balaam lifted up his eyes, and he saw Israel abiding in his tents according to their tribes;

and the spirit of God came upon him (Num. 24:2).

> And the spirit of the Lord came upon him, and
> he judged Israel, and went out to war: and the Lord
> delivered Chushanrishathaim king of Mesopotamia
> into his hand; and his hand prevailed against
> Chushanrishathaim (Judg. 3:10).

> And the Spirit of God came upon Azariah the
> son of Oded (2 Chron. 15:1).

These men or women were then enabled to perform incredible things for God. No power was able to resist them. They could not be stopped until God was through with them.

It was said to King Saul that "the spirit of the Lord will come upon thee, and thou shalt prophesy with them, and shalt be turned into another man" (1 Sam. 10:6). Literally, the Holy Spirit of God turned Saul into another man giving him abilities and powers for the calling of King of Israel that he did not have in himself. As long as this anointing was on King Saul he was invincible to the dark nations of evil that dwelt about Israel.

The Holy Ghost Is the Standard Bearer

Isaiah spoke of the restraining action of the Holy Ghost with this marvelous statement: "When the enemy shall come in like a flood, the Spirit of the Lord shall lift up a standard against him" (Isa. 59:19). The theology of this biblical truth is incredible. The word "standard" means a force or power superior to the enemy. It suggests to chase away, put to flight, or to vanquish. The believer or the church that dares to depend wholly on the Holy Spirit is destined to be a great power for God. The Holy Spirit alone is God's restraining power to vanquish all our enemies and we certainly need no other power.

The Holy Ghost and Pentecost

On the Day of Pentecost something happened in God's

economy to forever change His witnesses in the world. The epicenter of the Holy Spirit's activity had always been the throne of God or the heavenly sanctuary. While the Spirit is absolutely omnipresent (there is no place that He is not), the center of His presence and power was not within the First Testament church. He came upon men or women for special anointings and responsibilities. This illustration is probably crude and somewhat inadequate but let us say it is like being near a fire or being at a distance from a fire. You feel the heat in both cases, but there is an extreme difference. The First Testament church lived at a distance from the fire, but was certainly dependent upon its power and warmth. King David expressed that when he said, "Cast me not away from thy presence; and take not thy holy spirit from me" (Ps. 51:11).

On the Day of Pentecost the Holy Ghost moved His center of authority. Jesus had said,

> It is expedient for you that I go away: for if I go not away, the Comforter will not come unto you; but if I depart, I will send him unto you. And when he is come, he will reprove the world of sin, and of righteousness, and of judgment: Of sin, because they believe not on me; Of righteousness, because I go to my Father, and ye see me no more; Of judgment, because the prince of this world is judged. I have yet many things to say unto you, but ye cannot bear them now. Howbeit when he, the Spirit of truth, is come, he will guide you into all truth: for he shall not speak of himself; but whatsoever he shall hear, that shall he speak: and he will show you things to come. He shall glorify me: for he shall receive of mine, and shall show it unto you (John 16:7-14).

Jesus had much to say about himself and the Father sending back to the Church, or His earthly body, the person of the Holy Spirit. This was a major truth that Jesus taught His disciples. He was emphatic in telling them not to leave

Jerusalem until they had received this empowerment from Him. "And, behold, I send the promise of my Father upon you: but tarry ye in the city of Jerusalem, until ye be endued with power from on high" (Luke 24:49).

The Church, without the power of the Holy Spirit, becomes a joke. It is absolutely impossible to affect men spiritually and eternally if there is no anointing of the Spirit. Jesus said, "But ye shall receive power, after that the Holy Ghost is come upon you: and ye shall be witnesses unto me both in Jerusalem, and in all Judaea, and in Samaria, and unto the uttermost part of the earth" (Acts 1:8).

In the previous quote of Jesus about the purpose of the Holy Spirit baptism, He said, "When He is come, He shall reprove the world of sin, righteousness and judgment." The Holy Spirit alone can touch the spirit of man from which all spiritual life must flow. A person can be religious, dedicated to the church life, and even moral, and still have none of the true reality of Jesus Christ. Most of today's Church fits this category. The only way this can be different is when the restrainer is allowed to do His work in Christ's earthly body, the Church. There is no power to push back the darkness until the Spirit of Holiness, Spirit of Truth, or Spirit of Grace acts upon the human spirit. Until this takes place, you may have the preaching of truth, but it will be a dead letter, not a living epistle.

The Holy Spirit Reveals Jesus Christ

The Son of God cannot be known by flesh. Flesh cannot understand Jesus Christ nor have communion with Him. The heart of man is desperately wicked. His heart is alienated from God and all spiritual reality until acted upon by the restrainer of darkness. Paul said,

> But God hath revealed them unto us by his Spirit: for the Spirit searcheth all things, yea, the deep things of God. For what man knoweth the things of a man, save the spirit of man which is in

him? Even so the things of God knoweth no man, but the Spirit of God. Now we have received, not the spirit of the world, but the spirit which is of God; that we might know the things that are freely given to us of God (1 Cor. 2:10-12).

When the Restrainer Is Removed with the Bride

The picture is breathtaking. God the Father at the request of the Son sent the Holy Spirit to the Church to choose a Bride for the Son. For 2,000 years He has wooed, convicted, and converted millions to this brideship. Now the time has come to present that Bride to the Master's Son. All hell has marshaled its forces against the Bride, but the restrainer has reserved her from defilement. She is holy and undefiled, without spot or blemish and ready for Her crowning day. The Holy Ghost, at the word of the Father and the sound of the trumpet, unleashes the most incredible power known to mankind. Resurrection life invades the graves of the dead in Christ and changes every living member of the sanctified Bride.

In a moment, in the twinkling of an eye, at the last trump: for the trumpet shall sound, and the dead shall be raised incorruptible, and we shall be changed. For this corruptible must put on incorruption, and this mortal must put on immortality. So when this corruptible shall have put on incorruption, and this mortal shall have put on immortality, then shall be brought to pass the saying that is written, Death is swallowed up in victory (1 Cor. 15:52-54).

All the Father needs to do when the Rapture occurs is to call His Spirit to the throne. The Holy Spirit cannot move His epicenter to the heavenly sanctuary without the Bride being removed with Him. There will be no search-and-find effort necessary, for the Holy Spirit is the life of those ready for this day of victory and triumph. The Holy Spirit cannot leave without the Bride nor can the Bride leave without the Holy Spirit. "But if the Spirit of him that raised up Jesus from the dead dwell in you, he that raised up Christ from the dead shall also quicken your mortal bodies by his Spirit that dwelleth in you" (Rom. 8:11).

"Now, He That Letteth Will Let"

The mystery of iniquity or the spirit of Antichrist has been at work during the duration of the Church, but always limited and held at bay. This evil design has been on a leash until the Bride is secure and safe. The apostle Paul explains these facts clearly.

> And now ye know what withholdeth that he might be revealed in his time. For the mystery of iniquity doth already work: only he who now letteth will let, until he be taken out of the way. And then shall that Wicked be revealed, whom the Lord shall consume with the spirit of his mouth, and shall destroy with the brightness of his coming (2 Thess. 2:6).

There can be no doubt but that Satan and all the powers of hell are already at work. There is a growing spirit of wickedness, even a diabolical surge of an Antichrist spirit. Christianity is hated with a vengeance by an ever growing group of people. Satan is enlarging his kingdom and vying for the worship of the world. His present tactics are marvelously successful as men have become more humanistic and less discerning of the true realities of the spiritual world.

Even with this surge of evil and evil expressions there is still a clear sense that something or someone is holding back these wicked powers. The Bible calls Satan the god of this world. So, why does he not completely overrun all righteousness? He cannot, because the restrainer is greater in power and might and must be removed before this idiot god can at least try to fulfill his ugly will.

The word "letteth" as used in 2 Thessalonians 2 means

to hold fast in a spiritual sense or to detain or restrain. It means to hold possession of so that another power or person cannot siege. The inspiration of these words to the apostle Paul was perfect in describing the activities of the Holy Spirit. Soon this restrainer will be gone.

The Holy Spirit around the Throne

In the First Testament the Holy Spirit is seen as God's anointing imparted to individuals for specific ministries. When we moved to the Second Testament period, the Lord Jesus was given the Spirit without measure for His messianic and redemptive role. The church of Jesus Christ was then baptized with the Holy Ghost as He descended to dwell in the body of Christ. In Revelation, beginning with chapter four, John saw the future events that were clearly described as after the Church period. In this version we see the Holy Spirit around the throne of God in the heavenlies.

John describes this scene:

> And immediately I was in the spirit; and, behold, a throne was set in Heaven, and one sat on the throne. And he that sat was to look upon like a jasper and a sardine stone: and there was a rainbow round about the throne, in sight like unto an emerald. And round about the throne were four and twenty seats: and upon the seats I saw four and twenty elders sitting, clothed in white raiment; and they had on their heads crowns of gold. And out of the throne proceeded lightnings and thunderings and voices: and there were seven lamps of fire burning before the throne, which are the seven Spirits of God. And before the throne there was a sea of glass like unto crystal: and in the midst of the throne, and round about the throne, were four beasts full of eyes before and behind (Rev. 4:2-6).

It is clear that this picture is of events to occur immediately after the Rapture and before the marriage supper of the Bride and the Bridegroom. The Bride has just arrived around the throne. The heavenly participants are preparing for the actions of judgment against the wickedness of the enemies of God and for the cleansing of all evil that has defiled the Father's creation. Before judgment can occur, there must be worship, praise, and judicial preparation. The judge of eternal holiness does not act until all His kingdom has celebrated.

God the Father is on His throne. The sanctified Bride of the First and Second Testament church (24 elders) are gathered from the grave and the world and are present around the throne in resurrection glory. This glorious company is clothed in white raiment (righteousness) and have on their heads crowns of gold. This is not a mixed multitude of sinning *saints*, but a company of overcomers who have followed Jesus by way of the cross.

The angelic host are present, represented as four living creatures (beasts). There are apparently four orders of angels: archangels, cherubims, seraphims, and servant angels, and they are all present for this celebration.

Most importantly to this article is now seen the very essence of the awesome person of the omnipresent Spirit. His restraining powers and indescribable greatness is here seen as "seven lamps of fire burning before the Throne which are the seven Spirits of God" (Rev. 4:5). Nowhere in the Bible but Revelation is the Holy Ghost pictured in this fashion. His ministry has always been to give all glory to God and the Lord Jesus Christ. With His greatest work of all eternity accomplished, He is now described in the glory of His divine person. He is truly one with the Father and with the Son.

The complete number of seven is used because it pictures the Spirit in His perfect work. There is no weakness or limitation. He is God the Holy Spirit and the breadth and length of His powers are revealed as seven lamps of fire. This not only suggests His omnipresence, but His omnipotence and omniscience. He is truly one with Almighty God.

With His restraining powers now removed from the earth, Satan has a clear field to do his darkest deeds.

A World Without Restraint

When we speak of this world being without God we are not suggesting that God has forsaken it, but rather given it over for a very brief period for the final acts of evil and then His judgment. The Revelator John stated it clearly:

> Therefore rejoice, ye heavens, and ye that dwell in them. Woe to the inhabiters of the earth and of the sea! For the devil is come down unto you, having great wrath, because he knoweth that he hath but a short time (Rev. 12:12).

Satan will have his last effort to show himself to humankind. It will be his last hooray. He will make the most of it.

The Book of Revelation reveals a little bit of the diabolical events that will follow. I do not believe it is possible to realize the extent of this horrible hour. The bowels of hell will be opened upon the earth. Dark demon spirits will ascend from the bottomless pit after fettering in their wickedness for centuries or millenniums.

> And there came out of the smoke locusts upon the earth: and unto them was given power, as the scorpions of the earth have power. And it was commanded them that they should not hurt the grass of the earth, neither any green thing, neither any tree; but only those men which have not the seal of God in their foreheads. . . . And the shapes of the locusts were like unto horses prepared unto battle; and on their heads were as it were crowns like gold, and their faces were as the faces of men. . . . And they had breastplates, as it were breast-plates of iron; and the sound of their wings was as the sound of chariots of many horses running to

battle. And they had tails like unto scorpions, and there were stings in their tails: and their power was to hurt men five months. And they had a king over them, which is the angel of the bottomless pit, whose name in the Hebrew tongue is Abaddon, but in the Greek tongue hath his name Apollyon. One woe is past; and, behold, there come two woes more hereafter (Rev. 9:1-12).

What a picture! The bottomless pit is the darkest region of Hell. It suggests that these demon spirits and/or condemned men have been judged and reserved in the deepest regions of judgment. They represent hell's vilest inhabitants. Their fallen natures are corrupt to the worst degree.

This horde of wild creatures (beasts in nature) will be turned loose on mankind. They cannot kill and the men and women tormented cannot die. Though men seek death, it will be out of their reach. These creatures are called locusts, but appear as horses prepared to battle. Notice that their hair is as the hair of women and their teeth as that of lions. Their king is called Abaddon in Hebrew, but Apollyon in Greek. He is clearly a ranking angel of Lucifer and notorious in his evil nature. The second woe is even darker as the fury of hell grows stronger.

During the second woe, 200,000,000 spirits descend out of the regions of Babylon and the Euphrates River. Their geographic location is where Nimrod built his Tower of Babel and all pagan and evil religions had their beginnings. As we have learned, Satan turned Babylon into his unholy city just as the Father chose Jerusalem for the Holy City. These cities are clearly the antithesis of each other. Jerusalem is protected and kept by an innumerable host of angels. Babylon is the dwelling place of the greatest and best of Satan's wicked spirits.

Now, these spirits are unrestrained and turned loose on mankind. They are led by four generals from hell who have been restrained for centuries. Their anger is indescribable.

They ultimately kill one-third of mankind. That is close to two billion souls (2,000,000,000). Their evil abilities are terrible. These awesome creatures have breastplates of fire, jacinth and brimstone (creatures of fire) and their heads were said to be as the heads of lions. Out of their mouth issues fire, smoke, and brimstone.

The earth's inhabitants by this time have become so evil that even this display of hell's destruction does not turn them back to the true God. They are shown to be so committed to the worship of Satan that nothing will change their mind.

> And every island fled away, and the mountains were not found. And there fell upon men a great hail out of Heaven, every stone about the weight of a talent: and men blasphemed God because of the plague of the hail; for the plague thereof was exceeding great (Rev. 16:20-21).

Evil continues to grow and spread during the entire seven years of Tribulation. Men become so animated in their wickedness that restraint is impossible. Remember, there is now no power to hold back wickedness. Even the conscience of men inspired by the Holy Spirit has been released of all sense of right or wrong. The world is void of the spiritual values that biblical faith had previously created. The Holy Spirit did not describe the third woe, but simply said, "The second woe is past; and, behold, the third woe cometh quickly" (Rev. 11:14).

One can only imagine the extent of this final expression of evil. Satan will finally be seen in all his naked and evil nature.

The Unholy Trinity

Nothing reveals the design of Satan more than his unholy trinity that develops in Revelation 12 and 13. After he is cast to the earth and begins his rampage, he then reveals his unholy messiah and false religion leader. This truth is clearly his distorted version of the triune godhead.

He is determined to sit as God and rule the universe. His false messiah arrives as a beast out of the Great Sea (the Middle East) and immediately receives his power and authority from the dragon. A death and resurrection of this beast is simulated to represent Satan's version of a messianic sacrifice (Rev. 13:3-4). The world literally receives this beastly character as the true messianic promise and then celebrates the coming of their christ.

To aid in the final deception of all mankind there appears a second beast who is religious in nature and completes the unholy trinity. He has two horns like a lamb, but speaks as a dragon (Rev. 13:11-12). This is a picture of pious authority. The main purpose of this beast is to lead the world in worshipping the first beast (exactly as the Holy Spirit now leads us to worship Jesus Christ).

This unholy trinity is given to deception.

> And deceiveth them that dwell on the earth by the means of those miracles which he had power to do in the sight of the beast; saying to them that dwell on the earth, that they should make an image to the beast, which had the wound by a sword, and did live. And he had power to give life unto the image of the beast, that the image of the beast should both speak, and cause that as many as would not worship the image of the beast should be killed. And he causeth all, both small and great, rich and poor, free and bond, to receive a mark in their right hand, or in their foreheads: And that no man might buy or sell, save he that had the mark, or the name of the beast, or the number of his name. Here is wisdom. Let him that hath understanding count the number of the beast: for it is the number of a man; and his number is Six hundred threescore and six (Rev. 13:14-18).

The Restrainer Will Soon Be Gone

The most important conclusion of this chapter is to entreat you to prepare for this hour. The Holy Spirit is God the Spirit restraining evil and wickedness. When He is removed to the throne of God in heaven, this world will become a wilderness. You do not want to be here.

Your greatest need is to give your all to Jesus Christ. Confess every sin and rebellion against the Lord Jesus and His Holy Word. When you confess your sin or sins, He will forgive and cleanse you. Get into the Bible with great delight. Read and obey the Word.

Do not allow any influence in your life but that of the Word of God and the Holy Spirit. Both the Word and the Holy Spirit will lead you to Jesus Christ that He might be all in all.

If you have any doubt of what Satan is planning, you must continue. Satan is not unaware of the prophetic picture. He certainly does not know the hour but he does know his opportunity. In fact his followers are already boasting that his evil choir is rehearsing for the coming event.

Chapter 14

Hell Is Rehearsing for Armageddon

The term Armageddon appears in the Bible only one time (Rev. 16:16). It has reference to the concluding battle of the seven year tribulation period. It is a mistake if we fail to see that this battle actually represents the entire period that prepares the world for this concluding act of God's judgment. In other words, Armageddon is better represented as the entire end-time cataclysmic period which will end in the valley of Megiddo.[1] Please note the Holy Scripture that describes the preparation for this event.

> And I saw three unclean spirits like frogs come out of the mouth of the dragon, and out of the mouth of the false prophet. For they are the spirits of devils, working miracles, which go forth unto the kings of the earth and of the whole world, to gather them to the battle of that great day of God Almighty. Behold, I come as a thief. Blessed is he that watcheth, and keepeth his garments, lest he walk naked, and they see his shame. And he gathered them together into a place called in the Hebrew tongue Armageddon (Rev. 16:13-16).

I believe the preparation for this final judgment is already in progress. Satan's crowd must prepare and John the Revelator clearly described that fact. "For they are the spirits of devils working miracles, which go forth unto the kings of the earth and of the whole world, to gather them to the battle of the great day of God Almighty" (Rev. 16:14). Of course, this unholy trinity (Satan, Antichrist, and anti-spirit) believes that they can win against the great God Jehovah. We have interpreted a statement in Revelation 12:12, "he knoweth that he hath but a short time," to suggest he expects defeat. Instead it should be understood that he knows he has only a short time to win before God will conclude his last chance to take control of the world.

The entire one world government, one world religion, and one world economic system that Satan will promote and control is his grand scheme to create a world power. This he plans to use in defeating God and to then take His seat as the supreme authority. You may say it is crazy to believe that Satan is expecting to win. How can you read his grand design for world control, economic mastery (by his controlling all buying and selling), and the entire religious harlotry of biblical prophecy, and not believe Satan plans to win? Satan is preparing the ultimate effort to remove God from His throne, to defeat the Lord Jesus as the Saviour of men and to defile all humankind. We can believe the Word of God, Satan will lose.

The Satanists Are Preparing Their Followers

A noted author of pyramidology and occultist materials wrote the following in his book, *The Armageddon Script*.

> Their script is now written, subject only to last minute editing and stage direction. The stage itself, albeit as yet in darkness, is almost ready. Down in the pit, the subterranean orchestra is already tuning up. The last minute, walk-on parts are even now being filled. Most of the main actors, one suspects,

have already taken up their roles. Soon it will be time for them to come on stage, ready for the curtain to rise. The time for action will have come.[2]

Biblical terminology literally fills the writings and language of the New Agers and occultic leaders. They talk about the number 666, about saving the world (not souls), and about a harmonious, peace-loving age when everybody lives happily ever after. Read the following statements by these spirits of devils going forth to the whole world to gather them (world population) to this awesome hour of the final conflict between the true God and the idiot god, Satan. Read from several New Age writers.

> The blueprint for a peaceful, loving and harmonious world has been drawn. Prayer, meditation, positive affirmations, spiritual families and global healing events such as Live Aid and the December 31 World Peace Event all contribute to this blueprint. (*Harmonic Convergence Brochure*)

> I have come to believe firmly today that our future, peace, justice, and fulfillment, happiness, and harmony on this planet will not depend on world government but on divine or cosmic government . . . my great personal dream is to get a tremendous alliance between all major religions and the U.N. (*Robert Muller, former director general of the United Nations and now president of Peace University*).

> Humanity is on the verge of something entirely new, a further evolutionary step unlike any other: the emergence of the first global civilization. (*Thomas Berry, Catholic theologian*)

> I (see) images of a new heaven and a new earth. . . . THIS WORLD will be saved. The planet will be healed and harmonized. We can let the

kingdom come ... which means that THIS WORLD can be transformed into a heaven right now. . . . This is no fantasy. This is not scientific or religious fiction. This is the main event of our individual lives. (*John Randolph Price, organizer of the World Instant of Cooperation*)

Every major religion of the world has similar ideals of love, the same goal of benefiting humanity through spiritual practice. . . . The most important thing is to look at details of theology or metaphysics. . . . I believe that all the major religions of the world can contribute to world peace and work together for the benefit of humanity if we put aside subtle metaphysical differences, which are really the internal business of each religion. . . . The undying faith in religion clearly demonstrates the potency of religion as such. This spiritual energy and power can be purposefully used to bring about the spiritual conditions necessary for world peace. (*Dalai Lama*)

All human institutions, professions, programs, and activities must be judged primarily according to the extent they either obstruct and ignore or foster a mutually enhancing human-earth relationship. That is how good and evil will be judged in the coming years. (*Donald Keys, president of Planetary Citizens*)

A noted New Ager, José Arguelles, presented a 25-year plan to set up the New World Order. His plan began in 1987 at an event called "Harmonic Convergence." They promote a World Prayer Day every year on December 31. Every religious thought or faith is invited to participate. Their basic philosophy is an idea called global consciousness in which they teach that we all must learn to think by a new paradigm. God, to the New Ager like Arguelles, is not personal, but the global community of consciousness. If we can change our thought patterns to peace, harmony, and goodwill to everybody (except those religious maniacs called Jesus followers or fundamentalists) we can evolve to the next round on the evolutionary scale. It is called a paradigm shift in consciousness. It is nothing but satanic delusion. The word paradigm is the biggest new word in the language of the liberals. Beware of anyone who uses it. Please note the following timetable given by this leading New Ager under the following heading, "Campaign for the Earth."

Campaign for the Earth

José Arguelles in his publication, "The Crystal Earth Papers," has given the following timetable for a totally New World ruled by New Age powers. This campaign was inaugurated on August 18, 1987. The following is his dated schedule.

This is a ready-made peace mobilization plan. It is compromised of a "critical" minority selected from among the ranks of 550 million participating in or attuned to the Harmonic Convergence. These people will be the leaders of the five-year phase out of our present industrial civilization. The critical minority, combined with media and UN personnel will develop plans for economic battalions to be ready to begin to plan for re-distributions of wealth.

Summer 1988 - The Tibetan lama T'ai Situ Rinoche, is organizing a major spiritual Peace Event to become known as the World Peace Congress. Many world religious leaders will participate. It's the most critical step to development of a one world religion to date.

1989-1991 - Council of Gemants (pagan ritualists) will be set up on a global basis. They will coordinate all Earth rituals worldwide.

1992-1997 - Current government and political models will have been replaced. New values will stress: cooperation, collaboration and unification on behalf of the Spirit of the Earth.

1997-2002 - Known as the Era of Reseeding, it will thin out major population centers. The care of the planet will be entrusted to Shamanic exercises.

2007-2012 - This marks the Era of the New Harmony. All activities will be geared to Dec. 21, 2012 (Winter solstice North, Summer solstice South). The Crystal Kingdom of the Earth will be set up.[3]

These are certainly *close to target* and are moving forward with exhilarating activities.

Spiritual Warfare

While Satan is preparing his agents on a worldwide scale in a visible religious and political manner, there is a subtle but deadly warfare going on in the spirit world. It has always been a spiritual battle to obey the Holy Scripture and serve Jesus Christ as Lord. Scriptures are extremely clear that "we wrestle not against flesh and blood, but against principalities, against powers, against the rulers of the darkness of this world, against spiritual wickedness in high places" (Eph. 6:12). If this has been true in the past, how much greater is this warfare presently. Jesus clearly stated, "As the days of Noah were, so shall also the coming of the Son of man be" (Matt. 24:36). There were demons (sons of God) who appeared in visible form during Noah's day, who even co-habited with women producing giants and clearly terrorizing the last inhabitants before the terrible judgment of the flood.

I believe we are in for a flood of filth and wickedness that will be overwhelming to any man or woman that is not covered by the blood of Jesus and filled with the Holy Spirit. Fear and torment are already the scourge of this generation. Do not think that the bride of Christ will escape seeing the horrible prelude to the tribulation period. I am expecting Jesus to return any moment, but I know that until He returns there will be an ever increasing activity of satanism and his dark beguiling demons.

Any believer who expects to escape deception and confusion must submerge himself in the Holy Scripture and learn to lean on the abiding presence of God's Holy Spirit. Christians must refuse to listen or entertain, "the counsel of the ungodly" (Ps. 1:1-6). Do not spend a moment in any atmosphere where Jesus Christ is not Lord or the infallible Bible is not the final authority.

Increasing Demonic Activity: Warning to the Church

The prophecy of Revelation clearly describes this increasing tide of satanic powers. While this prophecy places the time period of the Tribulation after the Rapture has occurred, it certainly suggests that the early stages will be visible before the actual seven-year period begins. Notice chapter 16 and the verses I presented at the beginning of this chapter. In verse 12 the activity begins in the Euphrates River (Babylon sits on its original banks) and proceeds to show unclean spirits, like frogs, which proceed from the mouths of Satan, the Antichrist, and the false prophet. They go forth to deceive and prepare the world for this forthcoming war between heaven and hell. Then, suddenly, the Holy Spirit inspires John to speak to the church. "Behold I come as a thief. Blessed is he that watcheth and keepeth his garment [wedding attire] lest he walk naked, and they see his shame" (Rev. 16:15).

There is only one reason He placed this great warning in the midst of such a clear description of Satan's evil power that will reign in the dark period before the final battle of Armageddon. We in the church who are waiting for the Rapture are now witnessing the rise of these evil forces. They will continue to increase until the Rapture and then explode after the church Bride is gone. Paul was clear to state that the bride of Christ filled with the Holy Spirit is the only restraining power on this earth. Again, look at these powerful verses.

> And now ye know what withholdeth that he might be revealed in his time. For the mystery of iniquity doth already work: only he who now letteth will let, until he be taken out of the way. And then shall that Wicked be revealed, whom the Lord shall consume with the spirit of his mouth, and shall destroy with the brightness of his coming (2 Thess. 2:6-8).

This Scripture does not suggest that Satan cannot do anything toward his goal of world control before the bride of Christ is gone, but rather that he is limited. History will certainly confirm that he has had great power to destroy; but, also, that he has never been able to create a world domination like he will do when the restraints are lifted. Here is how the apostle Paul describes what will happen when the Bride has escaped.

> Even him, whose coming is after the working of Satan with all power and signs and lying wonders, and with all deceivableness of unrighteousness in them that perish; because they received not the love of the truth, that they might be saved. And for this cause God shall send them strong delusion, that they should believe a lie: that they all might be damned who believed not the truth, but had pleasure in unrighteousness (2 Thess. 2:9-12).

Whatever wickedness we can now identify, it will be many times worse after the first resurrection out from among the dead (Rapture). "If by any means I might attain unto the Resurrection of the dead [out from among the dead]" (Phil. 3:11). No wonder Paul constantly labored to be ready to escape the things coming to pass and to stand before the Lord.

Revelation 8 and 9

These two chapters describe in detail the flood of demons and their activity during the end. The entire picture is proceeded by an explanation of the power of prayer.

> And another angel came and stood at the altar, having a golden censor; and there was given him much incense, that he should offer it with the prayers of all saints upon the golden altar which was before the throne. And the smoke of the incense, which came with the prayers of the saints, ascended up before God out of the angel's hand. And the angel took the censor, and filled it with fire of the altar, and cast it into the earth: and there were voices, and thunderings, and lightnings, and an earthquake (Rev. 8:3-5).

It is evident that the seven trumpets which were mentioned in verse two before the scene of prayer power were held in check until the church was safe and her prayers remembered. We are always at the heart of His activities.

The seven trumpets all suggest great consternation upon the earth. The first four deal with the earth's resources and the heavenlies. Then follows the unleashing of the inhabitants of the damned and the spirits bound in their prisons. Jude stated, "And the angels which kept not their first estate, but left their own habitation, he hath reserved in everlasting chains under darkness unto the judgment of the great day" (Jude 6). These are very likely the sons of God who invaded Noah's world (notice Jude said, "left their habitation") and were shut up until the present to protect the earth from their utter destructive powers. Whoever they represent, they are to be released in the end to receive their justice in judgment.

The fifth and sixth trumpets deal with this region of darkness and open up their prison doors to the earth. The entire physical earth comes under siege from hell's inhabitants. Seal five describes an undisclosed number who are under the kingship of the angel of the bottomless pit. His name is Abaddon in Hebrew or Apollyon in the Greek tongue. These damned creatures take on the appearance of locusts who look like horses with destructive powers so great that the men they attack seek death as escape. John said, "And they had tails like scorpions, and there were stings in their tails, and their power was to hurt men five months" (Rev. 9:10). The sixth seal is worse. This second company of fallen creatures are connected with ancient Babylon and the deception of the ages. The entire picture is of an invasion out of the subterranean shadows of the earth where the wicked dead and fallen angels have festered with hatred, vileness and anger at everything within their reach. They will scourge the earth to torment and wreak havoc on all living creatures.

Preparing for the Final Battle

No question but that Satan is preparing for the end-time drama with the expectation of winning. It is evident that he will use all of his resources. The wicked living will serve him. The apostate church will offer their worship as he presents himself to them as their god. The Antichrist and false prophet will succeed in blinding and convincing the world for the new false trinity. Joining these will be the fallen angels, the wicked dead turned loose for a short period, and the army of demon spirits under Satan's control. It will be a dreadful company of the vilest creatures ever assembled. No wonder the name Armageddon holds such ominous vibrations. Even Satan's present followers on earth are anticipating this occasion.

Jesus Christ Returns to Fight

The mighty Redeemer becomes the warrior King. He appears out of the heavenlies like a God/Man with celestial attire. He rides an awesome stallion of spotless white and leads an army of triumphant saints. He is no longer the broken reed of Calvary, bleeding for sins' cleansing. He is now the judge of all who spurned His reconciling sacrifice. He comes to set right the rebellions of all creatures. It is time for righteousness to show its transcending authority. While He does tread the winepress of wrath and experience the bloodstain of battle, it is a quick victory and all rebellion is brought to judgment. Satan's well-planned schemes and his multitude of support has been of no avail. He is defeated and the King of kings begins His triumphant takeover.

> And I saw an angel come down from heaven, having the key of the bottomless pit and a great chain in his hand. And he laid hold on the dragon, that old serpent, which is the Devil, and Satan, and bound him a thousand years. And cast him into the bottomless pit, and shut him up, and set a seal upon him, that he should deceive the nations not more, till the thousand years should be fulfilled: and after that he must be loosed a little season (Rev. 20:1-3).

> Blessed and holy is he that hath part in the first resurrection: on such the second death hath no power, but they shall be priests of God and of Christ, and shall reign with him a thousand years (Rev. 20:6).

If you have ever doubted the evil and wickedness of Satan, I want to remove that doubt. His Antichrist and false prophet are called beasts because that is their character. Let us look at this beastly personage.

---

[1] James Strong, *Strong's Exhaustive Concordance* (Grand Rapids, MI: Baker Book House Co., 1979), Armageddon or Har-Meggiddon, Greek: 717 same as Mediddo, Hebrew: 4023,

[2] Peter LeMesurier, *The Armageddon Script* (Rockport, MA: Element, Inc., 1993).

[3] José Arguelles, "The Crystal Earth Papers." Reprinted from *NRI Trumpet,* July 1987.

Chapter 15

The Antichrist, a Beast from Hell

The consummate evil. A man so vile that he is called a beast and has for a name "blasphemy." He is seen on earth hurling blasphemies against God who is seated on His heavenly throne and he is angrily hurling the same at the saints already among the raptured. He receives his power (inherent ability), his seat (political religions), and his great authority (permission) from the dragon or Satan. Everything that he is, Satan equips him to be. The Bible describes only one type of person who can withstand his design, blinding deception or convincing leadership. John the Revelator said, "And all that dwell upon the earth shall worship him, whose names are not in the book of life of the Lamb slain from the foundation of the World" (Rev. 13:8).

Please read carefully John's full description of this evil genius.

And I stood upon the sand of the sea, and saw a beast rise up out of the sea, having seven heads and ten horns, and upon his horns ten crowns, and upon his heads the name of blasphemy. And the beast which I saw was like unto a leopard, and his feet were as the feet of a bear, and his mouth as the mouth of the lion: and the dragon gave him his power, and his seat, and great authority. And I saw one of his heads as it were wounded to death; and his deadly wound was healed: and all the world wondered after the beast. And they worshipped the dragon which gave power unto the beast: and they worshipped the beast, saying, Who is like unto the beast? who is able to make war with him? And there was given unto him a mouth speaking great things and blasphemies; and power was given unto him to continue forty and two months. And he opened his mouth in blasphemy against God, to blaspheme his name, and his tabernacle, and them that dwell in heaven. And it was given unto him to make war with the saints, and to overcome them: and power was given him over all kindreds, and tongues, and nations. And all that dwell upon the earth shall worship him, whose names are not written in the book of life of the Lamb slain from the foundation of the world. If any man have an ear, let him hear. He that leadeth into captivity shall go into captivity: he that killeth with the sword must be killed with the sword. Here is the patience and the faith of the saints (Rev. 13:1-10).

Several things are extremely important concerning these Scriptures. John is on the shore of the Mediterranean Sea (the great sea) where he has been exiled to the Isle of Patmos. There he sees this beast of a man arise from that same sea. As Daniel, Isaiah, Micah, and others before him, John identifies this man as a Middle Easterner coming to power where in the same region all prior world empires previously existed. This beast and his kingdom are the ultimate expression of all previous worldwide kingdoms. For that reason, this beast is a composite of all previous beasts representing the different kingdoms. He is like a leopard (Grecian), his feet are as of a bear (Medo-Persians), and his mouth is like a lion (Babylon). Daniel gave this same description in chapter 7, except the order was reversed. (We will discuss this later in the chapter.)

Nebuchadnezzar's dream was similar. The great image he saw stood on its feet and progressed downward. No part of these kingdoms has ceased to exist; although they have regressed in value (gold, silver, brass, iron, clay mingled with iron), and increased in fragility. Babylon has exported its vile paganism to every corner of the globe and is today more influential than ever. The developing worldwide religion is becoming more and more pure paganism. The Medes and Persians have existed in different political forms and under varying names, and still exist today as Iran. The Grecian kingdom was most noted for its intellectualism. One has only to read of Greek art, law, literature, and architecture to see the endless presence of this World Empire. It was a striking moment during the Gulf War to see the mayor of Athens, Greece, walking through the battle zones of Baghdad, Iraq. Greece, in an extremely reduced form, exists today as a sovereign nation. The last great kingdom in this dream embodies all the viciousness, wealth, paganism, lust, greed and filth of every part, past and present of the Babylonians, Media-Persians, Grecians, and Romans all under the control of the ultimate beast of a despot and dictator.

Satan Chooses His Man

Prophetic history has not chosen this man; he will be the personal choice of Satan himself. Satan has his children, his chosen family; just as God called the Jews; and he will use them until he manifests the man of perdition to give the world his own possessed messiah. Worldwide signs and biblical fulfillment would suggest that Satan's children may have already produced this individual and he is being readied for his fateful hour as though he were a Jesus in Nazareth waiting for a John to baptize him. "Son of Perdition" was the term used by the apostle Paul (2 Thess. 2:3) in warning that Jesus Christ could not establish His kingdom until Satan had a chance to produce a counterfeit to the Master. These words, "son of perdition," clearly establish that he will be prepared for this hour by evil design with utmost precision and Luciferian skill.

The worldwide rise of satanism, occultic activity, and New Age networking is no accident. Satan has been given space by the Eternal God to prepare his last effort. He failed in the past but this time he plans for it to be different. This counterfeit master must be able to convince the world that he is the real deliverer and that his trinity of gods is the true god of gods. This false messiah must be the best Satan and all his demonic family can produce, train, and empower. **"The world will wonder after the beast"** (Rev. 13:3). The Word of God is clear; Satan chooses and gives him all his characteristics, intelligence and authority. He is Satan's man/god just as Jesus Christ is the Father's God/Man.

Satan's Millennium Denies Final, Catastrophic Judgment

It is amazing to hear clergymen of the Evangelical and Charismatic ranks join the New Agers in calling for a new Millennium or crystal kingdom on the earth. Pat Robertson's new book, *The New Millennium, Megatrends of the 90's,* is described in his magazine with these words, "So, be forewarned, if you've already bought your Rapture robe, you probably won't want to buy this book." Pat is also quoted as saying, "Christianity will flourish worldwide in the Millennium"[1] When you deny the Rapture and make no provision for the total judgment of this wicked world, how do you promise a Christian Millennium?

Satanically inspired New Agers and trilateralist politicians are saying basically the same. José Arguelles has announced the "Crystal Kingdom on the Earth" to begin no later than December 21, 2012.[2] Political talk of a New World Order is engineered by the Dragon as he manipulates mankind in preparation for the Antichrist. You must understand that all of this represents the elaborate design of Lucifer with his determination to create his millennium ruled by himself and his unholy trinity.

The only thing this world is about to face is the final judgment. *The Rapture is hated because* it removes the *biblical crowd* from judgment danger and fixes the beginning of the darkest hour of God's wrath known to man. Jesus Christ, himself, described this hour:

> For then shall be great tribulation, such as was not since the beginning of the world to this time, no, nor ever shall be. And except those days should be shortened, there should no flesh be saved: but for the elect's sake those days shall be shortened. Then if any man shall say unto you, Lo, here is Christ, or there; believe it not. For there shall arise false Christs, and false prophets, and shall show great signs and wonders; insomuch that, if it were possible, they shall deceive the very elect (Matt. 24:21-24).

Nothing reveals the ruthlessness of Lucifer more than his use of the church and clergymen to prepare for his short last rule over humankind.

Daniel's Description of Satan's Last Fling

The Book of Daniel is Revelation's First Testament companion. Every truth in these two books synchronizes perfectly. The 13th chapter of Revelation describes the Antichrist with the words, leopard, bear, and lion all blended into an indescribable final beast. This is reversed in Daniel because he spoke prophetically before the facts, while John sees the view historically, after the facts. Here is how Daniel describes the scene.

> Daniel spake and said, I saw in my vision by night, and behold, the four winds of the heaven

strove upon the great sea. And four great beasts came up from the sea, diverse one from another. The first was like a lion, and had eagle's wings: I beheld till the wings thereof were plucked, and it was lifted up from the earth, and made stand upon the feet as a man, and a man's heart was given to it. And behold another beast, a second, like to a bear, and it raised itself on one side, and it had three ribs in the mouth of it between the teeth of it: and they said thus unto it, Arise, devour much flesh. After this I beheld, and lo another, like a leopard, which had upon the back of it four wings of a fowl; the beast had also four heads; and dominion was given to it. After this I saw in the night visions, and behold a fourth beast, dreadful and terrible, and strong exceedingly; and it had great iron teeth: it devoured and brake in pieces, and stamped the residue with the feet of it: and it was diverse from all the beasts that were before it; and it had ten horns (Dan. 7:2-7).

Again the last four major world kingdoms are beautifully pictured. In prophecy the first kingdom, Babylon, was politically in its death throes when Daniel received his vision. The next two are clearly the Medo-Persian and Grecian kingdoms followed by the Roman kingdom. The Roman Era is the worldwide kingdom existing in Christ's day, but surviving the centuries in broken form to emerge as the final political arm of Lucifer. This kingdom is not just the European Common Market. That represents part of the old Roman era but still clearly in a broken and imperfect form. The dragon, Antichrist, and false prophet (unholy trinity) will solidify the final stage creating their own one world kingdom.

John, in the Book of the Revelation (revelation means the unveiling or making manifest), painted a clear scene of this emerging One World Order that completes the Roman period. "And the ten horns which thou sawest are ten kings, which have received no kingdom as yet; but receive power as kings one hour with the beast. These have one mind, and shall give their power and strength unto the beast" (Rev. 17:12-13). The final ten kings which fulfill the ten toes of Daniel 2 (Nebuchadnezzar's dream) and ten horns of Daniel 7 (beast with ten horns) are not an existing political entity when the Antichrist appears. They have no kingdom or authority until they receive it from this final world leader. The Holy Scripture clearly states, "Which have received no kingdom as yet; but receive power as kings one hour with the beast." It is important that we do not look to any existing political order or form as the fulfillment of the Roman world empire. Once the Antichrist is on the scene, he will perfect that final stage of human governments.

Each of the first three of the last world empires existed in different forms and for considerable time until they finally centered in Babylon. It was at this point that they fulfilled the biblical requirement to be a world kingdom of prophecy. Babylon is the only acceptable capital for a one world government controlled by Satan.

Reverend G.H. Lang clarified this subject half of a century ago.

> Babylon had existed since the days of Nimrod (Gen. 10:10), but the ups and downs of that state during those hundreds of years do not matter *prophetically*. It was when Nebuchadnezzar made Babylon the centre of a world empire that the first kingdom of *prophecy* arose. The Medes and Persians had had an almost equally long history, but that is of no account *prophetically*. It was when Cyrus made Babylon the centre of his rule that the second kingdom of *prophecy* appeared. The Grecian states had been fighting, developing, colonizing for long centuries before Alexander, but prophecy takes no account of this also. It simply doesn't

matter. It was when Alexander made Babylon his world-centre that the third kingdom of *prophecy* became present (a reality). It is thus with the fourth empire, as might surely be expected. The mutations of its long course are of small concern *prophetically*. The divine interpretation and the profound interest concentrate on the closing days, when Antichrist will make Babylon his capital.[3]

The Roman period will be prophetically complete when Babylon becomes its center. Until then it is only iron or iron and clay awaiting the god of Babylon to elevate it to biblical fulfillment. It is interesting to note that the German leaders, especially Hitler, had already decided to make Babylon their headquarters when their conquest was finished. They spoke of the Third Reich kingdom lasting a thousand years.

Antichrist and Ultimate Religious Blasphemy

Nothing that the Antichrist does is more significant than his effort to duplicate the death and resurrection of Jesus Christ. When the dragon and his two beasts, the Antichrist and the false prophet, are finished with their religious deception and their fringed presentation of biblical Christianity, multiplied millions will be deceived beyond imagination. John describes it as the following, "And I saw one of his heads as it were wounded to death; and his deadly wound was healed: and all the world wondered after the beast" (Rev. 13:3). The master imitator will present biblical and Christ-like imitations, religious experiences, supernatural miracles, and double talk theology with convincing skills. "The world will wonder after the Beast" (Rev. 13:3).

He will have the ability to exalt and magnify himself above every god, except Jehovah God, but will be able to speak marvelous things against Him. The Hebrew word for "marvelous" means "to accomplish things beyond the bounds of human powers or expectation." Here are Daniel's words:

> And the king shall do according to his will;
> and he shall exalt himself, and magnify himself
> above every god, and shall speak marvellous things
> against the God of gods, and shall prosper till the
> indignation be accomplished: for that that is deter-
> mined shall be done (Dan. 11:36).

This beast of Satan will be an apostate with a family background of either the Jewish or Christian faith. Some of Satan's vilest work has been with individuals from a biblical heritage. Karl Marx, Charles Darwin, and Carl Jung are excellent examples. Daniel speaks to this fact. "Neither shall he regard the God of his fathers, nor the desire of women, nor regard any god: for he shall magnify himself above all" (Dan. 11:37).

The prophet, Ezekiel, spoke pointedly to the same subject.

> And thou, profane wicked prince of Israel,
> whose day is come, when iniquity shall have an
> end, Thus saith the Lord God; Remove the diadem,
> and take off the crown: this shall not be the same:
> exalt him that is low, and abase him that is high. I
> will overturn, overturn, overturn it: and it shall be
> no more, until he come whose right it is; and I will
> give it him (Ezek. 21:25-27).

This great prophetic statement confirms the words of Daniel. Ezekiel adds a clear statement that this false prince will be disposed and the true king, *Whose right it is* will be given the kingdom.

The force of this new religion that blasphemes everything in Holy Scripture is filling religious circles presently. Charismatic television ministers are leading personalities in this new deception. It looks real to undiscerning souls; it offers the perceived power of God and it titillates the flesh. Daniel called this explosion of religious titillation and fleshy emotions, *the god of forces.*

> But in his estate shall he honour the God of forces: and a god whom his fathers knew not shall he honour with gold, and silver, and with precious stones, and pleasant things. Thus shall he do in the most strong holds with a strange god, whom he shall acknowledge and increase with glory (Dan. 11:38-39).

This beast from hell with his false prophet (religious leader) will cause apostate church people to exclaim that the great revival is finally here. Already religious leaders who have rejected the Rapture and the Great Tribulation judgment, along with the separated holiness lifestyle, are predicting a revival so great that the ball games and sports events will be closed. They speak of an awakening that sweeps the world into Christianity. This cannot happen unless God suspends His infallible Word and changes the course of our present direction.

Great Demon Powers to Aid Satan

Immediately after the Rapture of the bride of Christ, a war will occur in the heavens. Michael and his angels cast Lucifer and his angels down to the earth.

> And there was war in heaven: Michael and his angels fought against the dragon; and the dragon fought and his angels, And prevailed not; neither was their place found any more in heaven. And the great dragon was cast out, that old serpent, called the Devil, and Satan, which deceiveth the whole world: he was cast out into the earth, and his angels were cast out with him. . . . Therefore, rejoice, ye heavens, and ye that dwell in them. Woe to the inhabitors of the earth and of the sea! for the devil is come down unto you, having great wrath, because he knoweth that he hath but a short time (Rev. 12:7-12).

There is literally an innumerable company of angels and one-third of them have joined Satan. They have had some limited access to the earth since their fall. Then they will be cast out of the second heaven and restricted in their presence and activity to the earth. John said, "Woe to the inhabitors of the earth." Not only does Satan have his unholy trinity, he has a multitude of powerful angels who are at his command. They are not limited to a bodily space nor the natural laws of the earth. They are as powerful as the holy angels, but totally debased and bent on destruction. Their service is to the Antichrist even as holy angels serve Jesus Christ.

The Antichrist will also have help from hell. These are angels and fallen men who have been locked up in the region of the damned. Jude 6 states, "And the Angels which kept not their first estate, but left their own habitation, he hath reserved in everlasting chains under darkness unto the judgment of the great day." In the original Greek, the word reserved means to guard; to keep the eye on; to prevent from escaping. There is a company of fallen angels who are so vile and abhorrent that God will not loose them in the earth before the Rapture. At the judgment of the great day which is the Tribulation period, God will loose them and they will unleash such filth, perversion, and ungodliness greater than men can now imagine.

They have had centuries to fester in their hatred for God and His Christ-centered kingdom. It is their battle to break the hold of the great God, Jehovah, and enthrone their god, Lucifer. They will spare no energy to make this earth an extension of hell. These are the servants of the Antichrist and join in a worldwide attack. The beast from hell will man an army with destructive power. The world will become a wilderness.

Isaiah describes what will result from this legion of evil led by Satan's messiah, the Antichrist.

Fear and the pit, and the snare, are upon thee,

O inhabitant of the earth. And it shall come to pass, that he who fleeth from the noise of the fear shall fall into the pit; and he that cometh up out of the midst of the pit shall be taken in the snare: for the windows from on high are open, and the foundations of the earth do shake. The earth is utterly broken down, the earth is clean dissolved, the earth is moved exceedingly. The earth shall reel to and fro like a drunkard, and shall be removed like a cottage; and the transgression thereof shall be heavy upon it; and it shall fall, and not rise again. And it shall come to pass in that day, that the Lord shall punish the host of the high ones that are on high, and the kings of the earth upon the earth. And they shall be gathered together, as prisoners are gathered in the pit, and shall be shut up in the prison, and after many days shall they be visited. Then the moon shall be confounded, and the sun ashamed, when the Lord of hosts shall reign in mount Zion, and in Jerusalem, and before his ancients gloriously (Isa. 24:17-23).

The Beast from Hell

Surely, such a picture is enough to warn the wicked and to excite the righteous. The great God does not allow this dragon because He desires man's destruction. Rather, wickedness is released to expose its vilest nature and to finish forever the debased schemes of godless men. The kingdom of Jesus Christ is waiting to fill the earth as waters cover the sea. Satan's last hour is the prelude of a cloudless eternity. Every believer ought to rejoice as the judgments near. The old saying is fitting, "The darkest hour is just before dawn."

Now we can ready ourselves for the grand finale. The earth is the Lord's and the impostor has been cast out. First, let us look at His chosen nation, Israel, as they finally experience the intended glory of His blessings.

[1] *The Christian American*, January/February 1991, page 11.

[2] José Arguelles, "The Crystal Earth Papers." Reprinted from *NRI Trumpet,* July 1987.

[3] G.H. Lang, *The Histories and Prophecies of Daniel* (Miami Springs, FL: Conley & Schoettle Publishing Co., Inc., 1985), p. 29.

Chapter 16

Israel — Master of the Middle East

Set in eternal concrete; prophesied by holy prophets, the nation of Israel and the throne of the great King David will be the final victor in this land of perpetual conflict. Not until these children of Abraham by the promised son Isaac have suffered their last and darkest period will this happen, but happen it will. The Holy Scripture which cannot fail has clearly established the scenario that we are now entering. The political noose around Israel will continue to tighten until she is forced to sign an agreement or covenant with an emerging One World Order. Israel has made one concession after the other as negotiations have continued with the Palestinians. Regardless of this action, the Arab nation asks for more. Nothing that Israel does will satisfy for a long period. As the pressure mounts, Israel will be more and more hard pressed to make more and more compromises. All of this will eventually represent a covenant with the new One World leader.

The new Jewish leaders are not the conservatives of the past. This has just changed in the 1996 elections. They want the favor of the world and world trade with the existing political powers. These liberals have no sense of the Jewish future or the biblical hope. They believe in a kind of Messianic age, but not a personal Messiah as do the Orthodox Jews. One of their key spokesmen is the former mayor of Jerusalem, Teddy Kollek, who constantly calls for the internationalization of this capital city. As we see in chapters 17 and 18, he also speaks of the Messiah, so he may differ from many of the more liberal Jews. There is no awareness of biblical fulfillment to these Jewish leaders and a covenant of peace will be to them a small price to pay for harmony with the world. A climate is presently developing that will make this covenant between Israel and the man who will emerge as Antichrist seem necessary. Watch for peace talks to become even more paramount between Israel's government and other political forces, even Saddam Hussein, as we move toward a one world government or New World Order. It must happen to fulfill the Word of God. The election of Benjamin Netanyahu seems to have slowed the Israeli rush to trade land for "peace."

The Abomination of Desolation

Israel's darkest hour of all her sufferings is ready to unfold. The Tribulation period of seven years will begin at the appropriate time of the covenant mentioned above. After 3-1/2 years of uneasy cooperation between the Jewish state and the one world builders, the agreement between them will fall apart. That is when the Antichrist breaks the covenant by entering the Jewish worship center and erecting an image to himself. Jesus spoke of this and described the horror of this dark hour.

> When ye therefore shall see the abomination of desolation, spoken of by Daniel the prophet, stand in the holy place, (whoso readeth, let him understand,) then let them which be in Judea flee into the mountains: let him which is on the housetop not come down to take any thing out of his house: neither let him which is in the field return

back to take his clothes. And woe unto them that are with child, and to them that give suck in those days! But pray ye that your flight be not in the winter, neither on the Sabbath day; for then shall be great tribulation, such as was not since the beginning of the world to this time, no, nor ever shall be. And except those days should be shortened, there should be no flesh be saved: but for the elect's sake those days shall be shortened (Matt. 24:15-22).

This event was foretold by Daniel with the following words, "And he shall confirm the covenant with many for one week [seven years]: and in the midst of the week he shall cause the sacrifice and the oblation to cease" (Dan. 9:27). Jeremiah added a significant description to this period.

And these are the words that the Lord spake concerning Israel and concerning Judah. For thus saith the Lord; we have heard a voice of trembling, of fear, and not of peace. Ask ye now, and see whether a man doth travail with child? wherefore do I see every man with his hands on his loins, as a woman in travail, and all faces turned into paleness? Alas! for that day is great, so that none is like it: it is even the time of Jacob's trouble; but he shall be saved out of it (Jer. 30:4-7).

Daniel made a very interesting observation when he quoted what a saint of God said to another saint:

Then I heard one saint speaking, and another saint said unto that certain saint which spake, How long shall be the vision concerning the daily sacrifice, and the transgression of desolation, to give both the sanctuary and the host to be trodden under foot? And he said unto me, Unto two thousand and three hundred days; then shall the sanctuary be cleansed (Dan. 8:13-14).

This quote put the Antichrist's unclean activities in the Jewish temple almost seven years. Could this suggest that the one world government is allowed to actually help build the temple as part of a covenant agreement? If so, it would explain why the area is trodden underfoot by unclean powers for almost the whole tribulation period. Daniel is clear (as seen above) that the actual abomination of desolation does not occur until the middle of this period.

When this happens in the middle of the seven-year Tribulation and the image of the Antichrist is erected in the temple, the Jews will flee Jerusalem for their last time. They will hasten to the wilderness of Moab, Ammon, and Edom where they will find refuge from their pursuers. The chosen people will find friends to shelter and protect them. Isaiah said, "Send ye the lamb to the ruler of the land from Sela [the Greek name *Petra* — rock — probably replaced the biblical name Sela[1]] to the wilderness, unto the mount of the daughter of Zion. . . . Let mine outcast dwell with thee Moab: be thou a covert to them from the face of the spoiler" (Isa. 16:1-4).

This prophecy affirms that the Jewish inheritance of Israel will be protected from the man of sin by the Moabites or present day Jordanians. The Ammonites are also modern Jordanians and will share in being what Isaiah calls coverts or a covering for the Jewish inhabitants. The land of Edom is also mentioned in this wilderness experience. Edom is the land of Esau and is presently located in areas controlled by either Jordan or Saudi Arabia. Some Edomites will share in protecting Israel while others will betray them.

Saved from the Antichrist

Because these Arab nations (descendants of Lot and Esau) befriend Israel in this dark hour God keeps His promise to "bless those that bless Jerusalem." Nothing escapes the omniscience of the Almighty. Daniel has already prophesied the protection. "He shall enter also into the glorious land, and many countries shall be overthrown: but these shall escape our of his hand even Edom and Moab, and the Chief of the children of Ammon" (Dan. 11:41-42). By some miraculous event this ruthless one world leader will be diverted from crossing over Jordan and the geographical line south of Jordan into the wilderness immediately east. The Jews who obey the Torah and prophets and flee as God has spoken will be protected. The rest of Israel will be viciously murdered and ravaged.

Two-Thirds of All Jews Will Be Killed

The prophet Zechariah has established what happens to both the two-thirds slain and the one-third who are delivered.

> And it shall come to pass that in all the land, saith the Lord, two parts therein shall be cut off and die; but the third shall be left therein. And I will bring the third part through the fire, and will refine them as silver is refined and will try them as gold is tried: they shall call on my name, and I will hear them: I will say, It is my people; and they shall say, the Lord is my God (Zech. 13:8-9).

This wilderness experience will break their stubbornness and haughty spirits and open their hearts to the Messiah Jesus Christ. The census in the *Jewish Directory and Almanac* states there are 14,527,150 Jews.[2] It has probably increased one million or more since that census was taken. That means approximately *10,000,000* plus Jews will be slaughtered and *5,000,000* will be ready to help establish the Kingdom of David. The 144,000 of the 12 tribes sealed in Revelation 7 will be evangelists to the Israeli nation and the world's Jewish population. These ministers will prepare their hearts for their Messiah.

Temple in Jerusalem to Be Cleansed Before the End of the Great Tribulation

One of the most thrilling things I have ever discovered is the cleansing of the temple in Jerusalem. It will actually happen about 8-1/2 months before the Battle of Armageddon as the Jews begin their heartfelt humility and repentance. God, the Holy Spirit, will be getting them ready to be converted and cleansed in one day. Daniel told the story of this happening.

> Yea, he magnified himself even to the prince of the host, and by him the daily sacrifice was taken away, and the place of his sanctuary was cast down. And a host was given him against the daily sacrifice by reason of transgression, and it cast down the truth to the ground; and it practised, and prospered. Then I heard one saint speaking, and another saint said unto that certain saint which spake, How long shall be the vision concerning the daily sacrifice, and the transgression of desolation, to give both the sanctuary and the host to be trodden under foot? And he said unto me, Unto two thousand and three hundred days; then shall the sanctuary be cleansed (Dan. 8:11-14).

Apparently, the Antichrist will be so occupied with his own troubles and the judgment of God falling on his head that he will not have time to maintain his hold of Jerusalem.

The 2,300 days include the first 3-1/2 years of daily sacrifices following the covenant with the impostor. Part of the seven-year covenant will be to return the Temple Mount to the Jews as their Holy Place. That is one of the reasons why the Antichrist must be connected to the Arab world. The next two years and 9-1/2 months will be while the sanctuary is trodden under foot by the prince of the host (verse 11) or this impostor posing himself as the high priest. During the last 8-1/2 months, the city of Jerusalem will be recaptured and the temple returned to Jewish control. When the first 3-1/2 years or 1,278 days are subtracted from 2,300 (Dan. 8:14), it leaves 1,022 days or 2 years and approximately 9-1/2 months. That leaves approximately 8-1/2 months to finish the last 3-1/2 years. The Holy Spirit never misses a detail. Every jot and tittle will be fulfilled.

Just exactly like Jesus promised, the days will be shortened for the elect, but not for the rest of the world. "And except those days should be shortened there should no flesh be saved; but for the elect's sake those days shall be shortened" (Matt. 24:22). While the Antichrist directs his New World Order from Babylon and his false prophets from Rome and Jerusalem, he will actually seek out every Jewish individual for death and will destroy over 10,000,000 of them. The Father will halt him before all of them are killed.

Jesus Returns to Defeat Gog and His Multitude

While the temple is being cleansed and the Jewish people are preparing for the returning Messiah, the Antichrist will be marshaling for the death blow against Jerusalem called Armageddon. He will be angry to the point of insanity due to the loss of Jerusalem and the re-instituting of Jewish worship in the Holy Place. His immense army will gather in Megiddo and prepare for the death blow, once and for all, of the State of Israel, Jerusalem, and every Jewish individual left. That is when the fury of God flies in his face.

> And I saw heaven opened, and behold a white horse; and he that sat upon him was called Faithful and True, and in righteousness he doth judge and make war. His eyes were as a flame of fire, and on his head were many crowns; and he had a name written, that no man knew, but he himself. And he was clothed with a vesture dipped in blood: and his name is called The Word of God. And the armies which were in heaven followed him upon white horses, clothed in fine linen, white and clean. And out of his mouth goeth a sharp sword, that with it he should smite the nations: and he shall rule them with a rod of iron: and he treadeth the winepress of the fierceness and wrath of Almighty God. And he hath on his vesture and on his thigh a name written,

KING OF KINDS, AND LORD OF LORDS. And I saw an angel standing in the sun; and he cried with a loud voice, saying to all the fowls that fly in the midst of heaven, Come and gather yourselves together unto the supper of the great God. That ye may eat the flesh of kings, and the flesh of captains, and the flesh of mighty men, and the flesh of horses, and of them that sit on them, and the flesh of all men, both free and bond, both small and great. And I saw the beast, and the kings of the earth, and their armies, gathered together to make war against him that sat on the horse, and against his army (Rev. 19:11-19).

The battle will reach the city of Jerusalem according to Zechariah.

Behold the day of the Lord cometh, and thy spoil shall be divided in the midst of thee. For I will gather all nations against Jerusalem to battle; and the city shall be taken, and the house rifled, and the women ravished; and half of the city shall go forth into captivity, and the residue of the people shall not be cut off from the city. Then shall the Lord go forth, and fight against these nations, as when he fought in the day of battle. And his feet shall stand in that day upon the Mount of Olives, which is before Jerusalem on the east, and the Mount of Olives shall cleave in the midst thereof toward the east and toward the west, and there shall be a very great valley; and half of the mountain shall remove toward the north, and half of it toward the south. And ye shall flee to the valley of the mountains; for the valley of the mountains shall reach unto Azal: yea, ye shall flee, like as ye fled from before the earthquake in the days of Uzziah king of Judah: and the Lord my God shall come, and all the saints with thee. And it shall come to pass in that day, that the light shall not be clear, nor dark; But it shall be one day which shall be known to the Lord, not day, nor night: but it shall come to pass, that at evening time it shall be light (Zech. 14:1-7).

We are discussing one of the most furious and destructive battles of human history. The Lord Jesus Christ will actually participate in combat as He trods the winepress of the wrath of God. It will take seven years for Israel to bury the dead.

All Israel to Be Cleansed and Saved

When the King of kings, riding His white stallion, has vanquished the army of this madman, He will immediately appear to the Jewish throng in Moab, Ammon, and Edom. They actually see and hear the pleading of their Messiah as He invites them to faith in Him. Isaiah describes this breathtaking moment.

> Who is this that cometh from Edom, with dyed garments from Bozrah? this that is glorious in his apparel, traveling in the greatness of his strength? I that speak in righteousness, mighty to save. Wherefore art thou red in this apparel, and thy garments like him that treadeth in the winevat? I have trodden the winepress alone; and of the people there was none with me: for I will tread them in mine anger, and trample them in my fury; and their blood shall be sprinkled upon my garments, and I will stain all my raiment. For the day of vengeance is in mine heart, and the year of my redeemed is come (Isa. 63:1-4).

Then He proceeds to the Eastern Gate of the Holy City, clothed in His blood stained apparel, where already the masons are removing the stones that have barred that entrance to the Temple Mount for centuries awaiting this Prince of Peace.

In one day all Israel will be converted to the Lord Jesus Christ and the land cleansed of all its defilement. Zechariah said:

> For behold the stone that I have laid before Joshua; upon one stone shall be seven eyes: behold, I will engrave the graving thereof, saith the Lord of hosts, and I will remove the iniquity of that land in one day. In that day, saith the Lord of hosts, shall ye call every man his neighbour under the vine and under the fig tree (Zech. 3:9-10).

The apostle Paul left no doubt in his inspiration by the Holy Spirit.

> For I would not, brethren, that ye should be ignorant of this mystery, lest ye should be wise in your own conceits, that blindness in part is happened to Israel, until the fulness of the Gentiles be come in. And so all Israel shall be saved: as it is written, There shall come out of Zion the Deliverer, and shall turn away ungodliness from Jacob: For this is my covenant unto them, when I shall take away their sins (Rom. 11:25-27).

The children of Abraham will finally prepare for their glorious kingdom. The borders of Israel will reach from the Mediterranean Sea to the Euphrates River. Every square inch promised to the father of faith will be the inheritance of these believing sons and daughters of Abraham, Isaac, and Jacob. God has promised "thy seed shall possess the gate of his enemies" (Gen. 22:17).

The Babylonians (Iraqis) will serve Israel as will other nations who have made slaves of the Jewish people. The land of promises will be a Garden of Eden and produce abundantly. Arid deserts will become as gardens and no man will lack for plenty. The Middle East is the cradle of civilization and will be the center of a worldwide theocracy ruled by the virgin born heir of David. Jesus will set up the kingdom of which He told His disciples in answer to their question, "Wilt thou at this time restore again the kingdom to Israel. He said, It is not for you to know the time and season which the Father hath put in His own power" (Acts 1:6-7). *The time has come!*

While Israel revels in the beauty of Jerusalem and their Garden of Eden, the whole earth becomes the place where His saints rule in honor. We, the *redeemed of the Lord,* will inherit all things and righteousness will cover the earth. One thousand years of glory will follow.

[1] *Britannica Encyclopedia,*15th edition, 1990, p. 9:339, 2b.
[2] The Jewish Information Center, New York, NY, 1983.

Chapter 17

The Millennium

The unfailing desire of humankind has been for a kingdom of peace, prosperity, lasting happiness, and dominion over his world. Deep in the human soul exists the dream that our Creator instilled when He intricately designed us and put us in His cosmos. We were created to reign over our environment, to be in charge of our future and the lesser creatures around us, and to offer all of this beauty back to the Heavenly Father for whose glory we were made. I believe we took the place in God's heart that Lucifer had filled but became void due to his fall from the love, power, and authority. If that is true, it certainly explains his hatred of mankind and the constant antagonism we have encountered.

God the Father instituted the reign of His children on earth and it was intended to be everything that we could ever long to know. It was a naturally supernatural world until sin was introduced by the usurper or interloper named Satan. The condition of the newly created world in Adam's day was just what it will be in the Millennium kingdom. A look at that world will start the process of understanding what we are waiting and longing for when Jesus returns to establish His earthly kingdom. The second Adam will do what the first Adam failed to do. "For as in Adam all die, even so in Christ shall all be made alive" (1 Cor. 15:22).

A statement in my first book, *Miracles, My Father's Delight,* describes the brand new world in which Adam and Eve found themselves.

> We must start with man's simple beginning and discover that everything God does is "naturally supernatural."
>
> Adam and Eve, as soon as they were created, had the entire resplendent, visible creation before them, both to enjoy and subdue. They were different from all the rest of God's creation. The Holy Trinity consulted about them and fashioned them in the image of their Creator.
>
> The work of creation was magnificent and complete. There were no defects or flaws. Adam and Eve were the crowning achievement, made just a little lower than the angels.
>
> Imagine what a supernatural lifestyle Adam and Eve enjoyed!
>
> They walked in a normal, yet totally miraculous (to our 20th century minds) existence "everyday!" God came down to the Garden to be with them, to have an intimate and personal fellowship with the man and woman He created.
>
> The Garden rested in a lush, canopied world — a greenhouse-like paradise shielded from the harsh, harmful rays of the sun. Adam and Eve, for the first time, were able to taste and discover each succulent, exotic fruit — from the glossy melons to the pebbled oranges.
>
> During mankind's very first parade, God brought each animal, beast, creeping thing, and fowl before His human creation, and allowed him to name each one. In this incredible, supernatural realm, Adam fit each species with the perfect biological characteristic as he labeled them —

from the shaggy, majestic lion, to the fluttering hummingbird, to the behemoth elephant, down to the chirping cricket.

Man and woman had dominion over an amazing, peaceful, "supernatural" paradise. They were created just a little lower than the celestial angels; they were able to walk in a problem-free garden without fear; they were with God — in person! It was exactly as the Father desired for a time.[1]

What a world that was and what a world it will soon be again. I love the term "naturally supernatural." As archeologists discover the relics of Erech (Uruk), Accad (Acade), Babel (Babylon) (Gen. 10:9-11), and other Sumerian cities, they are finding that this first civilization was highly cultured, extremely intelligent and profoundly artistic. The first language, according to secular history, archaeology, and the biblical fact, was Sumerian (Shinar in the Bible). This was the language of Adam, Eve, and their family and it was as highly intellectual as any language ever invented. Archaeologists have found incredible evidence dating back to 4000 B.C. of a civilization highly advanced and ingenious equal to any expression of human capacity.

This one language (Sumerian) was spoken by everyone until Babel (after the Flood) when God had to confuse their pagan design. Already in Adam's lifetime false religions were taking root. Erech, now called Uruk, dates back to approximately 3500 B.C. and sported a pagan temple/ ziggurat dedicated to Inanna (first female goddess). Adam and Eve probably lived or at least visited in this city and the murder of Abel by Cain may well have been inspired by his worship of Inanna at this very shrine. Babel was nothing but a larger version of this kind of temple tower used to promote a false god and to seduce the people to the sex orgies and crude celebrations designed by the mighty rebel Nimrod (called Gilgamesh in Sumerian history and folklore).

The world, as God created it, was perfect and inspired

by the Creator himself, an exclamation of perfection. "And God saw everything that he had made, and behold it was very good" (Gen. 1:31). Nothing existed that caused a curse, destructive behavior, or any action that reduced life from the lofty scale designed by the Creator. It was a beautiful and full world. Scientists, archaeologists, and anthropologists have documented support for an exotic world of sunshine, flowers, creatures of extreme size, and beauty; a place where life could be lived to the fullest. Into this world of such boundless life, sin entered; the first Adam sold our birthright and the consequence is apparent to everyone.

A New Heaven and a New Earth

Nothing short of remaking this universe can answer the problems caused by sin. Many political and religious leaders have dreamed of their New World Order. Past history has given us the Sumerians, Egyptians, Assyrians, Babylonians, Persians, Grecians, Romans, and the modern efforts of the Russians, French, British, Germans, and the United Nations. Numerous religious leaders have preached, written, and prophesied of a One World Order and man's right and capacity to take dominion over the earth. Pat Robertson, probably the most determined of all the present religious one worlders, said the following in his book, *The Secret Kingdom*:

> *Can there be a New World Order? Yes.*
>
> Later, during a time of fasting and prayer he said he heard God's voice and was told the following:
>
> "Let them have dominion." My eyes went over it several times. Then I knew the Lord's purpose. He wanted man to have dominion — then and now.
>
> It was very clear. This was a kingdom law. God wants man to have authority over the earth. He wants him to rule the way he was created to rule.

You cannot help but juxtapose this desire of God with today's reality. . . . Where is the blessing promised in the Bible from beginning to end? Was Jesus wrong when He said, "I will build my church; and the gates of hell shall not prevail against it?"

No, Jesus was not wrong. Hell will not prevail. But we are seeing an Old Testament warning lived out among the people of God, and indeed all mankind: "My people perish for want of knowledge." Men haven't been taught the Law of Dominion and the other principles of the kingdom. They are miserable.

But they can change immediately.

Almighty God wants us to recapture the dominion man held in the beginning. . . .

Remember, at the time of creation man exercised authority under God's sovereignty, over everything. He was God's surrogate, His steward or regent.

The Genesis account uses two colorful words to describe this. One, radah, we translate "dominion." Man was to have dominion. The word means to "rule over" or "tread down," as with grapes. It comes from a Hebrew root meaning "spread out" or "prostrate." The picture we get from it is one of all the creation spread out before man, whose dominion would extend wherever his feet trod.

The other word, kabash, is translated "subdue." Man was told to subdue the earth. The root means "to trample under foot," as one would do when washing dirty clothes. Therefore, in kabash we have in part the concept of separating good from evil by force.

With the first word, radah, God gives man the authority to govern all that is willing to be governed. With the second, kabash, He grants man authority over the untamed and the rebellious. In both instances, God gave man a sweeping and total mandate of dominion over this planet and everything in it.[2]

A classical Bible student can see immediately the fallacy of this logic. It completely bypasses man's sin and the consequences.

All of these political and religious leaders, sincere as they may be, have failed in the past and are failing in the present. The discussion in Scripture of dominion was a condition in God's plan that sin disrupted and now awaits the new heaven and earth for its fulfillment. Sinful mankind cannot take the dominion God originally planned until he and this universe are completely redeemed. Before that redemption, there must be the Great Tribulation/Judgment that Jesus announced. "For there shall be great tribulation such as was not since the beginning of the world [creation] to this time, no, nor ever shall be" (Matt. 24:21). The wickedness in our world is so pronounced and deep that a religious theocracy would be either no different or worse than a secular theocracy. The religious theocracy of Israel's Old Testament history is a case in point.

The Biblical Base of This Millennium

The Spirit of God gave Daniel an exact picture of how the human governments (secular or religious) would end.

> Thou, O king, sawest, and behold a great image. This great image, whose brightness was excellent, stood before thee; and the form thereof was terrible. This image's head was of fine gold, his breast and his arms of silver, his belly and his thighs of brass. His legs of iron, his feet part of iron and part of clay. Thou sawest till that a stone was cut out without hands, which smote the image upon his feet that were of iron and clay, and brake them to pieces. Then was the iron, the clay, the brass, the silver, and the gold, broken to pieces together, and

became like the chaff of the summer threshing-floors; and the wind carried them away, that no place was found for them: and the stone that smote the image became a great mountain, and filled the whole earth (Dan. 2:31-35).

And in the days of these kings shall the God of heaven set up a kingdom, which shall never be destroyed: and the kingdom shall not be left to other people, but it shall break in pieces and consume all these kingdoms, and it shall stand for ever. Forasmuch as thou sawest that the stone was cut out of the mountain without hands, and that it brake in pieces the iron, the brass, the clay, the silver, and the gold; the great God hath made known to the king what shall come to pass hereafter: and the dream is certain, and the interpretation thereof sure (Dan. 2:44-45).

There can be no doubt; this New World Order or Millennium kingdom is not the work of men. It is "cut out of the mountain without hands" and utterly destroys all governments, coalitions, empires, and political orders, religious or secular. The great God, as Daniel calls Him, is the sole Creator and executor. Later in Daniel's prophecies, he recounts a vision by declaring:

I beheld till the thrones [all earthly governments] were cast down, and the Ancient of days [Jehovah God, himself] did sit, whose garment was white as snow, and the hair of his head like the pure wool: his throne was like the fiery flame, and his wheels as burning fire ... I beheld then, because of the voice of the great words which the horn spake: I beheld even till the beast (the Antichrist and final representative of human government) was slain, and his body destroyed, and given to the burning flame (Dan. 7:9-11).

This kingdom is established by the Father himself and given to His Son Jesus Christ. Daniel describes the scene.

> I saw in the night visions, and, behold, one like the Son of man came to the Ancient of days, and they brought him near before him. And there was given him dominion, and glory, and a kingdom, that all people, nations, and languages, should serve him: his dominion is an everlasting dominion, which shall not pass away, and his kingdom that which shall not be destroyed (Dan. 7:13-14).

The glorified Son of God/Son of Man is clearly seen riding upon the clouds of heaven (His second return to earth) and coming to the Father himself who then presents the kingdoms of the world to His only begotten Son. The Creator, who has not walked upon His earth since He took Enoch home with himself (Gen. 5:24), now actually appears in Jerusalem to give the kingdom to the Second Adam. The first Adam brought sin and destruction, but the Second Adam brings life and righteousness. It is a heavenly dream finally fulfilled. The earth becomes the Father's garden again.

The Judgments of Sin Must Precede This Grand Finale

It is imperative to understand that this hour cannot transpire until sin is adjudicated. To talk about a New World Order without the seven years of earth's cleansing judgment is to question the holiness of God. The Psalmist had a clear view of this fact.

> Why do the heathen rage, and the people imagine a vain thing? The kings of the earth set themselves, and the rulers take counsel together, against the Lord, and against his Anointed, saying, Let us break their bands asunder, and cast away their cords from us. He that sitteth in the heavens

shall laugh: the Lord shall have them in derision. Then shall he speak unto them in his wrath, and vex them in his sore displeasure. Yet have I set my King upon my holy hill of Zion. I will declare the decree: the Lord hath said unto me, Thou art my Son; this day have I begotten thee. Ask of me, and I shall give thee the heathen for thine inheritance, and the uttermost parts of the earth for thy possession. Thou shalt break them with a rod of iron; Thou shalt dash them in pieces like a potter's vessel (Ps. 2:1-9).

Later He saw the King ruling in all His splendor.

Thy throne, O God, is for ever and ever: the sceptre of thy kingdom is a right sceptre. Thou lovest righteousness, and hatest wickedness: therefore God, thy God, hath anointed thee with the oil of gladness above thy fellows. All thy garments smell of myrrh, and aloes, and cassia, out of the ivory palaces, whereby they have made thee glad. Kings' daughters were among thy honourable women: upon thy right hand did stand the queen in gold of Ophir (Ps. 45:6-9).

This is a kingdom of righteousness and cannot coexist with an unjudged world. To talk about a righteous kingdom inaugurated in the midst of the present vileness and to suggest that some tele-evangelist, religious figure, or cheap politician would rule this worldwide government is scary.

Again, Daniel had perfect insight and gave a timetable for this hour of judgment.

Seventy weeks are determined upon thy people and upon thy holy city, to finish the transgression, and to make an end of sins, and to make reconciliation for iniquity, and to bring in everlasting righteousness, and to seal up the vision and prophecy, and to anoint the Most Holy (Dan. 9:24).

Documentation puts 69 of these 70 weeks ending at the crucifixion of Jesus Christ and then the seventieth week as the time of Israel's covenant.

> And he shall confirm the covenant with many for one week: and in the midst of the week he shall cause the sacrifice and the oblation to cease, and for the overspreading of abominations he shall make it desolate, even until the consummation, and that determined shall be poured upon the desolate (Dan. 9:27).

Jesus confirms that this covenant will be broken in the middle by the abomination of desolation. "When ye therefore shall see the abomination of desolation, spoken of by Daniel the prophet, stand in the holy place, (whoso readeth, let him understand)" (Matt. 24:15). The overspreading of filth and immoral sickness demands an unprecedented act of judgment.

The Revelator gives that picture.

> And I saw an angel standing in the sun; and he cried with a loud voice, saying to all the fowls that fly in the midst of heaven, Come and gather yourselves together unto the supper of the great God; That ye may eat the flesh of kings, and the flesh of captains, and the flesh of mighty men, and the flesh of horses, and of them that sit on them, and the flesh of all men, both free and bond, both small and great. And I saw the beast, and the kings of the earth, and their armies, gathered together to make war against him that sat on the horse, and against his army. And the beast was taken, and with him the false prophet that wrought miracles before him, and with which he deceived them that had received the mark of the beast, and them that worshipped his image. These both were cast alive into a lake of fire

burning with brimstone. And the remnant were slain with the sword of him that sat upon the horse, which sword proceeded out of his mouth: and all the fowls were filled with their flesh (Rev. 19:17-21).

God the Father has committed all judgment to the Son and He will tread the winepress of the awesome judgment of God. He will actually appear with blood on His garments when He reaches the sacred spot on Mount Moriah. Our universe will be purged of dark wickedness so that God's new world can emerge.

A New Place for a New World Order

The Millennium kingdom of Jesus Christ will be right here on this present earth but it will be a new earth completely renewed in creative righteousness. Isaiah, by the Spirit, stated, "For, behold, I create new heavens and a new earth" (Isa. 65:17). The word create (as used here) in Hebrew is *bara*, to choose or select that from which to create something or a formative process. In the beginning He created the heavens and earth from nothing, but here He creates a new heaven and earth from a broken one. This actually happens before the Millennium kingdom begins, not at the end. Isaiah speaks to this subject.

> For, behold, I create new heavens and a new earth: and the former shall not be remembered, nor come into mind. But be ye glad and rejoice for ever in that which I create: for, behold, I create Jerusalem a rejoicing, and her people a joy. And I will rejoice in Jerusalem, and joy in my people: and the voice of weeping shall be no more heard in her, nor the voice of crying. There shall be no more thence an infant of days, nor an old man that hath not filled his days: for the child shall die a hundred years old; but the sinner being a hundred years old shall be accursed. And they shall build houses, and inhabit

them; and they shall plant vineyards, and eat the fruit of them. They shall not build, and another inhabit; they shall not plant, and another eat: for as the days of a tree are the days of my people, and mine elect shall long enjoy the work of their hands. They shall not labour in vain, nor bring forth for trouble; for they are the seed of the blessed of the Lord, and their offspring with them. And it shall come to pass, that before they call, I will answer; and while they are yet speaking, I will hear. The wolf and the lamb shall feed together, and the lion shall eat straw like the bullock: and dust shall be the serpent's meat. They shall not hurt nor destroy in all my holy mountain, saith the Lord (Isa. 65:17-25).

A new earth certainly awaits those who are preparing to be part of the earthly kingdom of Jesus Christ. Let me list an array of changes clearly seen in Scripture:

1. Both the heavens and the earth will return to their pristine purity as existed before the fall of Satan and his deceptive work on earth.

2. There will be no more celestial disturbances, storms, hail stones, or even smog and other atmospheric pollutions. The heavenly bodies will reveal a beauty that we only now experience by the creativity of an artist.

3. The earth will be free of the results of sin. Sickness and disease cannot exist in a sin-free environment.

4. Seasons will be perfect and will provide an atmosphere absolutely perfect and conclusive to a garden-like world. "Behold, the days come, saith the Lord that the plowman shall overtake the reaper, and the treader of grapes him that soweth seed; and the mountains shall drop sweet wine, and all the hills shall melt" (Amos 9:13). (Exception:

All nations left of those who came against Jerusalem (Armageddon) will be required to go up yearly to the Feast of Tabernacles. If they refuse, it will not rain on them until they submit (Zech. 14:16-17).

5. There will be a change in length of life so that an infant shall die at 100 years (Isa. 65:20). Also a man who obeys God's laws shall live as long as the trees. "They shall not build, and another inhabit; they shall not plant, and another eat: for as the days of a tree are the days of my people, and mine elect shall long enjoy the work of their hands" (Isa. 65:22).

6. The animal kingdom will again become a joy of the earth completely dominated by man. There will be no viciousness between species and the shedding of blood (except God's judgment on disobedience) will be non-existent. "The wolf and the lamb shall feed together, and the lion shall eat straw like the bullock: and dust shall be the serpent's meat. They shall not hurt nor destroy in all my holy mountain, saith the Lord" (Isa. 65:25).

7. There will be universal prosperity with all natural resources equally available for creative and abundant living (Isa. 65:21).

8. All military hostility will cease. There will be no national identity to fight over and no dictators or human government to defend their turf. "And he shall judge among the nations, and shall rebuke many people: and they shall beat their swords into plowshares, and their spears into pruning hooks: nation shall not lift up sword against nation, neither shall they learn war any more" (Isa. 2:4).

9. Everyone will again speak the same pure language. "For then will I turn to the people a pure language, that they may all call upon the name of

the Lord, to serve him with one consent" (Zeph. 3:9). This alone will serve to unite mankind into one brotherhood of men. Adam's entire family probably had a photographic mind and communicated in pictorial thought. This fact is certainly suggested in the earliest writing available today. There were no alphabets, all was written with pictures. They apparently thought, spoke, and wrote in pictures rather than words. The alphabet was probably a regression rather than a progression.

10. The world will be worshippers of one God and will serve Him only. "And it shall come to pass, that every one that is left of all the nations which came against Jerusalem shall even go up from year to year to worship the King, the Lord of hosts, and to keep the feast of tabernacles" (Zech. 14:16).

11. Holiness and righteousness will be the spirit of the whole world. Holiness will reflect from every expression of life. The communication system, academy of arts, the writers, poets, journalists, and ministers alike will do everything for the glory of God. "In that day, shall there be upon the bells of the horses, HOLINESS UNTO THE LORD; and the pots in the Lord's house shall be like the bowls before the altar. Yea, every pot in Jerusalem and in Judah shall be holiness unto the Lord of hosts" (Zech. 14:20-21).

Jerusalem Will Be the Joy of the Earth

Jerusalem is the center of our cosmos. It is the city that was chosen by the Lord to be central for all His revelations. It is either loved or hated by every religious expression. No one can ignore Jerusalem. Zechariah, speaking for the Lord said:

Behold, I will make Jerusalem a cup of trembling unto all the people round about, when they shall be in the siege both against Judah and against Jerusalem. And in that day will I make Jerusalem a burdensome stone for all people: all that burden themselves with it shall be cut in pieces, though all the people of the earth be gathered together against it (Zech. 12:2-3).

It is the eternal city.

Former Vice President Dan Quayle made the following statement about the future of Jerusalem. This remark was made on December 12, 1990, at a dinner where former Mayor Teddy Kollek (Jerusalem) was honored. I do not have the complete text of the vice president's statement, but it is clearly prophetic of what God has planned for this chosen city. "Jerusalem can be the bridge to Arab-Israeli conciliation. And when that day comes — and in God's good time it will — the vision of David Ben-Gurion (the first prime minister of the State of Israel) and Teddy Kollek will stand vindicated and Jerusalem will be indeed 'a light unto the nations.' "

All nations shall flow into Jerusalem as this oft-destroyed city becomes the world's metropolis. Its boundaries will extend for miles as the multifarious inhabitants of the world delight and share the glory of the King of kings and Lord of lords. Its glory will extend unchecked until the New Jerusalem descends from God out of heaven at the end of one thousand years. The earthly city Jerusalem will probably be directly beneath New Jerusalem and the united cities will outshine the sun. "And the city (New Jerusalem) had no need of the sun to shine in it: for the glory of God did lighten it, and the Lamb is the light thereof" (Rev. 21:23).

The psalmist David sums up his revelation of future Jerusalem. He sees, by divine wisdom, a place where the King and the golden city seem to become indistinguishable. They reflect a heavenly glory that increases as the millennium progresses and finally as eternity begins.

Great is the Lord, and greatly to be praised in the city of our God, in the mountain of his holiness. Beautiful for situation, the joy of the whole earth, is mount Zion, on the sides of the north, the city of the great King. God is known in her palaces for a refuge (Ps. 48:1-3).

What a King and what a palace!

Conclusion

The Day of the Lord will come as a thief. That day or period starts with the Rapture of the firstfruits, and continues with seven years of judgment and the great Millennium kingdom. All elements of passing insignificance will be bound up by divine cleansing and new heavens and a new earth will emerge.

But the day of the Lord will come as a thief in the night; in the which the heavens shall pass away with a great noise, and the elements shall melt with fervent heat, the earth also and the works that are therein shall be burned up. Seeing then that all these things shall be dissolved, what manner of persons ought ye to be in all holy conversation and godliness, Looking for and hasting unto the coming of the day of God, wherein the heavens being on fire shall be dissolved, and the elements shall melt with fervent heat? Nevertheless we, according to his promise look for new heavens and a new earth, wherein dwelleth righteousness (2 Pet. 3:10-13).

This glorious kingdom was God's plan for Adam and Eve but they sold their inheritance. Jesus Christ, the Second Adam will not fail. He and His chosen will establish a New World Order or Millennium kingdom wherein dwelleth righteousness. He alone can inaugurate this glorious Millennium and careless souls will not be His co-regents. "Wherefore, beloved, seeing that ye look for such things, be diligent that ye may be found of him in peace, without spot, and blameless" (2 Pet. 3:14).

We must end this book with the two eternal Jerusalems. While Jerusalem, the city of David, is to be glorious beyond words, the New Jerusalem prepared for His bride is far beyond my power for description. It is a city of heavenly preparation that actually descends to the earth. Let us consider those two cities intimately connected for eternity.

[1] Joseph R. Chambers, *Miracles, My Father's Delight* (Cleveland, TN: Pathway Press, 1986), p. 11-12.

[2] Pat Robertson, *The Secret Kingdom* (Nashville, TN: Thomas Nelson Publishers, 1982), p. 15, 198-200

[3] Dan Quayle, Ethics and Public Policy Center Newsletter, Washington, DC, Winter 1991, p. 1.

Chapter 18

Jerusalem, the Eternal City

There is no place on earth both loved and hated as is the city of Jerusalem and the surrounding land promised to Abraham. The present State of Israel is a small part of the final geography that will constitute its completed territory. Jehovah God made an undisputed covenant to Abraham and gave him the basic perimeters of his final inheritance. The Jewish people, Abraham's seed, will soon take full possession. Jesus Christ will be seated on the reestablished throne of David and the glory and riches of the world will flow into this world capital.

From this golden city there will be established a righteous theocracy to ensure justice, equality, and mercy on a worldwide scale. Men have dreamed of a one world government ruled by man. This dream has always been the antithesis of God's future design. The rebuilt city of Babylon will be the last challenge to Jerusalem as the capital of a worldwide government. These two cities are the exact opposites. Jerusalem is the center of all spiritual revelation while Babylon is the springboard of every hateful and evil spirit.

Jerusalem, the Joy of the Whole Earth

While Abraham was still a wandering Bedouin, only recently having arrived from the land of heathens, Jerusalem had a king/priest named Melchizedek. He was called King of Salem, priest of the most high God, King of righteousness, and King of peace (Heb. 7:1-2). God had already chosen the city and its king and priest was described in language befitting a God. In fact, Jesus Christ, God's eternal Son, was made a priest after the order of Melchizedek, not after the order of Aaron. Very simply, Melchizedek predated Aaron and was of a spiritual order too expansive to describe here. It is clear that the Father himself had chosen this city. "But I have chosen Jerusalem, that my name might be there" (2 Chron. 6:6).

The children of Israel were the chosen heirs of Abraham and established Jerusalem as their capital under David, their second king. The Jebusites had made this city a military stronghold cleverly defended by a strong wall and situated on a hill surrounded by a continuous valley. It was called "the stronghold of Zion" (2 Sam. 5:6-9). In what appeared to be a military victory without firing an arrow, David took the city and renamed it the City of David. They immediately determined to bring the ark of the covenant to King David's new capital with great celebration. After a brief delay as described below, God's visible presence was in the chosen city and it became the source of great joy and blessing. Note the celebration and holiness this event describes.

> And David arose, and went with all the people that were with him from Baale of Judah, to bring up from thence the ark of God, whose name is called by the name of the Lord of hosts that dwelleth between the cherubim (2 Sam. 6:2).

> And David and all the house of Israel played before the Lord on all manner of instruments made of fir wood, even on harps, and on psalteries, and

on timbrels, and on cornets, and on cymbals. And when they came to Nachon's threshingfloor, Uzzah put forth his hand to the ark of God, and took hold of it; for the oxen shook it. And the anger of the Lord was kindled against Uzzah, and God smote him there for his error; and there he died by the ark of God. And David was displeased, because the Lord had made a breach upon Uzzah: and he called the name of the place Perez-Uzzah to this day. And David was afraid of the Lord that day, and said, How shall the ark of the Lord come to me? [The Ark was left at this location for a period of time] (2 Sam. 6:5-9).

And it was told king David, saying, The Lord hath blessed the house of Obed-edom, and all that pertaineth unto him, because of the ark of God. So David went and brought up the ark of God from the house of Obed-edom into the city of David with gladness. And it was so, that when they that bare the ark of the Lord had gone six paces, he sacrificed oxen and fatlings. And David danced before the Lord with all his might; and David was girded with a linen ephod. So David and all the house of Israel brought up the ark of the Lord with shouting, and with the sound of the trumpet. And as the ark of the Lord came into the city of David, Michal Saul's daughter looked through a window, and saw king David leaping and dancing before the Lord; and she despised him in her heart (2 Sam. 6:12-16).

Jesus and Jerusalem

Jesus was born in a small hamlet called Bethlehem just a few miles away from Jerusalem; but Jerusalem was the central city of His life. He was condemned and scourged in the same city of His earlier arrest. Final death by crucifixion and burial were immediately outside the walls. He ascended to Heaven from a mount overlooking the city and He will return to that same place, called the Mount of Olives. This golden city will be the location of His palace of residence and government headquarters. While Jerusalem has been God's chosen city with His name clearly associated in its rise and fall, now the city will see the glory which the great God intended. Human minds cannot envision the riches, grandeur and indescribable glory that will be its fortune. Only the New Jerusalem coming down from God out of heaven will eclipse its magnitude and splendor. In fact, I believe these two cities will be connected and serve to enhance each other. New Jerusalem will probably be suspended in the heavens above the earthly city and become the light overarching it as the fiery cloud did for Israel while camping in the wilderness.

Before arriving in Jerusalem, the returning Son of God will defeat the Antichrist in a glorious display of His position as Lord of Host. Zechariah describes His arrival at Jerusalem.

> And his feet shall stand in that day upon the mount of Olives, which is before Jerusalem on the east, and the mount of Olives shall cleave in the midst thereof toward the east and toward the west, and there shall be a very great valley; and half of the mountain shall remove toward the north, and half of it toward the south (Zech. 14:4).

> And it shall be in that day, that living waters shall go out from Jerusalem; half of them toward the former sea, and half of them toward the hinder sea; in summer and in winter shall it be. And the Lord shall be king over all the earth: in that day shall there be one Lord, and his name one. All the land shall be turned as a plain from Geba to Rimmon south of Jerusalem: and it shall be lifted up, and inhabited in her place, from Benjamin's gate unto the place of the first gate, unto the corner

gate, and from the tower of Hananeel unto the king's winepresses. And men shall dwell in it, and there shall be no more utter destruction; but Jerusalem shall be safely inhabited (Zech. 14:8-11).

The city will be greatly expanded as the topographical outlay is completely altered. Zechariah's description points clearly to the mountains moving in a northern and southern direction while the Mount of Olives moves in both of the opposite directions of east and west. The cleaving of the Mount of Olives will unleash a living fountain of waters that will flow from the great city toward the Dead Sea on the east and the Mediterranean Sea on the west. These waters actually flow from the Mount of Olives and through the temple altar or from the temple altar through the Mount of Olives, and then east and west. As they flow east to the Dead Sea, Ezekiel tells of the healing of this body of water and of all the deserts in the eastern direction. It will do the same to the deserts on all the sides of Jerusalem.

> Then said he unto me, These waters issue out toward the east country, and go down into the desert, and go into the sea: which being brought forth into the sea, the waters shall be healed. And it shall come to pass, that every thing that liveth, which moveth, whithersoever the rivers shall come, shall live: and there shall be a very great multitude of fish, because these waters shall come thither: for they shall be healed; and every thing shall live whither the river cometh (Ezek. 47:8-9).

This will create a great lush valley, "And there shall be a very great valley" (Zech. 14:4), which will change much of the landscape from mountainous terrain to a prosperous garden-like environment. Isaiah spoke of this grand day:

> The wilderness and the solitary place shall be glad for them; and the desert shall rejoice, and blossom as the rose. It shall blossom abundantly,

and rejoice even with joy and singing: the glory of Lebanon shall be given unto it, the excellency of Carmel and Sharon; they shall see the glory of the Lord, and the excellency of our God (Isa. 35:1-2).

The Garden of Eden was cut off because of Adam's sin. Now it is recreated and Jerusalem is its new center.

Ezekiel describes the extent of the city's new boundaries:

> And over against the border of the priests, the Levites shall have five and twenty thousand in length, and ten thousand in breadth: all the length shall be five and twenty thousand, and the breadth ten thousand. And they shall not sell of it, neither exchange, nor alienate the firstfruits of the land: for it is holy unto the Lord. And the five thousand, that are left in the breadth over against the five and twenty thousand, shall be a profane place for the city, for dwelling, and for suburbs: and the city shall be in the midst thereof. And these shall be the measures thereof; the north side four thousand and five hundred, and the south side four thousand and five hundred, and on the east side four thousand and five hundred, and the west side four thousand and five hundred. And the suburbs of the city shall be toward the north two hundred and fifty, and toward the south two hundred and fifty, and toward the east two hundred and fifty, and toward the west two hundred and fifty. And the residue in length over against the oblation of the holy portion shall be ten thousand eastward, and ten thousand westward: and it shall be over against the oblation of the holy portion; and the increase thereof shall be for food unto them that serve the city. And they that serve the city shall serve it out of all the tribes of Israel (Ezek. 48:13-19).

The city will be approximately 60 miles square with a 12-mile square inner city allowing a 24-mile perimeter on all four sides. This will stretch almost the entire distance from the Dead Sea to the Mediterranean. Many parts of the country are already becoming a garden, but not to compare with its future.

The psalmist David could see the future glory of his capital city and sang of that day in Psalm 48:1-3. "Great is the Lord, and greatly to be praised in the city of our God, in the mountain of his holiness. Beautiful for situation, the joy of the whole earth, is mount Zion, on the sides of the north, the city of the great King. God is known in her palaces for a refuge." David even details the hatred kings would feel in envy for this city. "For, lo, the kings were assembled, they passed by together. They saw it, and so they marveled; they were troubled, and hasted away. Fear took hold upon them there, and pain, as of a woman in travail" (Ps. 48:4-6). He also spoke of the city's eternal presence as the enduring city forever. "As we have heard, so have we seen in the city of the Lord of hosts, in the city of our God: God will establish it for ever. Selah" (Ps. 48:8).

Jerusalem, as it now exists, shall be attacked by the Antichrist, her temple desecrated by his false religion, and her palaces partially destroyed; but, immediately upon the triumph of the Messiah, she shall start her rise to greatness. The former mayor of Jerusalem, Teddy Kollek, recently stated that he had the greatest task in the world: to prepare Jerusalem for the Messiah. I believe this is the generation that will witness the final events that leads to the Millennium kingdom of the Son of God, Jesus Christ, and His rulership in this Eternal City. One can almost hear the words of Isaiah as they near fulfillment. "Awake, awake, put on thy strength, O Zion; put on thy beautiful garments, O Jerusalem, the holy city: for henceforth there shall no more come into thee the uncircumcised and the unclean" (Isa. 52:1). Ezekiel prophesies of Jerusalem, "And the name of the city from that day shall be, [Jehovah Shammah] The Lord is there" (Ezek. 48:35).

The Promise Land Stretching from Jerusalem

The great city of Jerusalem will be the capital of all the territory promised to Abraham. Her boundaries will eliminate several existing nations and she will finally experience peace with the two nations left on her borders. Assyria and Egypt will be her northern and southern allies, while the rest of the geography between the two is inhabited by the heirs of promise. The God that cannot lie has given His Word.

This is the promise as given to Abraham.

> In that same day the Lord made a covenant with Abram, saying, Unto thy seed have I given this land, from the river of Egypt unto the great river, the river Euphrates: the Kenites, and the Kenizzites, and the Kadmonites, and the Hittites, and the Perizzites, and the Rephaims, and the Amorites, and the Canaanites, and the Girgashites, and the Jebusites (Gen. 15:18-21).

Not only did Abraham receive this great assurance of his inheritance, but it was given with the cutting of a covenant unique to this promise. A great biblical scholar, G.H. Pember, details this covenant experience in breathtaking terms.

> In response, then, to the command of God, Abraham brought the prescribed animals, and proceeded to divide the beasts, laying each half opposite to that which corresponded with it.
>
> The birds he did not divide, being thus in accord with the later Mosaic ritual, but probably placed one on either side. And so, having completed his preparations, he waited for the arrival of the Other Party to the covenant, being watchful in the meanwhile to drive off the birds of prey that flew down upon the carcasses.

Now, when God had called him out of the tent, the stars were shining: at least, therefore, the time must have been very early morning. Hence the patriarch seems to have waited and watched during the whole of the long day, and still his faith was tried; for God did not yet appear to confirm the covenant. Just, however, as the sun was about to set, a deep sleep fell upon him, in which he experienced terror and great darkness. Then the gloom was pierced by the voice of God, and Abraham heard words by no means out of harmony with his direful circumstances, though ending in strains of far distant hope.

The sun had gone down, and Abraham seems to have awakened to a consciousness of his surroundings. It was dark, and he saw moving towards the carcasses an appearance in shape like to a cylindrical furnace, from which smoke was issuing, and a fiery flame streamed forth. It was the sign of God's presence, corresponding to the pillar of cloud and fire by which He subsequently manifested himself to Israel. In this form He passed between the pieces; but Abraham was not invited to follow Him. The reason of this departure from ordinary custom seems to lie in the fact that the covenant which God was about to establish involved an absolute promise, the fulfillment of which did not depend upon conditions to be required of Abraham.

After the Lord had thus passed between the pieces, He defined, in the plainest and most unmistakable terms, the extent of the territory which He had reserved for the children of Abraham. "Unto thy seed," He said, "have I given this land, from the river of Egypt unto the great river, the river Euphrates: the Kenite, and the Kenizzite, and the Kadmonite, and the Hittite, and the Perizzite, and the Rephaim,

and the Amorite, and the Canaanite, and the
Girgashite, and the Jebusite" (Gen. 15:18-21).

Such, then, is the memorable promise in which
the boundaries of the land of Israel were defined,
and its full extent made known. As we have before
remarked, it was given without any conditions:
consequently, no possible circumstances can prevent its ultimate fulfillment.[1]

The extent of the boundaries was set in unmistakable
terms. Israel was to drive out all its inhabitants and inherit
this entire territory when she returned from bondage in
Egypt. Instead, she bargained with her neighbor, started
serving their gods, intermarried with the heathens, and,
finally, ended in destruction and rejection by God. Nothing
that has happened in the 3,000 plus years since Abraham
heard from God has annulled God's faithfulness. Israel will
be chastened and scourged until her heart is humbled and
then the Messiah will come. "Then shall ye remember your
own evil ways, and your doings that were not good, and shall
loathe yourselves in your own sight for your iniquities and
for your abominations" (Ezek. 36:31). That day is fast
approaching.

Several additional Scriptures will help define the land
expanse involved in these promises.

From the wilderness and this Lebanon even
unto the great river, the river Euphrates, all the land
of the Hittites, and unto the great sea toward the
going down of the sun, shall be your coast (Josh.
1:4).

Every place whereon the soles of your feet
shall tread shall be yours: from the wilderness and
Lebanon, from the river, the river Euphrates, even
unto the uttermost sea shall your coast be (Deut.
11:24).

We can clearly define several areas: the wilderness

(Arabia, present Saudi Arabia, and several small Arab nations), Lebanon (controlled by Syria), to the river Euphrates (the portion of Iraq west of the Euphrates river), land of the Hittites (described below) with the Mediterranean Sea for the western boundary. All the land of the Hittites includes a large portion of eastern and southern Turkey and all of Syria is included in this promise. Other areas are described in the text from Genesis 15:18-21. *From the river of Egypt* is believed to represent the area from the north end of the Gulf of Suez going in a northwestern direction toward the Mediterranean Sea. It appears that the whole of the Sinai Desert and all of Jordan will belong to the Promised Land. The tribes of the Canaanites, all of which lived in Palestine, were dispossessed, either partially or entirely by Joshua and no longer exist in any natural form. This presents a fairly clear picture of the future possession of Israel. With the Mediterranean Sea as a western border, the southern lines of the Sinai and Arabian Desert as the southern border and going north along the Persian Gulf and the Euphrates River to embrace at least the southwestern half of Turkey from the Euphrates River to the regions running north of Syria and Lebanon and then ending again at the coast of the Great Sea. For Israel to speak of this kind of territorial design would be an act of war. Yet, God's promises that cannot fail are unquestionable in declaring Abraham's seed as the rightful heirs.

There are some areas of this territory that are to be judged and uninhabited at least until God creates a new heaven and a new earth and the former things are forever vanquished. I believe that the new creation begins at the start of the Millennium and will continue until all things are made new, and God the Father dwells with men in the New Jerusalem. It will all be final by the end of one thousand years when the bridal city descends from God to dwell among men. As the Millennium kingdom is established, righteousness and prosperity will fill the whole earth beginning in the new, greatly enlarged State of Israel.

Jewish People to Return after the Millennium Begins

Immediately after the return of Jesus Christ to end the Battle of Armageddon and to inaugurate His kingdom, there will be an influx of Jewish descendants from every corner of the globe. The return of the children of Abraham has begun, but is only a trickle compared to the future. The following prophecy given by Isaiah is clearly dated after the beginning of the thousand years of Christ's reign. A remnant is going home at present, but the entire seed of promise is soon to follow.

> And in that day there shall be a root of Jesse, which shall stand for an ensign of the people; to it shall the Gentiles seek: and his rest shall be glorious. And it shall come to pass in that day, that the Lord shall set his hand again the second time to recover the remnant of his people, which shall be left, from Assyria, and from Egypt, and from Pathros, and from Cush, and from Elam, and from Shinar, and from Hamath, and from the islands of the sea. And he shall set up an ensign for the nations, and shall assemble the outcasts of Israel, and gather together the dispersed of Judah from the four corners of the earth. The envy also of Ephraim shall depart, and the adversaries of Judah shall be cut off: Ephraim shall not envy Judah, and Judah shall not vex Ephraim. But they shall fly upon the shoulders of the Philistines toward the west; they shall spoil them of the east together: they shall lay their hand upon Edom and Moab; and the children of Ammon shall obey them. And the Lord shall utterly destroy the tongue of the Egyptian sea; and with his mighty wind shall he shake his hand over the river, and shall smite it in the seven streams, and make men go over dry-shod. And there shall be a highway for the remnant of his people, which shall be left, from Assyria; like as it was to Israel in

the day that he came up out of the land of Egypt (Isa. 11:10-16).

The multiplied city of Jerusalem and enlarged State of Israel will easily incorporate millions of Jewish citizens. The people of Israel represent a level of expertise and brain power unknown in any culture on earth. God has made them the most ingenious and creative people of all the nations of the world. This intellectual and creative ability will be mightily enhanced by the spiritual transformation of serving the glorified Messiah and now their new King, Jesus Christ. The glory that King David and Solomon dreamed about will be a stark reality as wealthy Jews bring all their riches to the Land of Promise. No longer will they be required to leave their accumulated possessions in the country from which they immigrate. It will now serve to increase the wealth of the Zion of God.

Information is now surfacing that there are millions more Jewish people in many countries of the world than previously believed. Debate has raged for decades over the ten tribes (Israel) that were deported into the Assyrian kingdom before the destruction of Jerusalem (Judah) and the deportation of its inhabitants to Babylon. I am not an authority on this subject, but I do believe millions will respond to the call when the Millennium kingdom is estab- lished. Isaiah clearly distinguished between the two groups with his prophecy. He said, "and shall assemble the outcasts of Israel and gather together the dispersed of Judah from the four corners of the earth" (Isa. 11:12). He called the people of Israel outcasts; that could refer to their rejection even by the present State of Israel. All of that will change when the Messiah is seated on the throne of David.

Israel to Possess Inhabitants of Babylon as Slaves

Citizens of Israel will not only be wealthy, they will possess the heathens for an inheritance. It will be a godly rule of justice and fairness, but the heathens will be their servants. Isaiah spoke of this day when Babylon would be destroyed as Sodom and Gomorrah. His words are as follows.

> For the Lord will have mercy on Jacob, and will yet choose Israel, and set them in their own land: and the strangers shall be joined with them, and they shall cleave to the house of Jacob. And the people shall take them, and bring them to their place: and the house of Israel shall possess them captives, whose captives they were; and they shall rule over their oppressors. And it shall come to pass in the day that the Lord shall give thee rest from thy sorrow, and from thy fear, and from the hard bondage wherein thou wast made to serve, that thou shalt take up this proverb against the king of Babylon, and say, How hath the oppressor ceased! the golden city ceased! The Lord hath broken the staff of the wicked, and the sceptre of the rulers. He who smote the people in wrath with a continual stroke, he that ruled the nations in anger, is persecuted, and none hindereth. The whole earth is at rest, and is quiet: they break forth into singing (Isa. 14:1-7).

The psalmist David saw this same reality in his prophetic utterances. He ties this historic future to the time when the King would sit upon the holy hill of Zion.

> Yet have I set my King upon my holy hill of Zion. I will declare the decree: the Lord hath said unto me, Thou art my Son; this day have I begotten thee. Ask of me, and I shall give thee the heathen for thine inheritance, and the uttermost parts of the earth for thy possession. Thou shalt break them with a rod of iron; thou shalt dash them in pieces like a potter's vessel (Ps. 2:6-9).

Our 20th century minds cannot grasp this kind of

thinking. We forget that God is just and all of us will reap exactly what we sow. Not only do individuals reap the fruit of their labour, but families and nations also answer for the corporate action of their past. The tribulation period will purge the earth of its wickedness, but those who survive this holocaust will be judged by their individual and corporate treatment of the Jewish nation. Their lot in the Millennium will be decided by their actions during Israel's darkest period of all history. Remember, these are natural people who manage to survive the seven years of tribulation. Three classes of people will share the Millennium kingdom: the Jewish nation, the glorified saints, and the natural people. Israelis will rule the new State of Israel, the saints will rule the rest of the world, and the natural people will serve both.

Assyria and Egypt to Be Partners with Israel

The promised land will stretch from Egypt on the south to Assyria on the north and east. Everything between these two nations will be possessed by the heirs of Isaac and Jacob. The Moabites, Ammonites (parts of modern Jordan), and Edomites will share the land given to them, but Israel will rule over them. A partnership will develop between Israel, Egypt, and Assyria that will give them control of the entire Middle East. Peace will finally come to this hot spot of the world.

Isaiah gave specific prophecy of this day.

> The burden of Egypt. Behold, the Lord rideth upon a swift cloud, and shall come into Egypt: and the idols of Egypt shall be moved at his presence, and the heart of Egypt shall melt in the midst of it (Isa. 19:1).

> And the Egyptians will I give over into the hand of a cruel lord; and a fierce king shall rule over them, saith the Lord, the Lord of hosts (Isa. 19:4).

> In that day shall Egypt be like unto women:

and it shall be afraid and fear because of the shaking of the hand of the Lord of hosts, which he shaketh over it. And the land of Judah shall be a terror unto Egypt, every one that maketh mention thereof shall be afraid in himself, because of the counsel of the Lord of hosts, which he hath determined against it (Isa. 19:16-17).

In that day shall there be an altar to the Lord in the midst of the land of Egypt, and a pillar at the border thereof to the Lord. And it shall be for a sign and for a witness unto the Lord of hosts in the land of Egypt: for they shall cry unto the Lord because of the oppressors, and he shall send them a saviour, and a great one, and he shall deliver them. And the Lord shall be known to Egypt, and the Egyptians shall know the Lord in that day, and shall do sacrifice and oblation; yea, they shall vow a vow unto the Lord, and perform it. And the Lord shall smite Egypt: he shall smite and heal it: and they shall return even to the Lord, and he shall be intreated of them, and shall heal them. In that day shall there be a highway out of Egypt to Assyria, and the Assyrian shall come into Egypt, and the Egyptian into Assyria, and the Egyptians shall serve with the Assyrians. In that day shall Israel be the third with Egypt and with Assyria, even a blessing in the midst of the land: whom the Lord of hosts shall bless, saying, Blessed be Egypt my people, and Assyria the work of my hands, and Israel mine inheritance (Isa. 19:19-25).

Prophecies of this magnitude always overwhelm me. When I was in Egypt in February 1990, my heart melted at the depression hanging like a cloud. When I arrived in my hotel the first night after a day of sightseeing and research, the Holy Spirit miraculously led me to these verses. Suddenly, the hope of my Messiah's (Jesus Christ) coming was more than escape. It was renewal, recreation, and glory for every part of God's earth, including Egypt.

These verses show that after Egypt and Assyria are judged, God will renew both and make them followers and worshippers of the King of Israel. They will share with Israel the blessings of the eternal kingdom. Israel will be a blessing in the midst of Egypt and Assyria. Egypt, He calls *My people*; Assyria, *the work of My hands*; and Israel, He calls *Mine inheritance*. Assyria and Egypt will be possessed by Israel's King, but not by Israel as a nation. It will be a unique partnership for eternity.

The New Center of Creation

Jerusalem, the Golden City, and the nation of Israel will be the center of God's new world. Its King will be the triumphant one who trod the winepress of God's wrath at Calvary and earned the right to rule. The old center of creation was Eden and the land of Shinar (Sumer) or Babylon. The people forfeited their position and God called a new nation by Abraham. Jerusalem took the place of Eden or Babylon before Abraham arrived in the land. Finally, after centuries of human failure, the promise will be final. The promise land will become the center of God's new world. For one thousand years, it will be perfectly ruled by the King of kings. What God designed for the first Adam will be enjoyed by the followers of the Second Adam.

> And they shall say, This land that was desolate is become like the garden of Eden; and the waste and desolate and ruined cities are become fenced, and are inhabited. Then the heathen that are left round about you shall know that I the Lord build the ruined places, and plant that that was desolate: I the Lord have spoken it, and I will do it (Ezek. 36:35-36).

It does not end with the Millennium kingdom. That is only the prelude to an eternity in the presence of God. The earthly Jerusalem and New Jerusalem coming down from God out of heaven will be the focus of God's entire cosmos. The Father himself will be with us for eternity. We will enjoy a *new heaven* and *new earth*. The glory of God and of the Lamb of God will enlighten and fill the sinless eternal existence of mankind.

And I saw a new heaven and a new earth: for the first heaven and the first earth were passed away; and there was no more sea (Rev. 21:1).

And I heard a great voice out of heaven saying, Behold, the tabernacle of God is with men, and he will dwell with them, and they shall be his people, and God himself shall be with them, and be their God (Rev. 21:3).

And I saw no temple therein: for the Lord God Almighty and the Lamb are the temple of it. And the city had no need of the sun, neither of the moon, to shine in it: for the glory of God did lighten it, and the Lamb is the light thereof (Rev. 21:22-23).

[1] G.H. Pember, *The Great Prophecies of the Centuries Concerning Israel and the Gentiles* (original publisher London: Hodder and Stoughton, 1909), p. 52-54

Conclusion

The future of this earth is glorious indeed. The two eternal cities of Jerusalem, the city of David and New Jerusalem coming down from God out of heaven, will be the everlasting joy of the whole earth. New Jerusalem will have in it the tree of life which was originally in the land of Shinar, where Babylon was built by Nimrod. Understand what the Garden of Eden and the tree of life meant to the first family and we can easily see that New Jerusalem replaces the lost paradise forfeited by Adam and his family.

Men have often talked about paradise lost. Even Satan's followers have bemoaned this ancient garden and spoke of re-discovering it by the powers of their idiot god. Their hopes are soon to be forever destroyed as Satan and his armies are judged.

The family of Jesus' chosen shall enjoy His renewed creation forever. The Jewish people will finally worship the true Messiah and dwell in the Promised Land of milk and honey. The bloodwashed throng of all nations will inherit the earth and New Jerusalem. It will be more than paradise regained.

The eternal Creator will enjoy His creation and His

creation will enjoy their God forever and ever.

But we speak the wisdom of God in a mystery, even the hidden wisdom, which God ordained before the world unto our glory: Which none of the princes of this world knew: for had they known it, they would not have crucified the Lord of glory. But as it is written, Eye hath not seen, nor ear heard, neither have entered into the heart of man, the things which God hath prepared for them that love him (1 Cor. 2:7-9).